Knit
great basics

Knit
great basics
Vicki Square

Brown Sheep Company

Published by Brown Sheep Company

Text, schematic and illustration © 2001 Vicki Square
Photography © 2001 Brown Sheep Company
Text for The Brown Sheep Story and About the Yarns © 2001 Brown Sheep Company

Book designer: Vicki Square
Photographer: Jason Reiff
Text editor: Joan Pickett
Pattern checkers: Caroline Yonker, Joan Pickett, Lois Eynon
Computer Graph: Elaine Sipes
Book Composition by Allentown Digital Services Division of RR Donnelley & Sons

All sample garments in this book are knit with Brown Sheep yarns.
Buttons provided by JHB.

Knitters: Heather Bean, Alice Bush, Lois Eynon, Nancy Hewitt, Kim Knight, Joan Pickett,
Christine Randazzo, MaryLee Rosen, Sharron Sala, Micky Shafer, Susan Shepard, and
Elaine Sipes

Models (adults): Morgan Barnes, Heidi Diehl, Cori Hixon, Gary Hixon, Justine Square, Reza Zedah
    (children): Tessa Bellin, Sophie Feavel, Mariah Green, Esther Romero

ISBN Number: 0-9711769-0-6

Library of Congress Card Catalog Number: 2001091963

Printed by RR Donnelley & Sons

For
Joan and Lois

for lighting the fire, standing firmly with me, praying for me

With Thanks

To all those involved in the creation of this book, I thank you.

To Peggy Wells for sharing my vision in the scope of the book, for all her support, and Harlan of Brown Sheep Company for this opportunity. To Joan, Derry, and Lois for all the reading they did of the manuscript, and to Caroline for checking all my numbers. To Elaine for sharing her computer savvy with me.

A big thank you to all my knitters for their many hours of fine work, without whom I would still be knitting . . . Alice, Lois, Nancy, Kim, Joan, Christine, MaryLee, Sharron, Micky, Susan, Heather, and Elaine. To my great models Morgan, Heidi, Cori, Gary, Justine, Reza, Tessa, Sophie, Mariah, and Esther for their beautiful smiles. Thanks to my Monday night knit group for always cheering me on.

I am fortunate to have Michelle Derkacs, Amy Eldridge, and Bethanne Ficzko at Allentown Digital Services Division of RR Donnelley & Sons for all their expertise and encouragment. Thanks to Jamie and Lance for their guidance.

A very special thank you to my husband, Johnny, and my children, Justine and Alex, for all their love, prayers, strength, and confidence in me.

I would do it all again, I've worked with such wonderful people.

Table of Contents

The Brown Sheep Story

The Legend and The Legacy

The dreamer and the doer, these are words that can be used to describe Harlan Brown, owner and founder of Brown Sheep Company, Inc. The dream began years ago with the purchase of an Ashford spinning wheel for his daughter at Christmas.

Harlan had farmed his grandfather's beloved Western Nebraska farm for 35 years. During that time he developed an extensive sheep feeding and wool production operation. He served his chosen field with commitment and dedication. He was an active member of the American Sheep Council and the Midwest Woolgrowers Association.

As the years went by Harlan became convinced than he needed to find a way to add value to the product that he already produced and understood—wool. As a member of the Midwest Woolgrowers Association, he understood the problems of the American wool market. The United States growers have continually been plagued with wide market fluctuations in price and demand.

Finally in 1980, a sale of spinning equipment from a mill in South Carolina was negotiated. Harlan and Janet drove their own semi truck and trailer down to retrieve the equipment. They returned home with a set of pin drafters, a spinning frame, and other miscellaneous equipment that they had not a clue how to use.

Six months later, on July 4, Harlan had his first ball of yarn in his hand. The first year was dedicated to perfecting one line of yarn, a single ply, 100% wool product that is still known today as Top of the Lamb. After producing a product that the Browns felt was marketable, they filled the trunk of their car and hit the road.

Making the product was one issue, but learning to market an unknown, untried yarn in an industry that is driven by past experience and reputation was a completely different issue. True to his pioneering spirit, Harlan Brown did not give up when he consistently heard the word "no". The natural salesman that he is, he convinced several individuals to give his new yarn a try. Soon his yarn was eating its way into the Southwest weaving industry and making a strong push into the world of hand knitters.

The second year, color was introduced, throwing the company into the world of science and chemistry and the world of art and fashion. Each year since new colors have been added, and new lines of yarns created until the company currently manufactures 12 lines of yarn and over 1000 different colors.

Yes, Harlan Brown has become a legend in the yarn industry. He created a textile mill where none was before; creating what he was told could not be done. You might think that at age 76, he would be ready to rest with his accomplishments. Not hardly! Each day finds Harlan buying wool, filling boxes, repairing equipment, and hatching new ideas.

I know, because I'm the daughter who received the spinning wheel, and I'm the daughter committed to carrying on the legacy. My husband, Robert and I have made the commitment to carry on the Brown Sheep Company name that represents both quality and service. We made a major commitment to the future of this company when we abandoned existing careers and moved our family from Colorado. We have been steadily learning the ropes.

It is our goal that Brown Sheep Company continue to be a leader of the finest natural fiber yarn produced in the United States. We are committed to utilizing American produced fiber when possible. Quality will continue to be our motto. It is our desire to provide excellent service as well as a quality product. We continue to seek new ways to grow our company and serve our growing list of faithful customers. We hope that this unique yarn design book can help all experience levels of knitters enjoy and utilize Brown Sheep yarn.

Peggy Jo Wells

Brown Sheep Yarns
at a Glance

When you choose wool and natural fiber yarns from the Brown Sheep Company, you are getting the finest quality and best value yarns available. Here is a quick description of the various lines of yarns that we manufacture for your knitting experience.

Top of the Lamb is the original 100% wool single yarn for Brown Sheep Company. The soft heathers and subtle to intense solid colors are available in worsted and sport weight in reeled skeins only.

Lamb's Pride is a blend of 85% pure, soft wool and 15% mohair and produces a garment of exquisite loft and softness. Both worsted and bulky weights are available in an assortment of bright, pastels, neutral tones and heathers.

Nature Spun brings together three of the most sought after qualities in 100% wool, traditional-plied yarn: softness, value, and a vast array of colors. A continual favorite among knitters and weavers, Nature Spun is available in three different weights, worsted, sport, and fingering.

Lamb's Pride Superwash is a 3 ply, 100% wool yarn that has been super washed, providing a soft, natural fiber that can be washed in the wash machine on gentle cycle. Available in worsted and bulky, it is a natural choice for anyone desiring easy care wool products.

Handpaint Originals colors are inspired by the earth, sea, and sky uniquely blended on our luxurious mohair and wool single ply worsted weight yarn. Each colorway consists if up to eight different hand-painted shades, applied to avoid unwanted patterning. Combine any of these beautiful blended colors with their complementing solid shades for a truly one-of-a-kind look.

Cotton Fleece and Cotton Fine are a light and airy blend of 80% cotton and 20% wool available in worsted and fine weights. This fiber blend is uniquely plied and cabled to provide a beautiful texture and drape for every knitted garment. Its soft touch and delightful resilience have other cotton yarns beat!

Kaleidoscope is the cotton/wool blend of Cotton Fleece that has been handpainted in several colorways. This yarn knits elegantly alone or coordinates beautiful with the solid colors of the Cotton Fleece.

Prairie Silk combines the luxury of silk with the wool you love to knit with the most. We took our Lamb's Pride, added a touch more mohair and just enough silk to make the sleekest and most satisfying blend of natural fibers into a worsted weight.

Wildfoote Luxury Sock is a washable wool and nylon blend that provides softness, warmth, easy care, and wearability. This yarn sports a variety of eye-catching solids and exciting bi and tri-color twists. This yarn is not for socks only, but if your feet could talk, they'd surely beg for socks made of Wildfoote!

Burly Spun is the 100% wool answer for a quick start-to-finish project. This extra bulky single has a soft hand perfect for garments, accessories, or knitting for home. The project is ready before the party can begin.

Country Classics: At the end of the day all those fibers that didn't make it through the complete process are gathered up, recarded and spun into this delightful economical natural fiber yarn. The fiber content may vary with wool, superwash wool, mohair, cotton, silk, and occasionally a little nylon. The blended color is a natural gray offered undyed or with color added to produce rich heathers.

Yarn Line	Fiber Content	Yards/Skein	No. of Plies	Recommended Needle Size	Average Gauge
Top of Lamb Worsted Sport	100% Wool	190 Yards 350 Yards	1 1	Size 8 Size 5	5 st/"—6 rw/" 12 st/"—8 rw/"
Lamb's Pride Worsted Bulky	85% Wool, 15% Mohair	190 Yards 125 Yards	1 1	Size 8 Size 10½	4 ½ st/"—6 rw/" 3 st/"—9 rw/2"
Lamb's Pride Superwash Worsted Bulky	100% Washable Wool	200 Yards 110 Yards	3 3	Size 8 Size 10 1/2	4½ st/" 3½ st/"
Nature Spun Worsted Sport Fingering	100% Wool	245 Yards 184 Yards 310 Yards	3 3 3	Size 7 Size 5 Size 3	5 st/"—6 rw/" 6 st/"—7 rw/" 7 st/"—9 rw/"
Handpaint Originals	70% Mohair 30% Wool	88 Yards	1	Size 8	4½ st/"
Cotton Fleece	80% Cotton 20% Wool	215 Yards	24	Size 6	5 st/"
Cotton Fine	80% Cotton 20% Wool	222 Yards	12	Size 2	6½ st/"
Kaleidoscope	80% Cotton 20% Wool	215 Yards	24	Size 6	5 st/"
Prairie Silk	72% Wool 18% Mohair 10% Silk	88 Yards	1	Size 8	4½ st/"
Wildfoote Luxury Sock	75% Washable Wool 25% Nylon	215 Yards	4	Size 1	8 st/"
Burly Spun	100% Wool	132 Yards	1	Size 13	2½ st/"
Country Classic Worsted Bulky	Blended Fibers	190 Yards 125 Yards	1 1	Size 8 Size 10½	4½ st/"—6 rw/" 3 st/"—9 rw/2"

Essentials

Before You Begin . . .

Great basic designs + great basic yarns = great wardrobe basics. Translation: a wardrobe basic is a 'must have' item that goes with almost everything and functions in many ways. Patterns need not be complex to accomplish great things. Hence, I designed a collection of basic garment styles with a contemporary flair. The lines are clean and the overall fit is relaxed. These basic designs provide a canvas on which to build and personalize your own knitted creations.

This book will help you choose any garment style and design options, choose any gauge, choose any size, and easily access all that information for a quick start to knitting using my simplified schematic instructions. As an artist, I always made drawings to visualize my concept. As a knitter, I recorded my numerical instructions in a streamlined manner. The result is a simplified schematic style I dub Speed Read. Text instructions also are given for those who prefer them.

Each chapter presents a garment style with design options and defined schematics for all the yarn weights,from fingering to bulky. Simple styling means the yarn truly makes the garment. Brown Sheep offers a wide range of beautiful, basic yarns in colors that are solid, heather, tweed, handpainted and richly blended. Yarns are singles, plied, and boucle using the natural fibers of wool, mohair, silk and cotton. Use any Brown Sheep yarn to make any garment variation and consider combining different yarns in a single piece. For example, knit the body in one yarn and the border in another (see the shawl collared coat), or knit with two yarns held together as one for textural innovation. All of the model garments pictured in the book are knitted with Brown Sheep yarns and illustrate possibilities nevertheless feel free to try your own handspun or other selection for a completely different look.

There are eight sizes ranging from child small to adult extra large. Always make your size selection according to the finished measurements, because small/medium/large labels are rather arbitrarily assigned and accomodate male and female. Each size and style has a schematic page of its own with measurement and gauge information.

Gauges are presented in pairs, i.e. 6½ • 7, 5 • 6, 4 • 4½, 3 • 3½ stitches per inch. Of these, the first number is the gauge corresponding to all left hand side numbers on the schematic. The second number is the gauge for all right hand side numbers. Draw an imaginary vertical line down the center of each line drawing to visually divide the gauge instructions. When there is only one number, as in the increase at the top of the ribbing, it is common to both gauges. In the Adult Small Vest example on the next page, for the 4 stitch per inch gauge use all the left hand side numbers as follows: to knit the back, with smaller needles cast on 71 stitches. Work in knit 1, purl 1 rib for 3 inches, increasing 10 stitches across last row of rib—total 81 stitches. Change to larger needles and continue in stockinette stitch for 15 inches. (Refer to measurement schematic on page 23 for lengths.) Shape armhole: bind off stitches at each armhole edge in the following sequence: 3 sts 2 times, 2 sts 1 time. Decrease 1 st 2 times, every other row. Continue even until armhole measures 9 inches. Place stitches on three holders, 16 for each shoulder and 29 for back neck.

Knit each body piece separately from hem to shoulder. Follow ball band instructions on chosen yarn

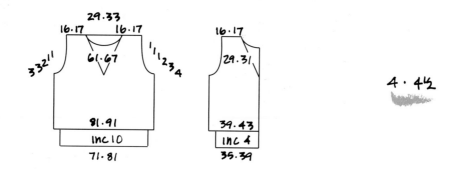

for guidelines on knitting needle size, or simply experiment with gauge until you have the look and feel you are after. For vest/waistcoat, pullover/cardigan, and jacket ribbings and borders, use a needle one or two sizes smaller than needle for gauge. After increase row on last row of rib, change to larger needle to complete knitting in stockinette stitch. I place shoulder stitches on hold and use a three needle bind off seam, my favorite, for finishing. Ribbed neck and armhole borders may be worked flat in rows, or done in the round to eliminate the need for seaming. Smaller sizes will require double pointed needles, larger sizes can be knit with a short length circular needle. For the styles with sleeves, I set the sleeve cap into armhole, using a crocheted seam. Then I sew side and sleeve seams using invisible weaving for stockinette. Look for different borders on various styles. Tunics should be knitted in a non-curling stitch, such as seed or garter stitch. Text instructions will clarify any procedural puzzles. For a first project, I recommend reading text instructions and following schematic directions for clarity. Once you've worked the method, you'll be able to jump start with schematics and use text for finishing details.

Use the following simple procedure to make the most of this book:

1• Choose garment style — i.e. vest, cardigan, jacket.

   1a• Choose design options — i.e. v-neck, curved armhole/shaped sleeve cap.

2• Choose garment size.

   2a• Rely on finished chest measurement to determine size. Note jackets and coats have more ease for each size.

3• Choose yarn.

   3a• See yarn amounts table at the beginning of each chapter. Yardage and recommended numbers of skeins of each yarn are approximate.

4• Knit gauge — The recommended gauge is a guideline only. You may want a softer hand for better drape, or a firmer, more stable jacket-like weight. Remember, it is your choice.

5• Choose Speed Read schematics for a quick start, or refer to text instructions. All finishing instructions are given in text.

If you are like me and many knitters I know, a lucious yarn will inspire you first. Then you will let the feel of the yarn determine the style you choose. The steps above are mixed up a bit. Just don't leave any steps out!

I hope this will be a resource for knitters to enjoy for years to come. My desire is for the book to serve as a tool for knitters, from beginner to experienced, to expand on their own creativity.

Vests
&
Waistcoats

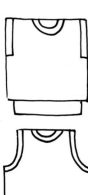

Choose:

- vest or waistcoat
- round or v-neck
- straight or curved armholes

	Child			Adult				
	S • 24"	M • 28"	L • 32"	XS • 36"	S • 40"	M • 44"	L • 48"	XL • 52"
6½ • 7 sts per inch yardage	400	550	750	950	1125	1300	1450	1650
Cotton Fine	2	3	4	5	6	6	7	8
Nature Spun (F)	2	2	3	4	4	5	5	6
Wildfoote	2	3	4	5	6	7	7	8
5 • 6 sts per inch yardage	300	400	600	700	850	950	1100	1250
Cotton Fleece	2	2	3	4	4	5	6	6
Kaleidoscope	3	6	7	9	11	13	14	16
Nature Spun (S)	2	3	4	6	7	7	8	9
Top of the Lamb (S)	1	2	2	2	3	3	4	4
4 • 4½ sts per inch yardage	250	350	500	600	750	850	950	1050
Country Classics (W)	2	2	3	4	4	5	5	6
Handpaint Originals	3	4	6	7	9	10	11	12
Lamb's Pride (W)	2	2	3	4	4	5	5	6
Lamb's Pride Superwash (W)	2	2	3	3	4	5	5	6
Nature Spun (W)	2	2	3	3	4	4	4	5
Prairie Silk	3	4	6	7	9	10	11	12
Top of the Lamb (W)	2	2	3	4	4	5	5	6
3 • 3½ sts per inch yardage	175	250	400	450	550	650	700	800
Country Classics (B)	2	2	4	4	5	6	6	7
Lamb's Pride (B)	2	2	4	4	5	6	6	7
Lamb's Pride Superwash (B)	2	3	4	5	5	6	7	8

(Yardage and skein estimates are approximations only.)

Child Small
finished chest circumference

24"

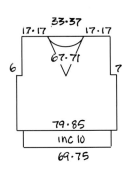 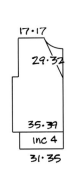

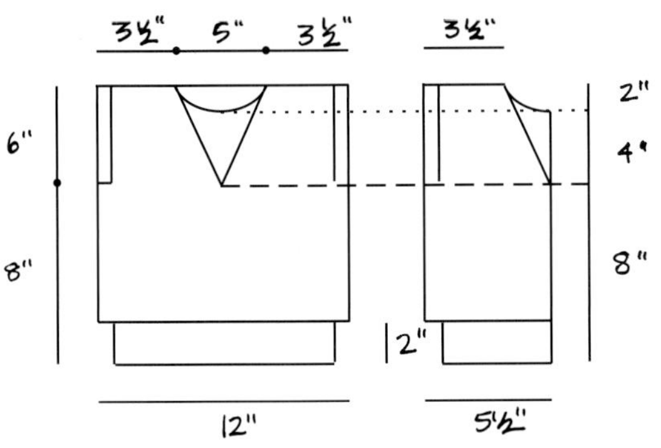

Top schematic measurements: 3½" 5" 3½" 3½" 6" 2" 4" 8" 8" 2" 12" 5½"

V   **W**

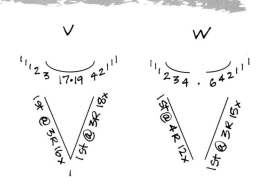

6½ · 7

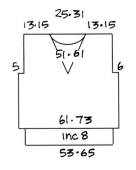 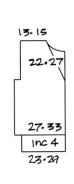

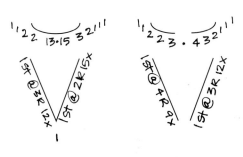

5 · 6

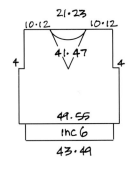 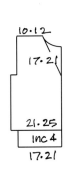

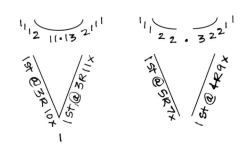

4 · 4½

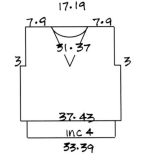 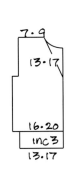

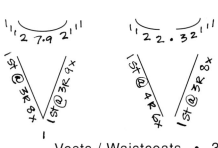

3 · 3½

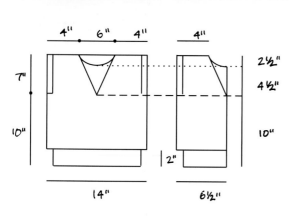

4"   6"   4"   4"

2½"

7"   4½"

10"   10"

2"

14"   6½"

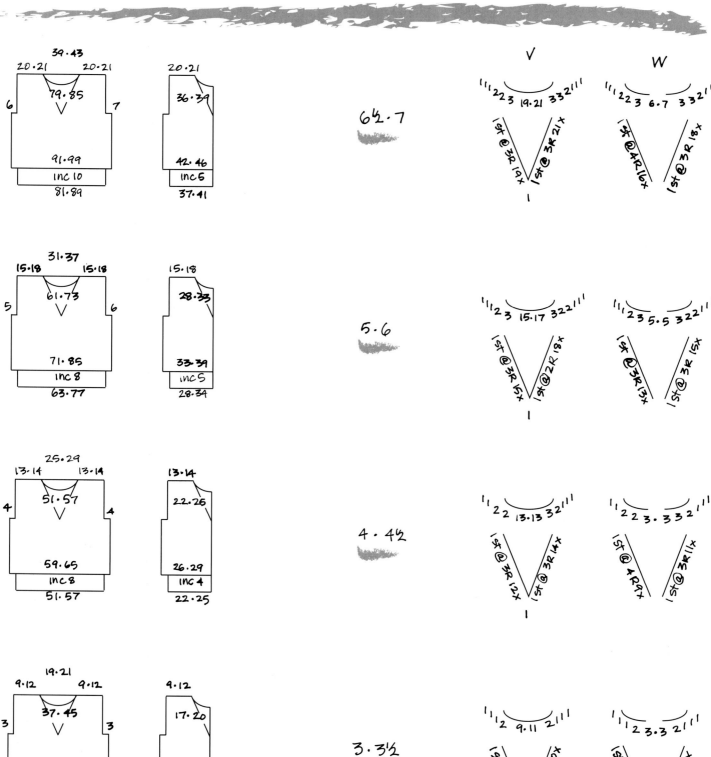

V   W

6½ · 7

39·43
20·21   20·21
6   7
79·85
V
91·99
inc 10
81·89

20·21
36·39
42·46
inc 5
37·41

¹¹₁₂₂₃ 19·21 ₃₃₂¹¹
1st @3R 19x   1st @ 3R 21x
1

¹¹₁₂₂₃ 6·7 ₃₃₂¹¹
1st @4R 16x   1st @ 3R 18x

5 · 6

31·37
15·18   15·18
5   6
61·73
V
71·85
inc 8
63·77

15·18
28·33
33·39
inc 5
28·34

¹¹₁₂₃ 15·17 ₃₂₂¹¹
1st @ 3R 15x   1st @2R 18x
1

¹¹₁₂₃ 5·5 ₃₂₂¹¹
1st @3R 13x   1st @3R 15x

4 · 4½

25·29
13·14   13·14
4   4
51·57
V
59·65
inc 8
51·57

13·14
22·26
26·29
inc 4
22·25

¹¹₁₂₂ 13·13 ₃₂¹¹
1st @ 3R 12x   1st @3R 14x
1

¹¹₁₂₂₃· ₃₃₂¹¹
1st @ 4R 9x   1st @3R 11x

3 · 3½

19·21
9·12   9·12
3   3
37·45
V
43·51
inc 6
37·45

9·12
17·20
20·23
inc 4
16·19

¹¹₁₂ 9·11 ₂¹¹
1st @3R 9x   1st @3R 10x
1

¹¹₁₂₃·3 ₂¹¹
1st @ 4R 8x   1st @4R 9x

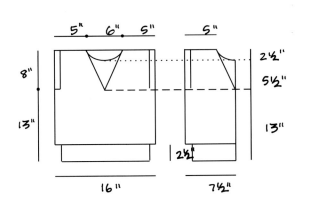

32"

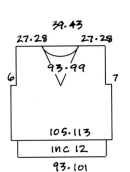

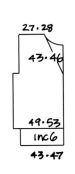

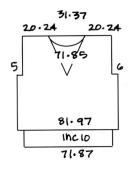

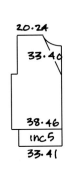

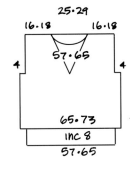

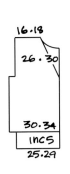

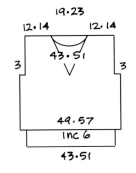

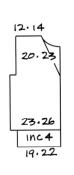

V   W

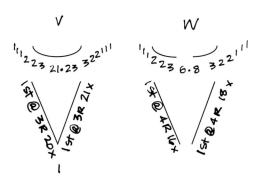

6½ . 7

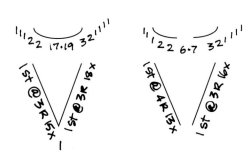

5 . 6

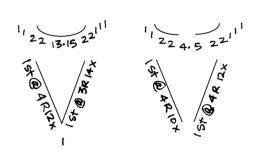

4 . 4½

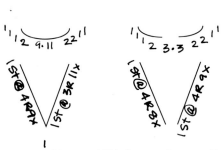

3 . 3½

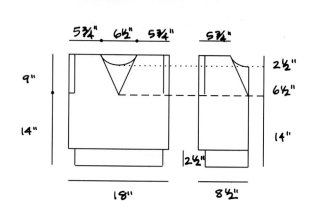

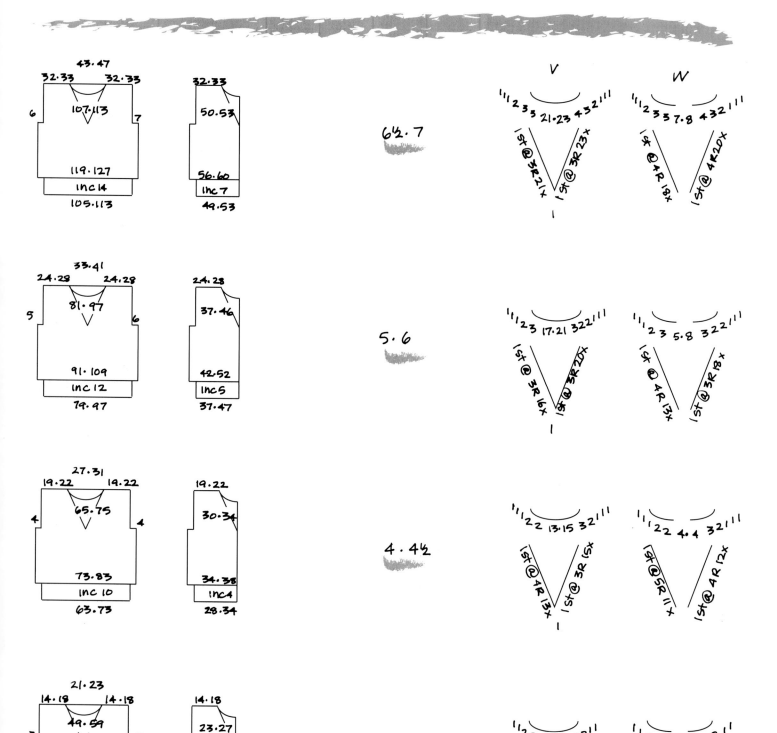

6 • Vicki Square

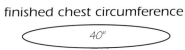
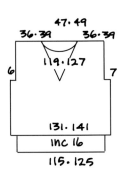

6½" 7" 6½"   6½"

10"

2½"

7½"

15"

15"

2½"

20"   9½"

V   W

47·49
36·39   36·39

119·127

6   7

131·141
inc 16
115·125

36·39

56·59

62·66
inc 7
55·59

6½·7

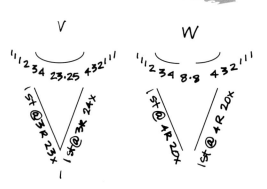
¹¹¹234 23·25 432¹¹¹   ¹¹¹234 8·8 432¹¹¹

1st @ 3R 24x   1st @ 4R 20x
1st @ 3R 23x
1
1st @ 4R 20x

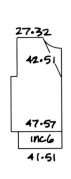

37·45
27·32   27·32

91·109

5   6

101·121
inc 14
87·107

27·32

42·51

47·57
inc 6
41·51

5·6

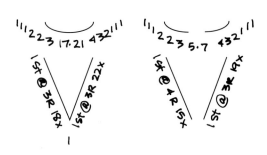
¹¹¹223 17·21 432¹¹¹   ¹¹¹223 5·7 432¹¹¹

1st @ 3R 22x   1st @ 3R 18x
1st @ 3R 18x
1
1st @ 4R 15x

29·33
22·25   22·25

73·83

4   4

81·91
inc 10
71·81

22·25

35·39

39·43
inc 4
35·39

4· 4½

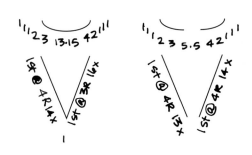
¹¹¹23 13·15 42¹¹¹   ¹¹¹23 5·5 42¹¹¹

1st @ 3R 14x   1st @ 4R 14x
1st @ 4R 14x
1
1st @ 4R 15x

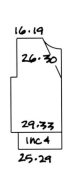

23·27
16·19   16·19

55·65

3   3

61·71
inc 8
53·63

16·19

26·30

29·33
inc 4
25·29

3· 3½

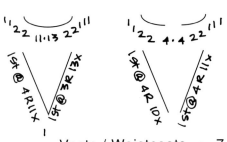
¹¹22 11·13 22¹¹   ¹¹22 4·4 22¹¹

1st @ 3R 13x   1st @ 4R 11x
1st @ 4R 11x
1
1st @ 4R 10x

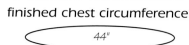
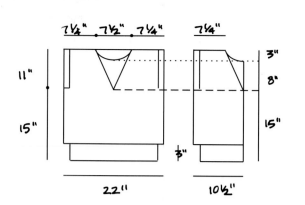

7¼" 7½" 7¼"   7¼"

11"

15"

3"

8"

15"

⅓"

22"   10½"

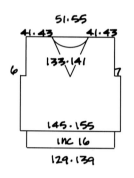

51·55

41·43   41·43

133·141

6   7

145·155

inc 16

129·139

41·43

62·67

68·74

inc 7

61·67

6½·7

V   W

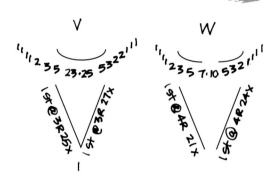

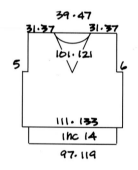

39·47

31·37   31·37

101·121

5   6

111·133

inc 14

97·119

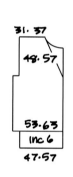

31·37

48·57

53·63

inc 6

47·57

5·6

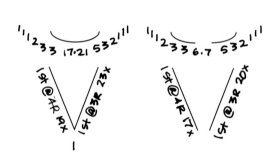

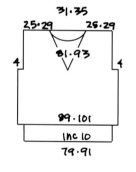

31·35

25·29   25·29

81·93

4   4

89·101

inc 10

79·91

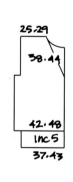

25·29

38·44

42·48

inc 5

37·43

4·4½

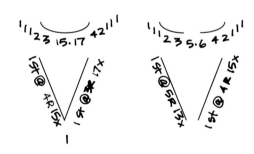

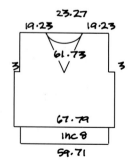

23·27

19·23   19·23

61·73

3   3

67·79

inc 8

59·71

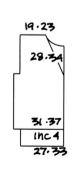

19·23

28·34

31·37

inc 4

27·33

3·3½

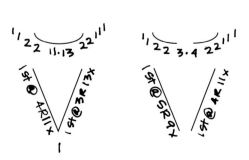

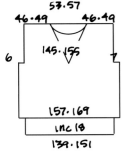

8" • 8" • 8"   8"

11½"

3"

8½"

15½"   15½"

3"

24   11½"

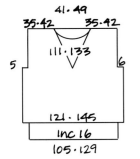

53·57
46·49   46·49
6   145·155   7
157·169
inc 18
139·151

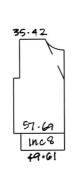

46·49
68·71
74·78
inc 9
65·69

6½·7

V
'''2 3 5   27·29   5 3 2'''
1st @ 4R 24x   1st @ 3R 28x

W
'''2 3 5   9·10   5 3 2'''
1st @ 4R 22x   1st @ 4R 24x

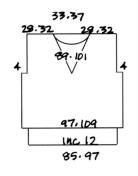

41·49
35·42   35·42
5   111·133   6
121·145
inc 16
105·129

35·42
57·69
inc 8
49·61

5·6

V
'''2 2 3   21·25   4 3 2'''
1st @ 4R 20x   1st @ 3R 24x

W
'''2 2 3   7·9   4 3 2'''
1st @ 4R 17x   1st @ 3R 21x

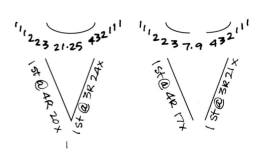

33·37
28·32   28·32
4   89·101   4
97·109
inc 12
85·97

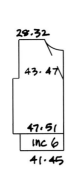

28·32
43·47
47·51
inc 6
41·45

4·4½

V
'''2 3   17·19   4 2'''
1st @ 4R 16x   1st @ 3R 18x

W
'''2 4   6·6   4 2'''
1st @ 4R 15x   1st @ 4R 15x

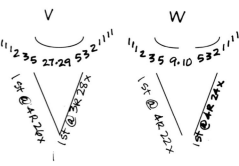

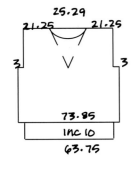

25·29
21·25   21·25
3   V   3
73·85
inc 10
63·75

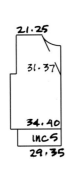

21·25
31·37
34·40
inc 5
29·35

3·3½

V
'''2 2   13·15   2 2'''
1st @ 4R 12x   1st @ 3R 14x

W
'''2 2   4·5   2 2'''
1st @ 3R 10x   1st @ 4R 12x

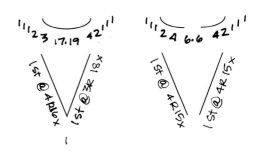

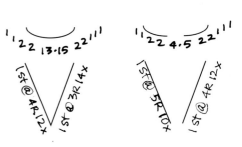

52"

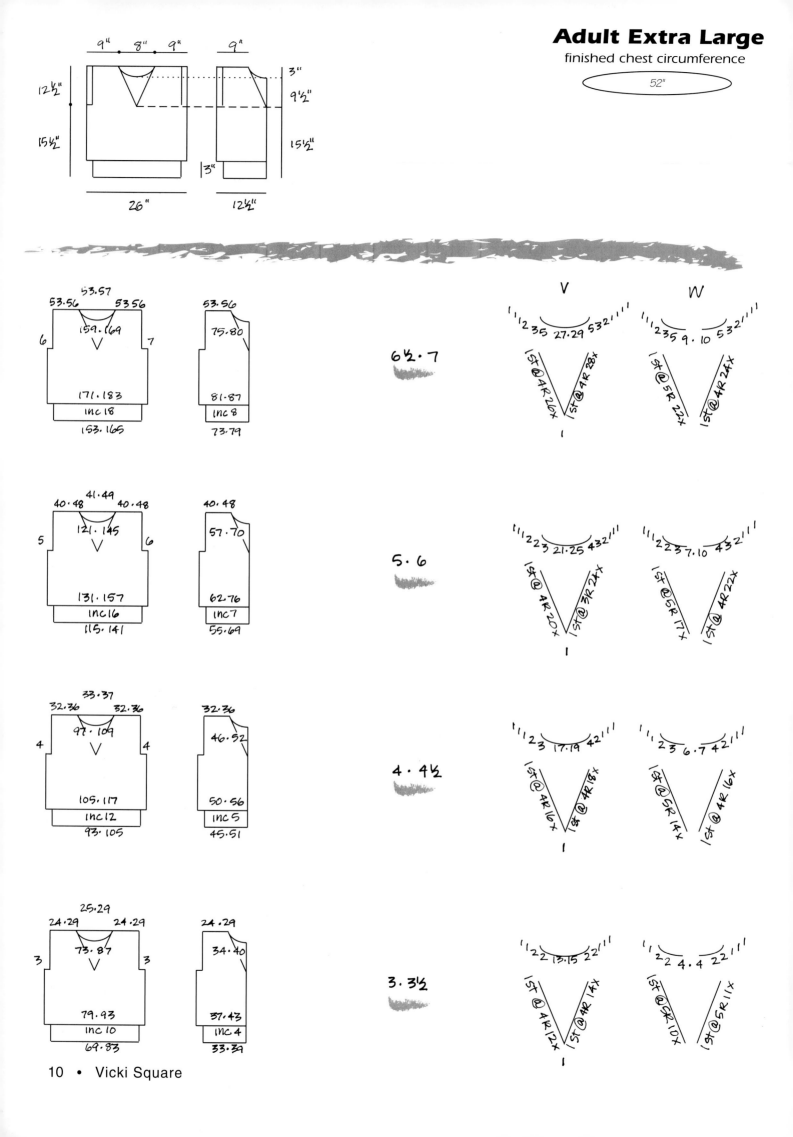

Top schematic:

9" 8" 9"   9"

12½"   3"

9½"

15½"   15½"

3"

26"   12½"

Row 1 (6½·7):

53.57
53.56   5356
159.169
6   7
171.183
inc 18
153.165

53.56
75.80
81.87
inc 8
73.79

6½·7

V
1 2 3 5 27·29 5 3 2
1st @ 4R 26x   1st @ 4R 28x
1

W
1 2 3 5 9·10 5 3 2
1st @ 5R 22x   1st @ 4R 24x

Row 2 (5·6):

41.49
40·48   40·48
121·145
5   6
131·157
inc16
115·141

40·48
57·70
62·76
inc7
55·69

5·6

1 2 2 3 21·25 4 3 2
1st @ 4R 20x   1st @ 3R 24x
1

1 2 2 3 7·10 4 3 2
1st @ 5R 17x   1st @ 4R 22x

Row 3 (4·4½):

33·37
32·36   32·36
97·109
4   4
105·117
inc12
93·105

32·36
46·52
50·56
inc 5
45·51

4·4½

1 1 2 3 17·19 4 2
1st @ 4R 16x   1st @ 4R 18x
1

1 2 3 6·7 4 2
1st @ 5R 14x   1st @ 4R 16x

Row 4 (3·3½):

25·29
24·29   24·29
73·87
3   3
79·93
inc 10
69·83

24·29
34·40
37·43
inc 4
33·39

3·3½

1 2 2 13·15 2 2
1st @ 4R 12x   1st @ 4R 14x
1

1 2 2 4·4 2 2
1st @ 5R 10x   1st @ 5R 11x

6½ • 7 sts per inch

	Child			Adult				
	S • 24"	M • 28"	L • 32"	XS • 36"	S • 40"	M • 44"	L • 48"	XL • 52"

BACK VEST/WAISTCOAT

	S • 24"	M • 28"	L • 32"	XS • 36"	S • 40"	M • 44"	L • 48"	XL • 52"
With smaller needles, cast on __ sts.	69•75	81•89	93•101	105•113	115•125	129•139	139•151	153•165
Work 1/1 rib for __ inches,	2	2	2½	2½	2½	3	3	3
increasing __ sts across last row of rib,	10	10	12	14	16	16	18	18
__ sts.	79•85	91•99	105•113	119•127	131•141	145•155	157•169	171•183
Change to larger needles and work in st st until piece meas __ inches.	8	10	13	14	15	15	15½	15½

Choose armhole style.

Straight armhole: shape notch for armhole ribbing: bind off __ sts at beg of next 2 rows. Cont even.

	S • 24"	M • 28"	L • 32"	XS • 36"	S • 40"	M • 44"	L • 48"	XL • 52"
	6•7	6•7	6•7	6•7	6•7	6•7	6•7	6•7

OR

Curved armhole: Bind off sts at each armhole edge in the foll sequence:

	S • 24"	M • 28"	L • 32"	XS • 36"	S • 40"	M • 44"	L • 48"	XL • 52"
					6 | 6	6 | 7	8 | 10	10 | 11
	| 3	3 | 4	5 | 6	6 | 6	3 | 4	4 | 4	5 | 5	6 | 6
	4 | 3	3 | 2	3 | 3	3 | 3	2 | 2	3 | 3	3 | 3	4 | 4
	2 | 2	2 | 2	2 | 2	2 | 2	2x2 | 1x3	2 | 2	2 | 2	2 | 2
	1x3 | 1x2	1x2 | 1x3	1x3 | 1x3	1x3 | 1x3	1x4 | 1x4	1x5 | 1x5	1x5 | 1x5	1x5 | 1x5

	S • 24"	M • 28"	L • 32"	XS • 36"	S • 40"	M • 44"	L • 48"	XL • 52"
Cont even until armhole meas __ inches. Place all sts on hold for later finishing.	6	7	8	9	10	11	11½	12½

FRONT VEST

Work as for back, including armhole shaping.
AT SAME TIME, choose neckline style.

V-neck: When work meas __ inches, mark center st. Knit to within 3 sts of center st, k2tog, k1. Place center st on hold, join second ball of yarn, k1, SSK, knit to end. Work each side separately, decreasing 1 st at neck edge every __ row __ times.

	S • 24"	M • 28"	L • 32"	XS • 36"	S • 40"	M • 44"	L • 48"	XL • 52"
When work meas __ inches	8	10	13	14	15	15	15½	15½
every __ row	3•3	3•3	3•3	3•3	3•3	3•3	4•3	4•4
__ times	16•18	19•21	20•21	21•23	23•24	25•27	26•28	26•28

OR

Round neck: When work meas __ inches, mark center __ sts. Knit to marker, place center sts on hold, join second ball of yarn and knit to end. Working each side separately, at neck edge every other row, bind off in foll sequence:

	S • 24"	M • 28"	L • 32"	XS • 36"	S • 40"	M • 44"	L • 48"	XL • 52"
When work meas __ inches	12	14½	18½	20½	22½	23	24	25
mark center __ sts	17•19	19•21	21•23	21•23	23•25	23•25	27•29	27•29

	S • 24"	M • 28"	L • 32"	XS • 36"	S • 40"	M • 44"	L • 48"	XL • 52"
							5	
	|	3 | 3	3 | 3	3 | 4	4 | 4	4 | 4	5 | 3	5 | 5
	3 | 4	2 | 3	2 | 2	3 | 3	3 | 3	3 | 3	3 | 3	3 | 3
	2 | 2	2 | 2	2 | 2	2 | 2	2 | 2	2 | 2	2 | 2	2 | 2
	1x3 | 1x3	1x3 | 1x3	1x3 | 1x3	1x3 | 1x3	1x3 | 1x3	1x4 | 1x3	1x3 | 1x4	1x3 | 1x4

When work meas same as back, place sts on hold for later three needle bind-off seaming.

FRONT WAISTCOAT

	S • 24"	M • 28"	L • 32"	XS • 36"	S • 40"	M • 44"	L • 48"	XL • 52"
With smaller needles, cast on __ sts.	31•35	37•41	43•47	49•53	55•59	61•67	65•69	73•79
Work 1/1 rib for __ inches,	2	2	2½	2½	2½	3	3	3
increasing __ sts across last row of rib —	4	5	6	7	7	7	9	8
__ sts.	35•39	42•46	49•53	56•60	62•66	68•74	74•78	81•87
Change to larger needles and work in st st until piece meas __ inches.	8	10	13	14	15	15	15½	15½

Work armhole as for back.
AT SAME TIME, choose neckline style.

V-neck: When work meas __ inches, dec at neck edge 1 st every __ row __ times.

	S • 24"	M • 28"	L • 32"	XS • 36"	S • 40"	M • 44"	L • 48"	XL • 52"
When work meas __ inches	8	10	13	14	15	15	15½	15½
every __ row	4•3	4•3	4•4	4•4	4•4	4•4	4•4	5•4
__ times	12•15	16•18	16•18	18•20	20•20	21•24	22•24	22•24

OR

Round neck: When work meas __ inches, at neck edge bind off in foll sequence:

	S • 24"	M • 28"	L • 32"	XS • 36"	S • 40"	M • 44"	L • 48"	XL • 52"
When work meas __ inches	12	14½	18½	20½	22½	23	24	25
		6 | 7	6 | 8	7 | 8	8 | 8	7 | 10	9 | 10	9 | 10
	4 | 6	3 | 3	3 | 3	3 | 4	4 | 4	4 | 4	5 | 5	5 | 5
	3 | 4	2 | 2	2 | 2	2 | 3	3 | 3	3 | 3	3 | 3	3 | 3
	2 | 2	2 | 2	2 | 2	2 | 2	2 | 2	2 | 2	2 | 2	2 | 2
	1x3 | 1x3	1x3 | 1x3	1x3 | 1x3	1x3 | 1x3	1x3 | 1x3	1x4 | 1x4	1x3 | 1x4	1x3 | 1x4

Cont even until piece meas same as back. Place sts on hold for later three needle bind-off seaming.

	6½ • 7 sts per inch	Child			Adult				
		S • 24"	M • 28"	L • 32"	XS • 36"	S • 40"	M • 44"	L • 48"	XL • 52"

FINISHING
Work three needle bind off seaming for shoulders, leaving back neck sts on hold. For all the following ribbed borders, use smaller circular or dp needles and pick up sts from right side.

VEST v-neck border: Beg at left shoulder, pick up __ sts along left front neck edge, place marker, knit center st through back of loop, place marker, pick up sts along right front neck edge as for left front, knit across back neck sts — __ sts. Work 1/1 rib for one inch, decreasing 1 st before first marker (SSK) and 1 st after second marker (K 2 tog) every other row. Bind off loosely in pattern.

	S • 24"	M • 28"	L • 32"	XS • 36"	S • 40"	M • 44"	L • 48"	XL • 52"
	42·45	49·53	55·60	62·67	68·74	75·81	79·85	85·92
	118·128	138·150	152·164	162·182	184·198	202·218	212·228	224·242

VEST round neck border: Beg at left shoulder, pick up __ sts along left front neck curve, knit across center front sts, pick up sts along right front neck curve as for left front, knit across back neck sts — __ sts. Work 1/1 rib for one inch. Bind off loosely in pattern.

	S • 24"	M • 28"	L • 32"	XS • 36"	S • 40"	M • 44"	L • 48"	XL • 52"
	16·17	21·22	21·22	23·24	24·26	27·29	27·29	27·29
	82·90	100·108	100·108	110·118	118·126	128·138	134·144	134·144

WAISTCOAT v-neck border: Mark placement for buttonholes, with first at beg of v-neck shaping, the last ¾ inch from lower edge, and __ others spaced evenly between. Mark on right front for female, and on left front for male. Beg at lower right front edge, pick up __ sts along center front edge, __ sts along right front v-neck, knit across back neck sts, along left front v-neck and left center front edge pick up sts as for right front — __ sts.
NOTE: The border may be worked in two parts, dividing and seaming at left shoulder seam.
Work 1/1 rib for one inch, bind off loosely in pattern.
AT SAME TIME, when border meas half or total width, work buttonholes at markers. (I like the eyelet buttonhole for bulky yarns, and the one row buttonhole for worsted and finer yarns.)

	S • 24"	M • 28"	L • 32"	XS • 36"	S • 40"	M • 44"	L • 48"	XL • 52"
	1	2	3	3	3	3	4	4
	52·56	65·70	85·91	91·98	98·105	98·105	101·109	101·109
	42·45	49·53	55·59	61·66	68·74	75·80	78·84	85·91
	221·239	267·289	321·343	347·375	379·407	397·425	411·443	425·457

WAISTCOAT round neck border: Beg at center front right neck edge, pick up __ sts along right neck curve, knit back neck sts, pick up sts along left neck curve as for right neck. Work 1/1 rib for one inch. Bind off loosely in pattern. Mark placement for buttonholes, with the first ½ inch from top edge, the last ¾ inch from lower edge, and __ others spaced evenly between. Mark on right front for female, and on left front for male. Pick up __ sts along each center front edge and work 1/1 rib for one inch. Bind off loosely in patt.
AT SAME TIME, when buttonhole border meas half of total width, work buttonholes at markers. (Eyelet for bulky, one-row buttonhole for worsed and finer.)

	S • 24"	M • 28"	L • 32"	XS • 36"	S • 40"	M • 44"	L • 48"	XL • 52"
	20·22	25·27	25·27	28·30	31·33	33·36	36·39	40·43
	73·81	89·97	89·97	99·107	109·115	117·127	125·135	133·143
	3	3	4	5	6	6	6	6
	85·91	101·109	127·137	139·151	153·165	157·167	163·175	169·183

VEST/WAISTCOAT armhole border:
Notched armhole: Pick up __ sts evenly along front and back armhole selvage edge only. Work 1/1 rib until even with side edge. Bind off loosely in patt. Seam selvage edge of rib to bound off edge of notched armhole. Sew side seam.
Curved armhole: Pick up __ sts evenly along front and back armhole edge. To work in the round, sew side seam first. Work 1/1 rib for one inch. Bind off loosely in patt. If knit flat in rows, sew side seam now. Sew on buttons. Block, using the wet towel method.

	S • 24"	M • 28"	L • 32"	XS • 36"	S • 40"	M • 44"	L • 48"	XL • 52"
	78·84	90·98	104·112	116·126	130·140	142·154	148·160	162·175
	88·94	107·115	120·130	130·140	150·161	162·175	175·189	195·210

(spiral logo) *5 • 6 sts per inch*

	Child			Adult				
	S • 24"	M • 28"	L • 32"	XS • 36"	S • 40"	M • 44"	L • 48"	XL • 52"

BACK VEST/WAISTCOAT

With smaller needles, cast on __ sts.
Work 1/1 rib for __ inches,
increasing __ sts across last row of rib,
__ sts.
Change to larger needles and work in st st until piece meas __ inches.
Choose armhole style.
Straight armhole: shape notch for armhole ribbing: bind off __ sts at beg of next 2 rows. Cont even.
OR
Curved armhole: Bind off sts at each armhole edge in the foll sequence:

	S • 24"	M • 28"	L • 32"	XS • 36"	S • 40"	M • 44"	L • 48"	XL • 52"
cast on	53·65	63·77	71·87	79·97	87·107	97·119	105·129	115·141
rib inches	2	2	2½	2½	2½	3	3	3
increasing sts	8	8	10	12	14	14	16	16
sts	61·73	71·85	81·97	91·109	101·121	111·133	121·145	131·157
piece meas inches	8	10	13	14	15	15	15½	15½
straight bind off	5·6	5·6	5·6	5·6	5·6	5·6	5·6	5·6
curved seq 1						/ 7	6 / 7	7 / 8
curved seq 2			3 / 4	3 / 4	5 / 6	6 / 4	4 / 4	4 / 6
curved seq 3	3 / 4	3 / 4	3 / 3	3 / 3	3 / 4	4 / 2	2 / 3	3 / 4
curved seq 4	2 / 2	2 / 2	2 / 2	2 / 2	2 / 2	2 / 2	2 / 2	2 / 2
curved seq 5	1x2 / 1x3	1x3 / 1x3	1x2 / 1x3	1x2 / 1x3	1x3 / 1x3	1x3 / 1x4	1x4 / 1x5	1x4 / 1x4

Cont even until armhole meas __ inches. Place all sts on hold for later finishing.

	S • 24"	M • 28"	L • 32"	XS • 36"	S • 40"	M • 44"	L • 48"	XL • 52"
armhole meas inches	6	7	8	9	10	11	11½	12½

FRONT VEST

Work as for back, including armhole shaping.
AT SAME TIME, choose neckline style.
V-neck: When work meas __ inches, mark center st. Knit to within 3 sts of center st, k2tog, k1. Place center st on hold, join second ball of yarn, k1, SSK, knit to end. Work each side separately, decreasing 1 st at neck edge every __ row __ times.
OR
Round neck: When work meas __ inches, mark center __ sts. Knit to marker, place center sts on hold, join second ball of yarn and knit to end. Working each side separately, at neck edge every other row, bind off in foll sequence:

	S • 24"	M • 28"	L • 32"	XS • 36"	S • 40"	M • 44"	L • 48"	XL • 52"
V-neck work meas inches	8	10	13	14	15	15	15½	15½
dec every __ row	3·2	3·2	3·3	3·3	3·3	4·3	4·3	4·3
__ times	12·15	15·18	15·18	16·20	18·22	19·23	20·24	20·24
Round neck work meas inches	12	14½	18½	20½	22½	23	24	25
center __ sts	13·15	15·17	17·19	17·21	17·21	17·21	21·25	21·25

Round neck bind-off sequence (values shown 5 sts/inch / 6 sts/inch, top to bottom):
- S • 24": 2 / 3, 2 / 2, 1x2 / 1x3
- M • 28": (top / 3), 3 / 2, 2 / 2, 1x3 / 1x3
- L • 32": 2 / 3, 2 / 2, 1x3 / 1x4
- XS • 36": 3 / 2, 2 / 2, 1x3 / 1x3
- S • 40": 3 / 3, 2 / 2, 2 / 2, 1x3 / 1x3
- M • 44": 3 / 4, 2 / 3, 2 / 2, 1x3 / 1x3
- L • 48": 3 / 4, 2 / 3, 2 / 2, 1x3 / 1x3
- XL • 52": 3 / 4, 2 / 3, 2 / 2, 1x3 / 1x3

When work meas same as back, place sts on hold for later three needle bind-off seaming.

FRONT WAISTCOAT

With smaller needles, cast on __ sts.
Work 1/1 rib for __ inches,
increasing __ sts across last row of rib —
__ sts.
Change to larger needles and work in st st until piece meas __ inches.
Work armhole as for back.
AT SAME TIME, choose neckline style.
V-neck: When work meas __ inches, dec at neck edge 1 st every __ row __ times.
OR
Round neck: When work meas __ inches, at neck edge bind off in foll sequence:

	S • 24"	M • 28"	L • 32"	XS • 36"	S • 40"	M • 44"	L • 48"	XL • 52"
cast on	23·29	28·34	33·41	37·47	41·51	47·57	49·61	55·69
rib inches	2	2	2½	2½	2½	3	3	3
increasing sts	4	5	5	5	6	6	8	7
sts	27·33	33·39	38·46	42·52	47·57	53·63	57·69	62·76
piece meas inches	8	10	13	14	15	15	15½	15½
V-neck work meas inches	8	10	13	14	15	15	15½	15½
dec 1 st every __ row	4·3	3·3	4·3	4·3	4·3	4·3	4·3	5·4
__ times	9·12	13·15	13·16	13·18	15·19	17·20	17·21	17·22
Round neck work meas inches	12	14½	18½	20½	22½	23	24	25

Round neck bind-off sequence (values shown 5 sts/inch / 6 sts/inch, top to bottom):
- S • 24": 3 / 4, 2 / 3, 2 / 2, 1x2 / 1x3
- M • 28": (top / 5), 5 / 3, 3 / 2, 2 / 2, 1x3 / 1x3
- L • 32": 6 / 7, 2 / 3, 2 / 2, 1x3 / 1x4
- XS • 36": 5 / 3, 3 / 2, 2 / 2, 1x3 / 1x3
- S • 40": (top / 8), 5 / 3, 3 / 2, 2 / 2, 1x3 / 1x3
- M • 44": 6 / 7, 3 / 5, 2 / 3, 2 / 2, 1x3 / 1x3
- L • 48": 7 / 9, 3 / 4, 2 / 3, 2 / 2, 1x3 / 1x3
- XL • 52": 7 / 10, 3 / 4, 2 / 3, 2 / 2, 1x3 / 1x3

Cont even until piece meas same as back. Place sts on hold for later three needle bind-off seaming.

	S • 24"	M • 28"	L • 32"	XS • 36"	S • 40"	M • 44"	L • 48"	XL • 52"
FINISHING Work three needle bind off seaming for shoulders, leaving back neck sts on hold. For all the following ribbed borders, use smaller circular or dp needles and pick up sts from right side.								
VEST v-neck border: Beg at left shoulder, pick up __ sts along left front neck edge, place marker, knit center st through back of loop, place marker, pick up sts along right front neck edge as for left front, knit across back neck sts — __ sts. Work 1/1 rib for one inch, decreasing 1 st before first marker (SSK) and 1 st after second marker (k 2 tog) every other row. Bind off loosely in pattern.	32·39 90·110	38·46 108·130	43·51 118·140	48·57 130·156	53·63 144·172	58·70 156·188	61·73 164·196	66·79 174·208
VEST round neck border: Beg at left shoulder, pick up __ sts along left front neck curve, knit across center front sts, pick up sts along right front neck curve as for left front, knit across back neck sts— __ sts. Work 1/1 rib for one inch. Bind off loosely in pattern.	13·16 64·78	16·20 78·94	16·20 78·94	17·20 84·102	19·22 92·110	21·25 98·118	21·25 104·124	21·25 104·124
WAISTCOAT v-neck border: Mark placement for buttonholes, with first at beg of v-neck shaping, the last 3/4 inch from lower edge, and __ others spaced evenly between. Mark on right front for female, and on left front for male. Beg at lower right front edge, pick up __ sts along center front edge, __ sts along right front v-neck, knit across back neck sts, along left front v-neck and left center front edge pick up sts as for right front— __ sts. NOTE: The border may be worked in two parts, dividing and seaming at left shoulder seam. Work 1/1 rib for one inch, bind off loosely in pattern. AT SAME TIME, when border meas half of total width, work buttonholes at markers. (I like the eyelet buttonhole for bulky yarns, and the one row buttonhole for worsted and finer yarns.)	1 40·48 32·39 169·205	2 50·60 38·45 207·247	3 65·78 42·51 245·295	3 70·84 47·57 267·323	3 75·90 53·63 293·351	3 75·90 58·69 305·365	4 78·93 60·72 317·379	4 78·93 65·78 327·391
WAISTCOAT round neck border: Beg at center front right neck edge, pick up __ sts along right neck curve, knit back neck sts, pick up sts along left neck curve as for right neck __ sts. Work 1/1 rib for one inch. Bind off loosely in pattern. Mark placement for buttonholes, with the first ½ inch from top edge, the last ¾ inch from lower edge, and __ others spaced evenly between. Mark on right front for female, and on left front for male. Pick up __ sts along each center front edge and work 1/1 rib for one inch. Bind off loosely in patt. AT SAME TIME, when buttonhole border meas half of total width, work buttonholes at markers. (Eyelet for bulky, one-row buttonhole for worsted and finer.)	16·19 56·69 3 65·78	20·23 71·83 3 77·93	20·23 71·83 4 97·117	22·26 77·93 5 107·129	24·28 85·101 6 117·141	26·31 91·109 6 121·145	28·33 97·115 6 125·151	31·37 103·123 6 131·157
VEST/WAISTCOAT armhole border: **Notched** armhole: Pick up __ sts evenly along front and back armhole selvage edge only. Work 1/1 rib until even with side edge. Bind off loosely in patt. Seam selvage edge of rib to bound off edge of notched armhole. Sew side seam. **Curved** armhole: Pick up __ sts evenly along front and back armhole edge. To work in the round, sew side seam first. Work 1/1 rib for one inch. Bind off loosely in patt. If knit flat in rows, sew side seam now. Sew on buttons. Block, using the wet towel method.	60·72 67·81	70·84 82·99	80·96 92·111	90·108 100·120	100·120 115·138	110·132 125·150	114·138 135·162	125·150 150·180

	Child			Adult				
	S • 24"	M • 28"	L • 32"	XS • 36"	S • 40"	M • 44"	L • 48"	XL • 52"

BACK VEST/WAISTCOAT

	S • 24"	M • 28"	L • 32"	XS • 36"	S • 40"	M • 44"	L • 48"	XL • 52"
With smaller needles, cast on __ sts.	43•49	51•57	57•65	63•73	71•81	79•91	85•97	93•105
Work 1/1 rib for __ inches,	2	2	2½	2½	2½	3	3	3
increasing __ sts across last row of rib,	6	8	8	10	10	10	12	12
__ sts.	49•55	59•65	65•73	73•83	81•91	89•101	97•109	105•117
Change to larger needles and work in st st until piece meas __ inches.	8	10	13	14	15	15	15½	15½

Choose armhole style.

Straight armhole: shape notch for armhole ribbing: bind off __ sts at beg of next 2 rows. Cont even.

	S • 24"	M • 28"	L • 32"	XS • 36"	S • 40"	M • 44"	L • 48"	XL • 52"
	4•4	4•4	4•4	4•4	4•4	4•4	4•4	4•4

OR

Curved armhole: Bind off sts at each armhole edge in the foll sequence:

	S • 24"	M • 28"	L • 32"	XS • 36"	S • 40"	M • 44"	L • 48"	XL • 52"
				⎪ 3	3 ⎪ 4	4 ⎪ 6	6 ⎪ 6	6 ⎪ (top 6)
	2 ⎪ 2	3 ⎪ 3	3 ⎪ 4	3 ⎪ 3	3 ⎪ 3	3 ⎪ 4	3 ⎪ 4	4 ⎪ 2
	2 ⎪ 2	2 ⎪ 2	2 ⎪ 2	2 ⎪ 2	2 ⎪ 2	2 ⎪ 2	2 ⎪ 2	2 ⎪ 2
	1x2 ⎪ 1x2	1x2 ⎪ 1x3	1x2 ⎪ 1x3	1x3 ⎪ 1x2	1x2 ⎪ 1x3	1x3 ⎪ 1x3	1x3 ⎪ 1x4	1x4 ⎪ 1x4

	S • 24"	M • 28"	L • 32"	XS • 36"	S • 40"	M • 44"	L • 48"	XL • 52"
Cont even until armhole meas __ inches. Place all sts on hold for later finishing.	6	7	8	9	10	11	11½	12½

FRONT VEST

Work as for back, including armhole shaping.

AT SAME TIME, choose neckline style.

V-neck: When work meas __ inches, mark center st. Knit to within 3 sts of center st, k2tog, k1. Place center st on hold, join second ball of yarn, k1, SSK, knit to end. Work each side separately, decreasing 1 st at neck edge every __ row __ times.

	S • 24"	M • 28"	L • 32"	XS • 36"	S • 40"	M • 44"	L • 48"	XL • 52"
When work meas __ inches	8	10	13	14	15	15	15½	15½
every __ row	3•3	3•3	4•3	4•3	4•3	4•3	4•3	4•4
__ times.	10•11	12•14	12•14	13•15	14•16	15•17	16•18	16•18

OR

Round neck: When work meas __ inches, mark center __ sts. Knit to marker, place center sts on hold, join second ball of yarn and knit to end. Working each side separately, at neck edge every other row, bind off in foll sequence:

	S • 24"	M • 28"	L • 32"	XS • 36"	S • 40"	M • 44"	L • 48"	XL • 52"
When work meas __ inches	12	14½	18½	20½	22½	23	24	25
mark center __ sts	11•13	13•13	13•15	13•15	13•15	15•17	17•19	17•19

	S • 24"	M • 28"	L • 32"	XS • 36"	S • 40"	M • 44"	L • 48"	XL • 52"
		2 ⎪ 3	2 ⎪ 2	2 ⎪ 2	2 ⎪ 3	3 ⎪ 4	3 ⎪ 4	3 ⎪ 4
	2 ⎪ 2	2 ⎪ 2	2 ⎪ 2	2 ⎪ 2	2 ⎪ 2	2 ⎪ 2	2 ⎪ 2	2 ⎪ 2
	1x3 ⎪ 1x3	1x2 ⎪ 1x3	1x2 ⎪ 1x3	1x2 ⎪ 1x3	1x3 ⎪ 1x3	1x3 ⎪ 1x3	1x3 ⎪ 1x3	1x3 ⎪ 1x3

When work meas same as back, place sts on hold for later three needle bind-off seaming.

FRONT WAISTCOAT

	S • 24"	M • 28"	L • 32"	XS • 36"	S • 40"	M • 44"	L • 48"	XL • 52"
With smaller needles, cast on __ sts.	17•21	22•25	25•29	30•34	35•39	37•43	41•45	45•51
Work 1/1 rib for __ inches,	2	2	2½	2½	2½	3	3	3
increasing __ sts across last row of rib —	4	4	5	4	4	5	6	5
__ sts.	21•25	26•29	30•34	34•38	39•43	42•48	47•51	50•56
Change to larger needles and work in st st until piece meas __ inches.	8	10	13	14	15	15	15½	15½

Work armhole as for back.

AT SAME TIME, choose neckline style.

V-neck: When work meas __ inches, dec at neck edge 1 st every __ row __ times.

	S • 24"	M • 28"	L • 32"	XS • 36"	S • 40"	M • 44"	L • 48"	XL • 52"
When work meas __ inches	8	10	13	14	15	15	15½	15½
1 st every __ row	4•4	4•3	4•4	5•4	4•4	5•4	4•4	5•4
__ times.	7•9	9•11	10•12	11•12	13•14	13•15	15•15	14•16

OR

Round neck: When work meas __ inches, at neck edge bind off in foll sequence:

	S • 24"	M • 28"	L • 32"	XS • 36"	S • 40"	M • 44"	L • 48"	XL • 52"
When work meas __ inches	12	14 1/2	18½	20½	22½	23	24	25

	S • 24"	M • 28"	L • 32"	XS • 36"	S • 40"	M • 44"	L • 48"	XL • 52"
	⎪ 3	3 ⎪ 3	4 ⎪ 5	4 ⎪ 4	5 ⎪ 5	5 ⎪ 6	6 ⎪ 6	6 ⎪ 7
	2 ⎪ 2	2 ⎪ 3	2 ⎪ 2	2 ⎪ 3	3 ⎪ 4	3 ⎪ 4	4 ⎪ 4	3 ⎪ 4
	2 ⎪ 2	2 ⎪ 2	2 ⎪ 2	2 ⎪ 2	2 ⎪ 2	2 ⎪ 2	2 ⎪ 2	2 ⎪ 2
	1x3 ⎪ 1x2	1x2 ⎪ 1x3	1x2 ⎪ 1x2	1x3 ⎪ 1x3	1x3 ⎪ 1x3	1x3 ⎪ 1x3	1x3 ⎪ 1x3	1x3 ⎪ 1x3

Cont even until piece meas same as back. Place sts on hold for later three needle bind-off seaming.

	Child			Adult				
4 • 4½ sts per inch	S • 24"	M • 28"	L • 32"	XS • 36"	S • 40"	M • 44"	L • 48"	XL • 52"

FINISHING

Work three needle bind off seaming for shoulders, leaving back neck sts on hold. For all the following ribbed borders, use smaller circular or dp needles and pick up sts from right side.

	Child			Adult				
	S • 24"	M • 28"	L • 32"	XS • 36"	S • 40"	M • 44"	L • 48"	XL • 52"
VEST v-neck border: Beg at left shoulder, pick up __ sts along left front neck edge, place marker, knit center st through back of loop, place marker, pick up sts along right front neck edge as for left front, knit across back neck sts — __ sts. Work 1/1 rib for one inch, decreasing 1 st before first marker (SSK) and 1 st after second marker (k 2 tog) every other row. Bind off loosely in pattern.	26•29	30•34	34•38	38•43	42•47	46•52	48•54	52•59
	74•82	86•98	94•106	104•118	114•128	124•140	130•146	138•156
VEST round neck border: Beg at left shoulder, pick up __ sts along left front neck curve, knit across center front sts, pick up sts along right front neck curve as for left front, knit across back neck sts — __ sts. Work 1/1 rib for one inch. Bind off loosely in pattern.	10•11	12•15	12•15	14•15	15•17	16•16	17•19	17•19
	52•58	62•72	62•72	68•76	72•82	78•88	84•94	84•94
WAISTCOAT v-neck border: Mark placement for buttonholes, with first at beg of v-neck shaping, the last 3/4 inch from lower edge, and __ others spaced evenly between. Mark on right front for female, and on left front for male. Beg at lower right front edge, pick up __ sts along center front edge, __ sts along right front v-neck, knit across back neck sts, along left front v-neck and left center front edge pick up sts as for right front — __ sts. *NOTE: The border may be worked in two parts, dividing and seaming at left shoulder seam.* Work 1/1 rib for one inch, bind off loosely in pattern. **AT SAME TIME,** when border meas half of total width, work buttonholes at markers. (I like the eyelet buttonhole for bulky yarns, and the one row buttonhole for worsted and finer yarns.)	1	2	3	3	3	3	4	4
	32•36	40•45	52•59	56•63	60•68	60•68	62•70	62•70
	26•29	30•34	34•38	38•42	42•47	42•52	48•54	52•58
	137•153	165•183	197•223	215•241	233•263	241•275	253•285	261•293
WAISTCOAT round neck border: Beg at center front right neck edge, pick up __ sts along right neck curve, knit back neck sts, pick up sts along left neck curve as for right neck. Work 1/1 rib for one inch. Bind off loosely in pattern. Mark placement for buttonholes, with the first 1/2 inch from top edge, the last 3/4 inch from lower edge, and __ others spaced evenly between. Mark on right front for female, and on left front for male. Pick up __ sts along each center front edge and work 1/1 rib for one inch. Bind off loosely in patt. **AT SAME TIME,** when buttonhole border meas half of total width, work buttonholes at markers. (Eyelet for bulky, one-row buttonhole for worsted and finer.)	13•14	16•18	16•18	18•19	19•21	20•23	22•25	25•28
	47•51	57•65	57•65	63•69	67•75	71•81	77•87	83•93
	3	3	4	5	6	6	6	6
	51•59	61•69	77•87	87•97	95•105	97•109	101•113	105•117
VEST/WAISTCOAT armhole border: Notched armhole: Pick up __ sts evenly along front and back armhole selvage edge only. Work 1/1 rib until even with side edge. Bind off loosely in patt. Seam selvage edge of rib to bound off edge of notched armhole. Sew side seam.	48•54	56•62	64•72	72•80	80•90	88•98	92•103	100•112
Curved armhole: Pick up __ sts evenly along front and back armhole edge. To work in the round, sew side seam first. Work 1/1 rib for one inch. Bind off loosely in patt. If knit flat in rows, sew side seam now. Sew on buttons. Block, using the wet towel method.	54•61	66•77	74•83	80•90	92•103	100•112	108•121	120•135

3 • 3½ sts per inch

	Child			Adult				
	S • 24"	M • 28"	L • 32"	XS • 36"	S • 40"	M • 44"	L • 48"	XL • 52"
BACK VEST/WAISTCOAT								
With smaller needles, cast on __ sts.	33·39	37·45	43·51	47·57	53·63	59·71	63·75	69·83
Work 1/1 rib for __ inches,	2	2	2½	2½	2½	3	3	3
increasing __ sts across last row of rib,	4	6	6	8	8	8	10	10
__ sts.	37·43	43·51	49·57	55·65	61·71	67·79	73·85	79·93
Change to larger needles and work in st st until piece meas __ inches.	8	10	13	14	15	15	15½	15½
Choose armhole style. **Straight** armhole: shape notch for armhole ribbing: bind off __ sts at beg of next 2 rows. Cont even. OR	3·3	3·3	3·3	3·3	3·3	3·3	3·3	3·3
Curved armhole: Bind off sts at each armhole edge in the foll sequence:	2 / 1x3 · 2 / 1x3	2 / 1x3 · 2 / 2 / 1x2	2 / 2 / 1x3 · 3 / 2 / 1x2	2 / 2 / 1x2 · 3 / 2 / 1x3	3 / 2 / 1x2 · 4 / 2 / 1x3	4 / 2 / 1x3 · 4 / 2 / 2 / 1x3	4 / 3 / 2 / 1x2 · 5 / 3 / 2 / 1x3	4 / 3 / 2 / 1x3 · 6 / 4 / 2 / 1x3
Cont even until armhole meas __ inches. Place all sts on hold for later finishing.	6	7	8	9	10	11	11½	12½
FRONT VEST Work as for back, including armhole shaping. **AT SAME TIME, choose neckline style.** **V-neck:** When work meas __ inches, mark center st. Knit to within 3 sts of center st, k2tog, k1. Place center st on hold, join second ball of yarn, k1, SSK, knit to end. Work each side separately, decreasing	8	10	13	14	15	15	15½	15½
1 st at neck edge every __ row	3·3	3·3	4·3	4·3	4·3	4·3	4·3	4·4
__ times. OR	8·9	9·10	9·11	10·11	11·13	11·13	12·14	12·14
Round neck: When work meas __ inches, mark	12	14½	18½	20½	22½	23	24	25
center __ sts. Knit to marker, place center sts on hold, join second ball of yarn and knit to end. Working each side separately, at neck edge every other row, bind off in foll sequence:	2 / 1x3 · 2 / 1x3	2 / 1x3 · 2 / 1x3	2 / 1x3 · 2 / 2 / 1x2	2 / 2 / 1x2 · 2 / 2 / 1x2	2 / 2 / 1x2 · 2 / 2 / 1x2	2 / 2 / 1x2 · 2 / 2 / 1x3	2 / 2 / 1x2 · 2 / 2 / 1x3	2 / 2 / 1x2 · 2 / 2 / 1x3
center __ sts (round neck mark)	7·9	9·11	9·11	9·11	11·13	11·13	13·15	13·15
When work meas same as back, place sts on hold for later three needle bind-off seaming.								
FRONT WAISTCOAT With smaller needles, cast on __ sts.	13·17	16·19	19·22	23·27	25·29	27·33	29·35	33·39
Work 1/1 rib for __ inches,	2	2	2½	2½	2½	3	3	3
increasing __ sts across last row of rib —	3	4	4	3	4	4	5	4
__ sts.	16·20	20·23	23·26	26·30	29·33	31·37	34·40	37·43
Change to larger needles and work in st st until piece meas __ inches. Work armhole as for back. **AT SAME TIME, choose neckline style.** **V-neck:** When work meas __ inches, dec at neck	8	10	13	14	15	15	15½	15½
V-neck work meas __ inches	8	10	13	14	15	15	15½	15½
edge 1 st every __ row	4·3	4·4	4·4	4·4	4·4	5·4	5·4	5·5
__ times. OR	6·8	8·8	8·9	9·9	10·11	9·11	10·12	10·11
Round neck: When work meas __ inches, at neck	12	14½	18½	20½	22½	23	24	25
edge bind off in foll sequence:	2 / 2 / 1x2 · 3 / 2 / 1x3	3 / 2 / 1x3 · 3 / 2 / 1x3	3 / 2 / 1x3 · 3 / 2 / 2 / 1x2	3 / 2 / 2 / 1x2 · 3 / 2 / 2 / 1x2	4 / 2 / 2 / 1x2 · 4 / 2 / 2 / 1x2	3 / 2 / 2 / 1x2 · 4 / 2 / 2 / 1x3	4 / 2 / 2 / 1x2 · 5 / 2 / 2 / 1x3	4 / 2 / 2 / 1x2 · 4 / 2 / 2 / 1x3
Cont even until piece meas same as back. Place sts on hold for later three needle bind-off seaming.								

◉ 3 • 3½ sts per inch	Child			Adult				
	S • 24"	M • 28"	L • 32"	XS • 36"	S • 40"	M • 44"	L • 48"	XL • 52"

FINISHING
Work three needle bind off seaming for shoulders, leaving back neck sts on hold. For all the following ribbed borders, use smaller circular or dp needles and pick up sts from right side.

VEST v-neck border: Beg at left shoulder, pick up __ sts along left front neck edge, place marker, knit center st through back of loop, place marker, pick up sts along right front neck edge as for left front, knit across back neck sts — __ sts. Work 1/1 rib for one inch, decreasing 1 st before first marker (SSK) and 1 st after second marker (k 2 tog) every other row. Bind off loosely in pattern.

	S • 24"	M • 28"	L • 32"	XS • 36"	S • 40"	M • 44"	L • 48"	XL • 52"
	19·23	23·27	26·30	29·33	32·37	35·41	36·42	39·46
	56·66	66·76	72·84	80·90	88·102	94·110	98·114	104·122

VEST round neck border: Beg at left shoulder, pick up __ sts along left front neck curve, knit across center front sts, pick up sts along right front neck curve as for left front, knit across back neck sts— __ sts. Work 1/1 rib for one inch. Bind off loosely in pattern.

	S • 24"	M • 28"	L • 32"	XS • 36"	S • 40"	M • 44"	L • 48"	XL • 52"
	8·9	10·11	10·11	11·12	11·13	12·14	12·14	12·14
	40·46	48·54	48·54	52·58	56·66	58·68	62·72	62·72

WAISTCOAT v-neck border: Mark placement for buttonholes, with first at beg of v-neck shaping, the last 3/4 inch from lower edge, and __ others spaced evenly between. Mark on right front for female, and on left front for male. Beg at lower right front edge, pick up __ sts along center front edge, __ sts along right front v-neck, knit across back neck sts, along left front v-neck and left center front edge pick up sts as for right front — __ sts.
NOTE: The border may be worked in two parts, dividing and seaming at left shoulder seam.
Work 1/1 rib for one inch, bind off loosely in pattern.
AT SAME TIME, when border meas half of total width, work buttonholes at markers. (I like the eyelet buttonhole for bulky yarns, and the one row buttonhole for worsted and finer yarns.)

	S • 24"	M • 28"	L • 32"	XS • 36"	S • 40"	M • 44"	L • 48"	XL • 52"
	1	2	3	3	3	3	4	4
	24·28	30·35	39·46	42·49	45·53	45·53	47·54	47·54
	19·22	23·27	25·30	28·33	32·37	35·41	36·42	39·45
	103·119	125·145	147·175	161·187	177·207	183·215	191·221	197·227

WAISTCOAT round neck border: Beg at center front right neck edge, pick up __ sts along right neck curve, knit back neck sts, pick up sts along left neck curve as for right neck. Work 1/1 rib for one inch. Bind off loosely in pattern. Mark placement for buttonholes, with the first ½ inch from top edge, the last ¾ inch from lower edge, and __ others spaced evenly between. Mark on right front for female, and on left front for male. Pick up __ sts along each center front edge and work 1/1 rib for one inch. Bind off loosely in patt.
AT SAME TIME, when buttonhole border meas half of total width, work buttonholes at markers. (Eyelet for bulky, one-row buttonhole for worsted and finer.)

	S • 24"	M • 28"	L • 32"	XS • 36"	S • 40"	M • 44"	L • 48"	XL • 52"
	9·11	12·14	12·14	13·15	14·16	15·18	17·19	19·22
	35·41	43·49	43·49	47·53	51·59	53·63	59·67	63·73
	3	3	4	5	6	6	6	6
	39·45	47·55	59·69	65·75	71·83	73·85	75·87	79·91

VEST/WAISTCOAT armhole border:
Notched armhole: Pick up __ sts evenly along front and back armhole selvage edge only. Work 1/1 rib until even with side edge. Bind off loosely in patt. Seam selvage edge of rib to bound off edge of notched armhole. Sew side seam.
Curved armhole: Pick up __ sts evenly along front and back armhole edge. To work in the round, sew side seam first. Work 1/1 rib for one inch. Bind off loosely in patt. If knit flat in rows, sew side seam now. Sew on buttons. Block, using the wet towel method.

	S • 24"	M • 28"	L • 32"	XS • 36"	S • 40"	M • 44"	L • 48"	XL • 52"
	36·42	42·48	48·56	54·62	60·70	66·76	69·80	75·87
	41·47	49·57	55·65	60·70	69·81	75·87	81·91	90·105

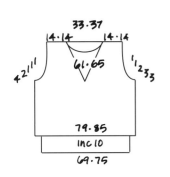
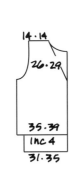
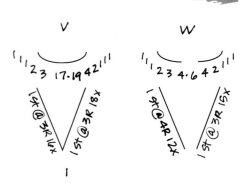

Top schematic measurements: 2⅛" 5" 2⅛"   2⅛"   6"   9¼"   2"   4"   4"   8"   8"   12"   5½"   2"

Row 1

33·37

14·14   14·14   14·14

42 | 1   61·65   1 | 1 2 3 3   26·29

79·85   35·39

inc 10   inc 4

69·75   31·35

6½·7

V   W

1 | 1 2 3   17·19 4 2 | 1 1   1 | 1 2 3 4·6 4 2 | 1 1

1st @ 3R 16x   1st @ 3R 18x   1st @ 4R 12x   1st @ 3R 15x

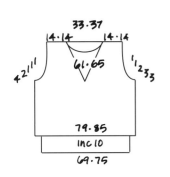
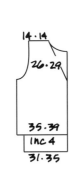
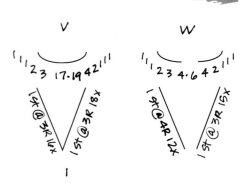

Row 2

25·31

11·12   11·12   11·12

32 | 1   47·55   1 | 1 1 2 4   20·24

61·73   27·33

inc 8   inc 4

53·65   23·29

5·6

1 | 1 2 2   13·15 3 2 | 1 1   1 | 1 2 2 3·4 3 2 | 1 1

1st @ 3R 12x   1st @ 2R 15x   1st @ 4R 9x   1st @ 3R 12x

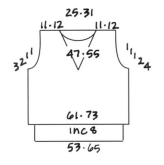
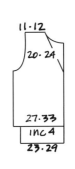
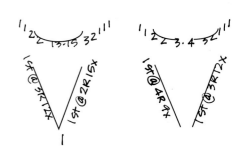

Row 3

21·23

8·10   8·10   8·10

22 | 1   37·43   1 | 1 2 2   15·19

49·55   21·25

inc 6   inc 4

43·49   17·21

4·4½

V   W

1 | 1 2   11·13 2 | 1 1   1 | 1 2 2·2·3 2 2 | 1 1

1st @ 3R 10x   1st @ 3R 11x   1st @ 4R 7x   1st @ 4R 7x

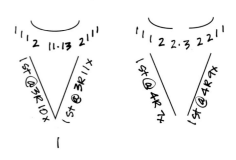

Row 4

17·19

5·7   5·7   5·7

2 | 1   27·33   1 | 1 2   11·15

37·43   16·20

inc 4   inc 3

33·39   13·17

3·3½

1 | 1 2   7·9 2 | 1 1   1 | 1 2 2·3 2 | 1 1

1st @ 3R 9x   1st @ 3R 8x   1st @ 4R 6x   1st @ 3R 8x

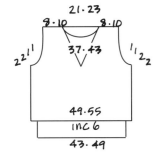

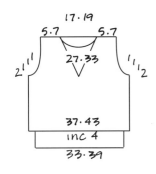
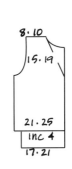
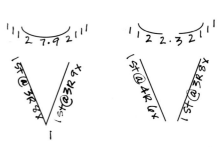

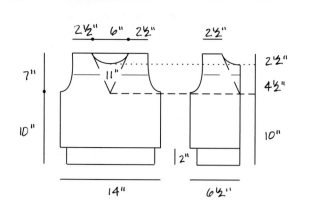

2½" 6" 2½"   2½"

7"

11"

2½"

4½"

10"

10"

2"

14"   6½"

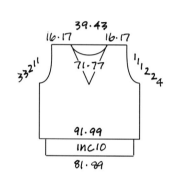

39.43

16.17   16.17

32"   71.77   "224

91.99

INC 10

81.89

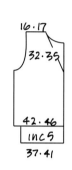

16.17

32.35

42.46

INC 5

37.41

6½.7

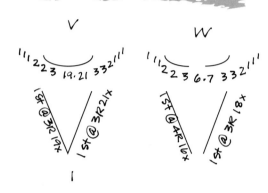

V   W

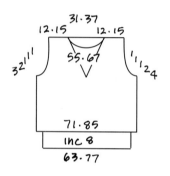

31.37

12.15   12.15

32"   55.67   "124

71.85

Inc 8

63.77

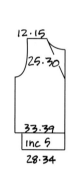

12.15

25.30

33.39

Inc 5

28.34

5.6

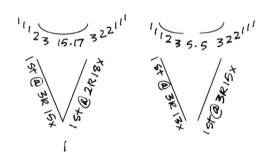

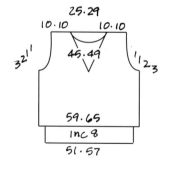

25.29

10.10   10.10

32"   45.49   "23

59.65

Inc 8

51.57

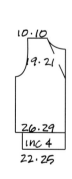

10.10

19.21

26.29

Inc 4

22.25

4.4½

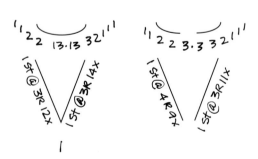

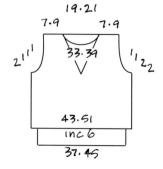

19.21

7.9   7.9

2"   33.39   "22

43.51

Inc 6

37.45

7.9

15.17

20.23

Inc 4

16.19

3.3½

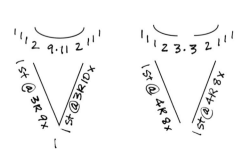

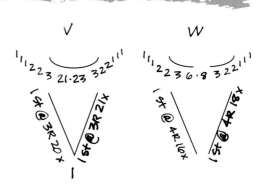

32"

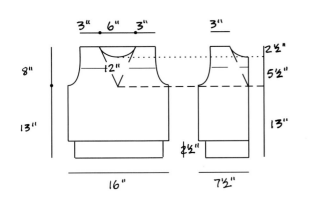

3" · 6" · 3"   3"

8"

12"

2½"

5½"

13"   13"

4½"

16"   7½"

V   W

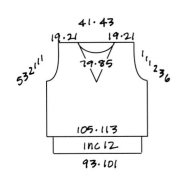

41·43
19·21   19·21
532'"   29·85   '"236
105·113
inc 12
93·101

19·21
36·39
49·53
inc 6
43·47

6½·7

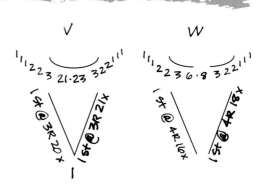

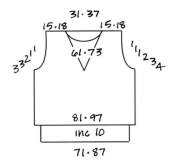

31·37
15·18   15·18
332'"   61·73   '"234
81·97
inc 10
71·87

15·18
28·34
38·46
inc 5
33·41

5·6

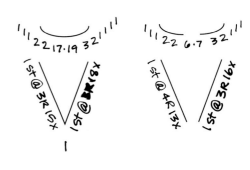

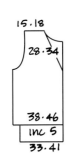

25·29
12·13   12·13
32'"   49·55   '"24
65·73
inc 8
57·65

12·13
22·25
30·34
inc 5
25·29

4·4½

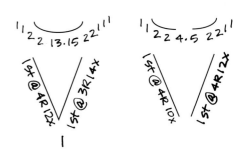

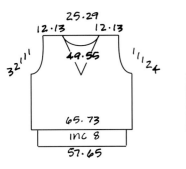

19·23
9·10   9·10
22'"   37·43   '"23
49·57
inc 6
43·51

9·10
17·19
23·26
inc 4
19·22

3·3½

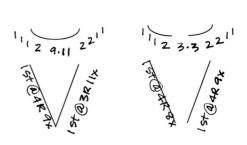

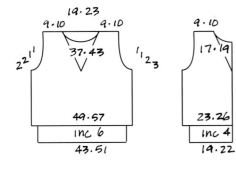

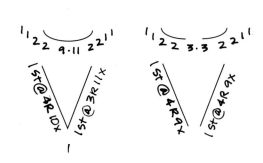

36"

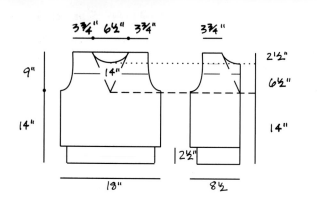

3¾" 6½" 3¾"   3¾"

9"

14"

14"

2½"
6½"
14"

18"   8½

2½"

Row 1

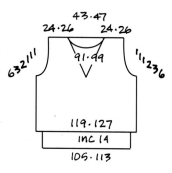

43·47
24·26   24·26
632¹¹¹   91·99   ¹¹¹236
119·127
INC 14
105·113

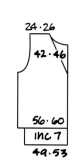

24·26
42·46
56·60
INC 7
49·53

6½·7

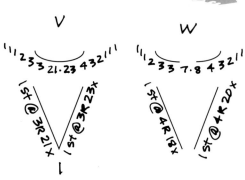

V   W

Row 2

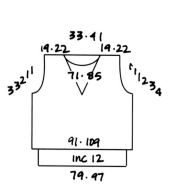

33·41
19·22   19·22
332¹¹   71·85   ¹¹¹234
91·109
INC 12
79·97

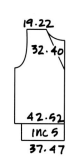

19·22
32·40
42·52
INC 5
37·47

5·6

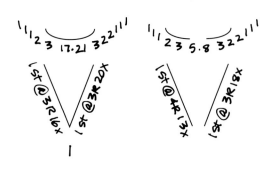

Row 3

27·31
15·16   15·16
32¹¹   57·63   ¹¹233
73·83
INC 10
63·73

15·16
26·28
34·38
INC 4
30·34

4·4½

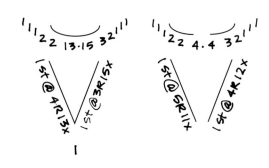

Row 4

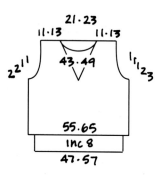

21·23
11·13   11·13
22¹¹   43·49   ¹¹¹23
55·65
INC 8
47·57

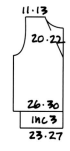

11·13
20·22
26·30
INC 3
23·27

3·3½

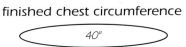

40"

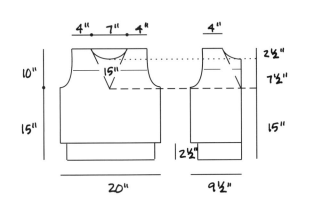

4"   7"   4"   4"

10"

15"

2½"

7½"

15"

15"

2½"

20"   9½"

V   W

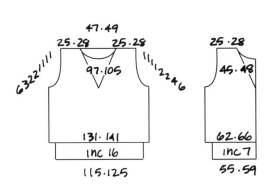

47·49

25·28   25·28

97·105

6322/111   1112246

25·28

45·48

131·141

inc 16

115·125

62·66

inc 7

55·59

6½·7

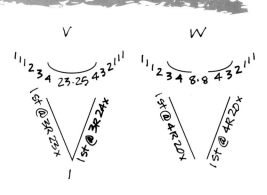

1112 3 4   23·25   4 3 2 111

1st @ 3R 23x   1st @ 3R 24x

l

1112 3 4   8·8   4 3 2 111

1st @ 4R 20x   1st @ 4R 20x

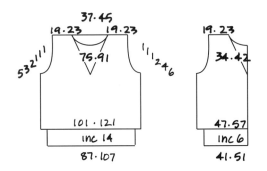

37·45

19·23   19·23

75·91

532/11   111246

19·23

34·42

101·121

inc 14

87·107

47·57

inc 6

41·51

5·6

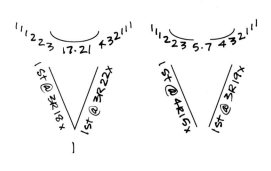

1112 23   17·21   4 3 2 111

1st @ 3R 18x   1st @ 3R 22x

l

1112 23   5·7   4 3 2 111

1st @ 4R 16x   1st @ 3R 19x

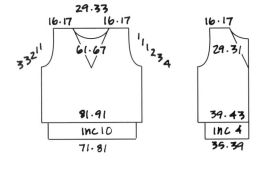

29·33

16·17   16·17

61·67

332/1   11123 4

16·17

29·31

81·91

inc 10

71·81

39·43

inc 4

35·39

4·4½

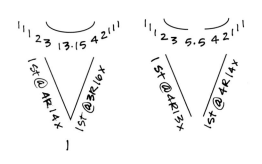

1112 3   13·15   4 2 111

1st @ 4R 14x   1st @ 3R 16x

l

1112 3   5·5   4 2 111

1st @ 4R 13x   1st @ 4R 14x

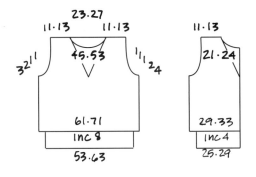

23·27

11·13   11·13

45·53

32/1   1112 4

11·13

21·24

61·71

inc 8

53·63

29·33

inc 4

25·29

3·3½

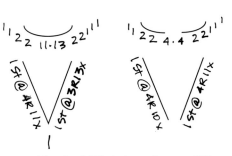

1112 2   11·13   2 2 111

1st @ 4R 11x   1st @ 3R 13x

l

1112 2   4·4   2 2 111

1st @ 4R 10x   1st @ 4R 11x

Adult Medium
finished chest circumference

44"

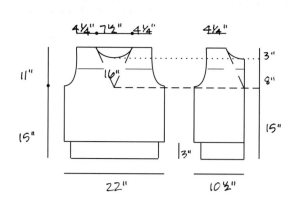

4¼" 7½" 4¼"   4¼"

11"

16"   3"

8"

15"   15"

3"

22"   10½"

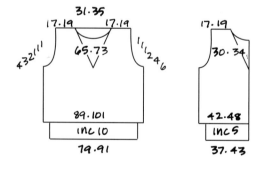

51·55
27·29   27·29
6432'''   105·113   '''2347
145·155
inc 16
129·139

27·29
48·53
68·74
inc 7
61·67

6½·7

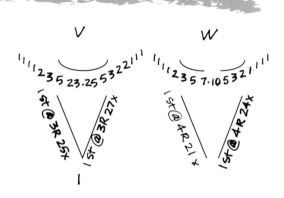

V   W

'''235 23·25 5322'''   '''2357·10532'''
1st@3R25x   1st@3R27x   1st@4R21x   1st@4R24x
I

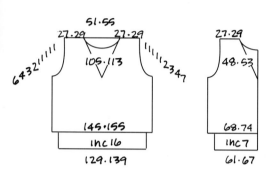

39·47
21·25   21·25
642'''   81·97   '''2247
111·133
inc 14
97·119

21·25
38·45
53·63
inc 6
47·57

5·6

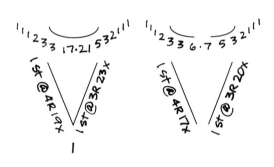

'''1233 17·21 532'''   '''12336·7532'''
1st@4R19x   1st@3R23x   1st@4R17x   1st@3R20x
I

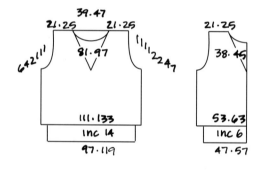

31·35
17·19   17·19
432'''   65·73   '''246
89·101
inc 10
79·91

17·19
30·34
42·48
inc 5
37·43

4·4½

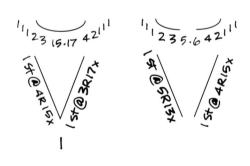

'''123 15·17 42'''   '''235·642'''
1st@4R15x   1st@3R17x   1st@5R13x   1st@4R15x
I

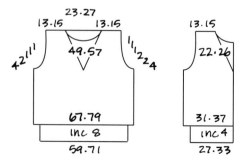

23·27
13·15   13·15
42'''   49·57   '''224
67·79
inc 8
59·71

13·15
22·26
31·37
inc 4
27·33

3·3½

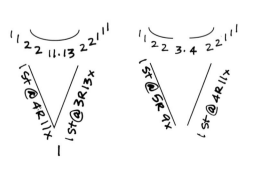

'''22 11·13 22'''   '''22 3·4 22'''
1st@4R11x   1st@3R13x   1st@5R9x   1st@4R11x
I

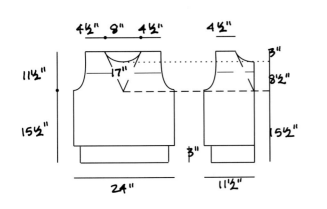

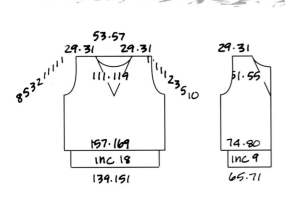

6½·7

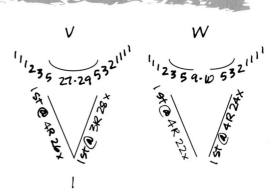

V   W

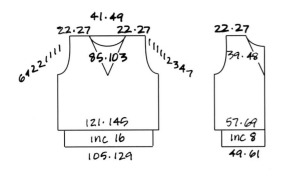

5·6

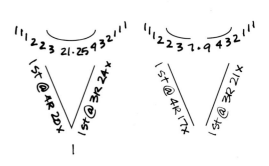

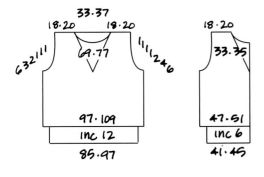

4·4½

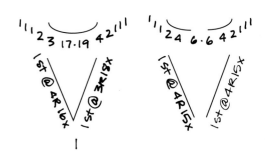

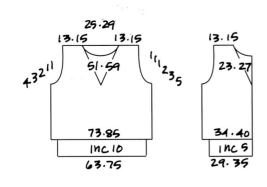

3·3½

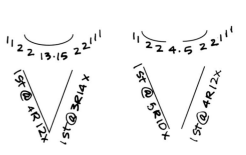

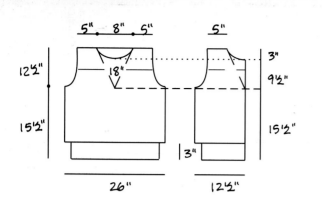

5" 8" 5"   5"

12½"   18"   3"

                        9½"

15½"   15½"

                    3"

26"   12½"

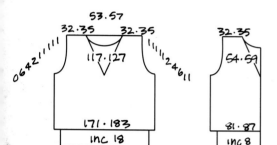

53.57

32.35   32.35   32.35

06421111   117·127   111124611   54·59

171·183   81·87

inc 18   inc 8

153·165   73·79

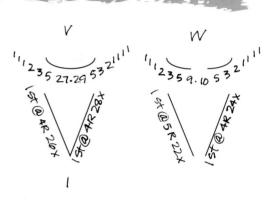

V   W

1112 3 5 27·29 5 3 2 111   1112 3 5 9·10 5 3 2 111

1st @ 4R 28x   1st @ 5R 22x

1st @ 4R 26x   1st @ 4R 24x

6½·7

41·49

25.30   25.30   25.30

74321111   91·109   111124 68   42·52

131·157   62·76

inc 16   inc 7

115·141   55·69

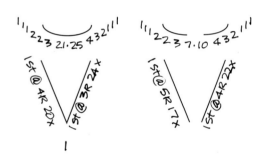

1112 2 3 21·25 4 3 2 111   1112 2 3 7·10 4 3 2 111

1st @ 3R 24x   1st @ 4R 22x

1st @ 4R 20x   1st @ 5R 17x

5·6

33·37

20·22   20·22   20·22

64211111   73·81   11112246   34·38

105·117   50·56

inc 12   inc 5

93·105   45·51

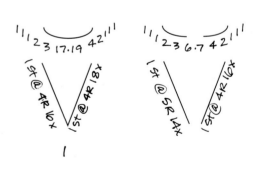

1112 3 17·19 4 2 111   1112 3 6·7 4 2 111

1st @ 4R 18x   1st @ 4R 16x

1st @ 4R 16x   1st @ 5R 14x

4·4½

25·29

15·17   15·17   15·17

4321111   55·63   111246   25·29

79·93   37·43

inc 10   inc 4

69·83   33·39

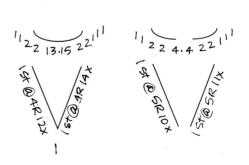

1112 2 13·15 2 2 111   111 2 2 4·4 2 2 111

1st @ 4R 14x   1st @ 5R 11x

1st @ 4R 12x   1st @ 5R 10x

3·3½

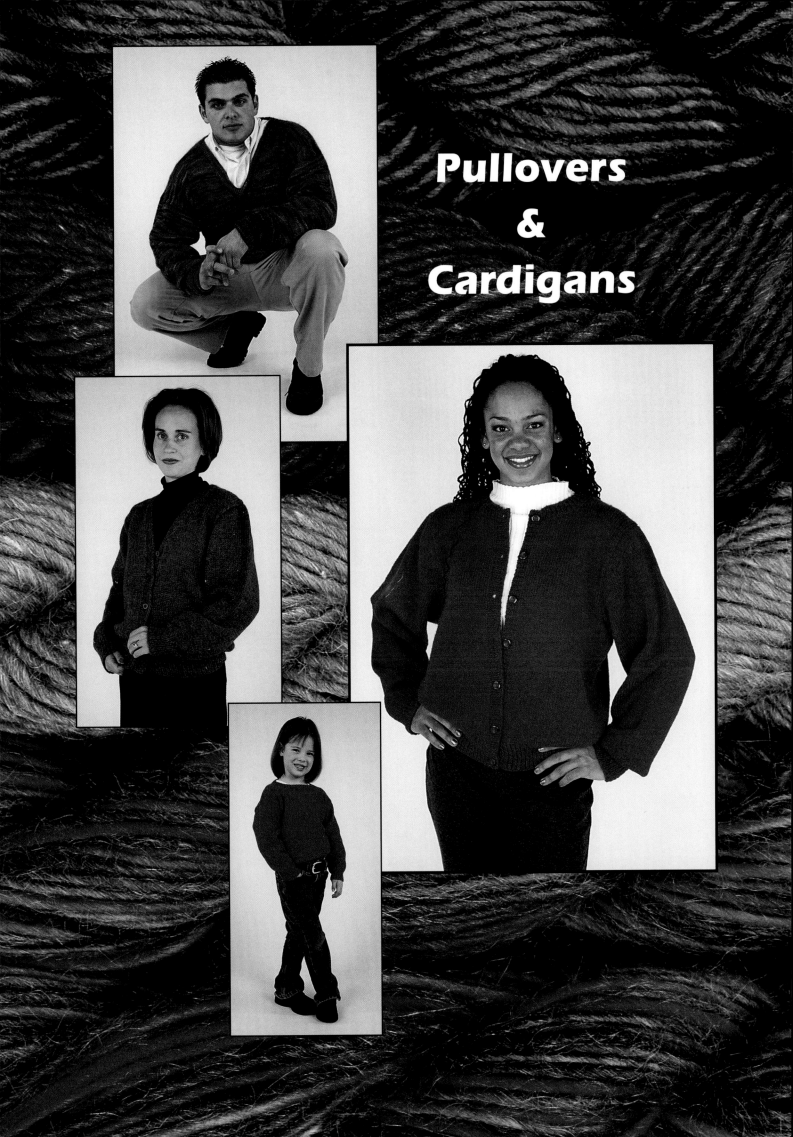

Pullovers & Cardigans

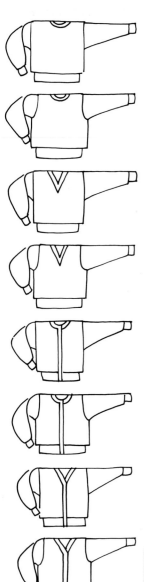

	Child			Adult				
	S • 24"	M • 28"	L • 32"	XS • 36"	S • 40"	M • 44"	L • 48"	XL • 52"
6½ • 7 sts per inch yardage	750	1000	1450	1800	2100	2500	2700	3000
Cotton Fine	4	5	7	9	10	12	13	14
Nature Spun (F)	3	4	5	6	7	9	9	10
Wildfoote	4	5	7	9	10	12	13	14
5 • 6 sts per inch yardage	550	800	1100	1400	1600	1900	2100	2300
Cotton Fleece	3	4	6	9	8	9	10	11
Kaleidoscope	6	8	11	14	15	18	20	22
Nature Spun (S)	3	5	6	8	9	11	12	13
Top of the Lamb (S)	2	3	4	4	5	6	6	7
4 • 4½ sts per inch yardage	500	650	1000	1200	1400	1600	1800	2000
Country Classics (W)	3	4	6	7	8	9	10	11
Hand paint Originals	6	8	12	14	16	19	21	23
Lamb's Pride (W)	3	4	6	7	8	9	10	11
Lamb's Pride Superwash (W)	3	4	5	6	7	8	9	10
Nature Spun (W)	2	3	4	5	6	7	8	9
Prairie Silk	6	8	12	14	16	19	21	23
Top of the Lamb (W)	3	4	6	7	8	9	10	11
3 • 3½ sts per inch yardage	350	500	700	900	1000	1200	1300	1500
Country Classics (B)	3	4	6	8	8	10	11	12
Lamb's Pride (B)	3	4	6	8	8	10	11	12
Lamb's Pride Superwash (B)	4	5	7	9	10	11	12	14

(Yardage and skein estimates are approximations only.)

Choose:

• pullover or cardigan

• round or v-neck

• straight or curved armholes with straight or shaped sleeve caps

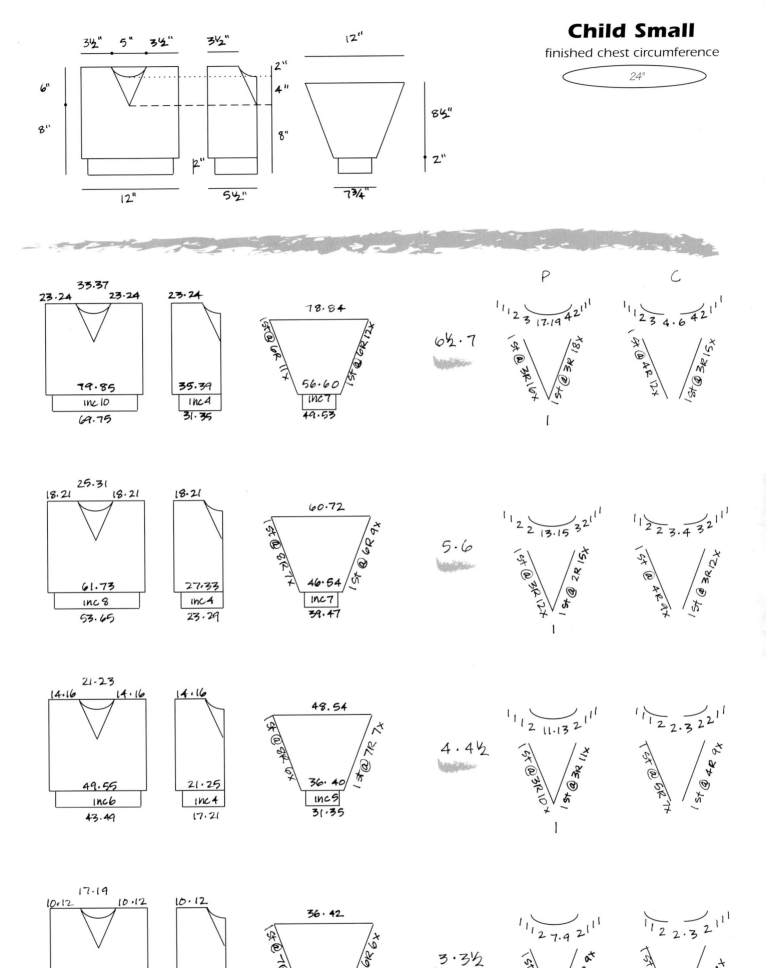

Child Medium

finished chest circumference

28"

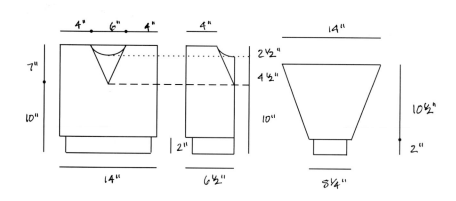

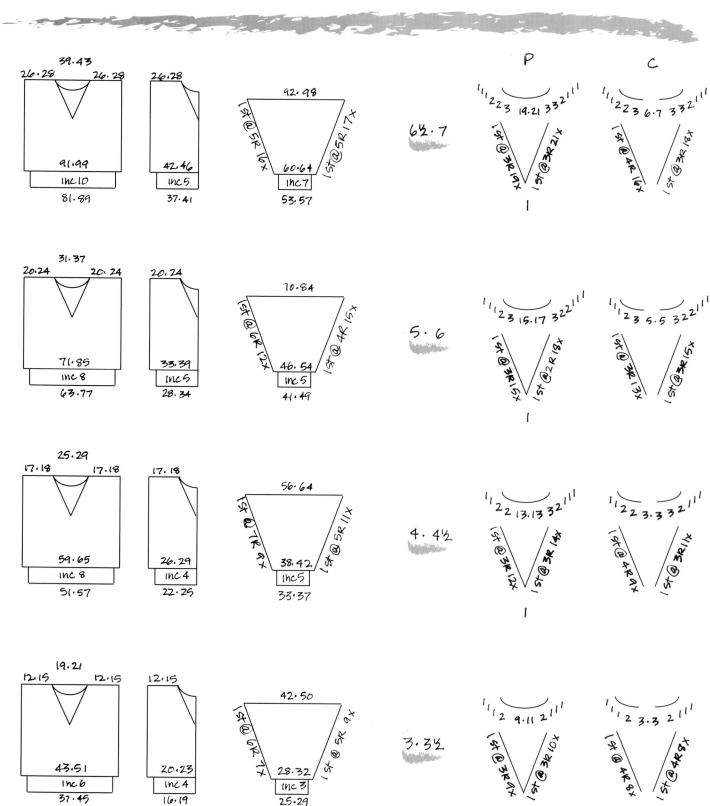

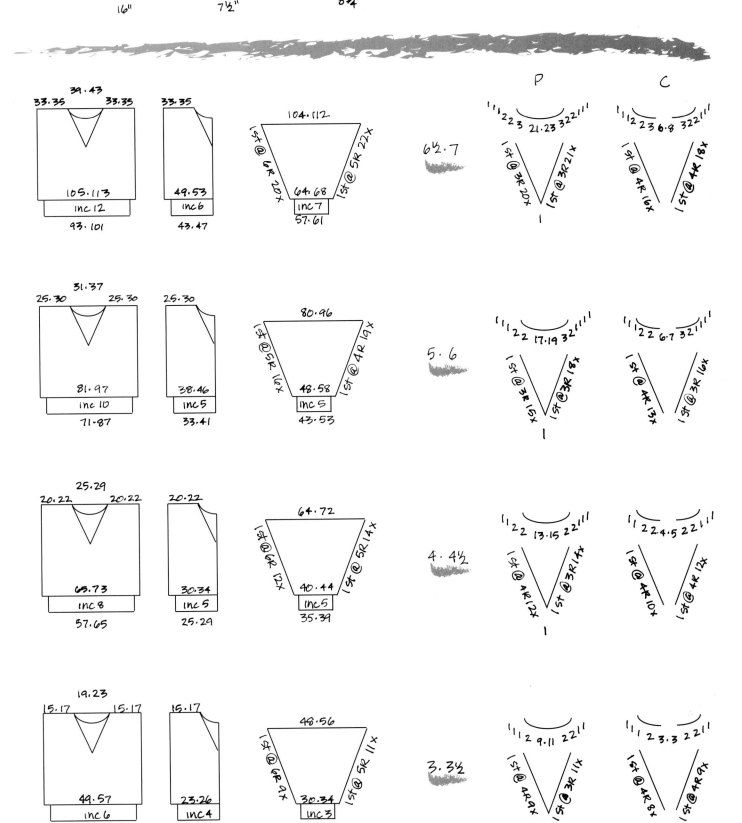

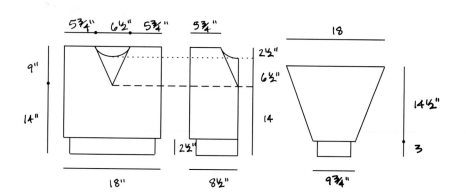

Adult Extra Small

finished chest circumference

36"

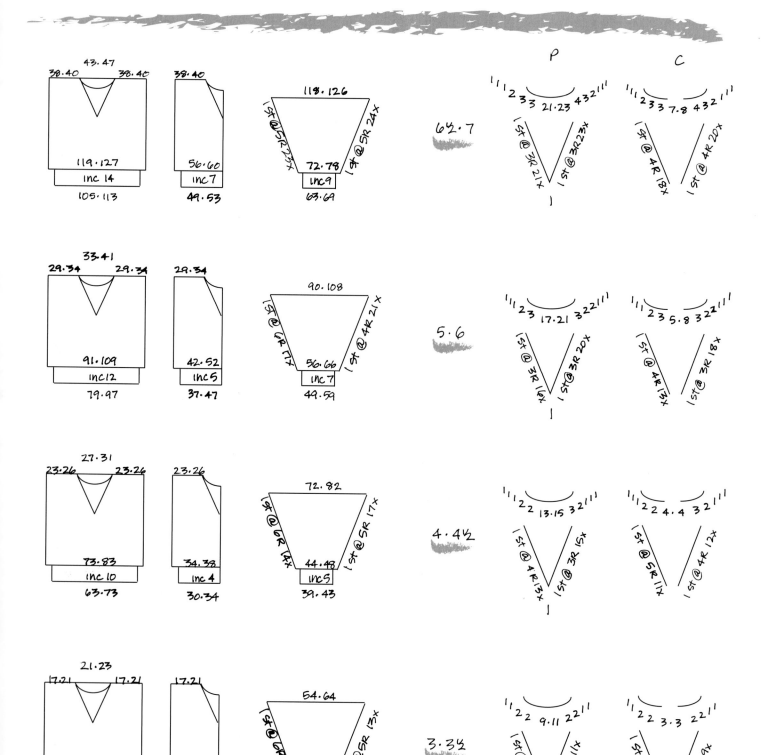

6½" 7" 6½" 6½" 20"

10" 2½" 7½" 15"

15" 15" 3"

20" 9½" 2½" 10½"

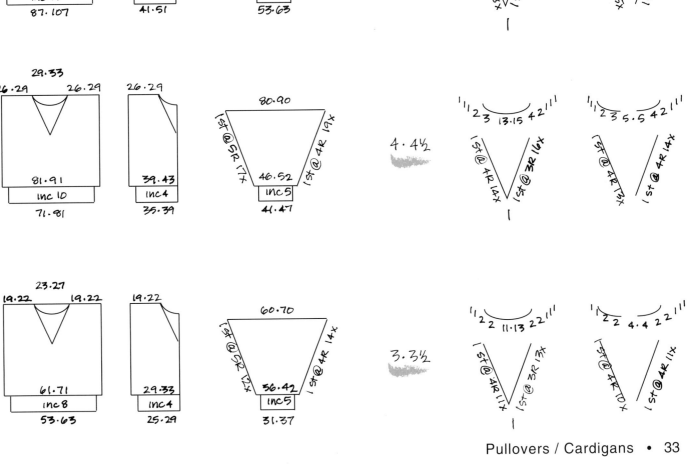

P C

47.49
42.46 42.46 42.46

131.141 62.66

inc 16 inc 7

115.125 55.59

130.140

1st @ SR 26x 78.82 1st @ 4R 29x

inc 9

69.73

6½.7

''1 2 3 4 23.25 4 3 2 1''
1st @ 3R 23x 1st @ 3R 24x

''1 2 3 4 8.8 4 3 2 1''
1st @ 4R 20x

37.45
32.38 32.38 32.38

101.121 47.57

inc 14 inc 6

87.107 41.51

100.120

1st @ SR 20x 60.70 1st @ 4R 25x

inc 7

53.63

5.6

''1 2 2 3 17.21 4 3 2 1''
1st @ 3R 18x 1st @ 3R 22x

''1 2 2 3 5.7 4 3 2 1''
1st @ 4R 19x

29.33
26.29 26.29 26.29

81.91 39.43

inc 10 inc 4

71.81 35.39

80.90

1st @ SR 17x 46.52 1st @ 4R 19x

inc 5

41.47

4.4½

''1 2 3 13.15 4 2 1''
1st @ 4R 14x 1st @ 3R 16x

''1 2 3 5.5 4 2 1''
1st @ 4R 14x

23.27
19.22 19.22 19.22

61.71 29.33

inc 8 inc 4

53.63 25.29

60.70

1st @ SR 12x 56.42 1st @ 4R 14x

inc 5

31.37

3.3½

''1 2 2 11.13 2 2 1''
1st @ 4R 11x 1st @ 3R 13x

''1 2 2 4.4 2 2 1''
1st @ 4R 11x

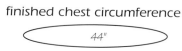
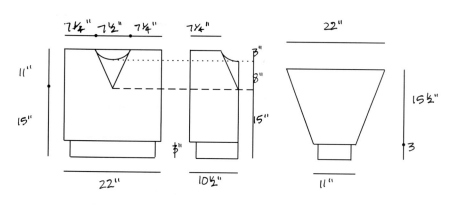

7¼" 7½" 7¼"   7¼"   22"

11"   3"
                       8"
15"   15"   15½"

22"   10½"   11"   3

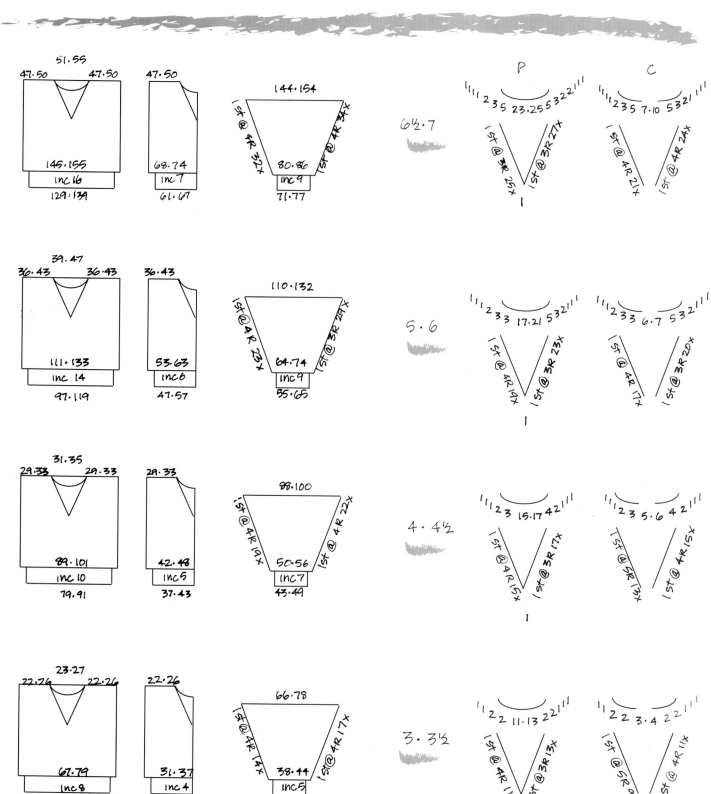

51·55
47·50   47·50   47·50   144·154

                                        1st @ 4R 34x
145·155   68·74   80·86
inc 16   inc 7   inc 9
129·139   61·67   71·77

1st @ 4R 32x   1st @ 4R 32x

6½·7

P   C

111 2 3 5 23·25 5 5 3 2 2 111   111 2 3 5 7·10 5 3 2 111

1st @ 3R 27x   1st @ 4R 24x
1st @ 3R 26x   1st @ 3R 27x   1st @ 4R 21x

1

39·47
36·43   36·43   36·43   110·132

111·133   53·63   64·74
inc 14   inc 6   inc 9
97·119   47·57   55·65

1st @ 4R 23x   1st @ 3R 29x

5·6

111 2 3 3 17·21 5 3 2 111   111 2 3 3 6·7 5 3 2 111

1st @ 3R 23x   1st @ 3R 20x
1st @ 4R 19x   1st @ 4R 17x

1

31·35
29·33   29·33   29·33   88·100

89·101   42·48   50·56
inc 10   inc 5   inc 7
79·91   37·43   43·49

1st @ 4R 19x   1st @ 4R 22x

4·4½

111 2 3 15·17 4 2 111   111 2 3 5·6 4 2 111

1st @ 3R 17x   1st @ 4R 15x
1st @ 4R 15x   1st @ 3R 13x

1

23·27
22·26   22·26   22·26   66·78

67·79   31·37   38·44
inc 8   inc 4   inc 5
59·71   27·33   33·39

1st @ 4R 14x   1st @ 4R 17x

3·3½

111 2 2 11·13 2 2 111   11 2 2 3·4 2 2 11

1st @ 3R 13x   1st @ 4R 11x
1st @ 4R 11x   1st @ 5R 9x

1

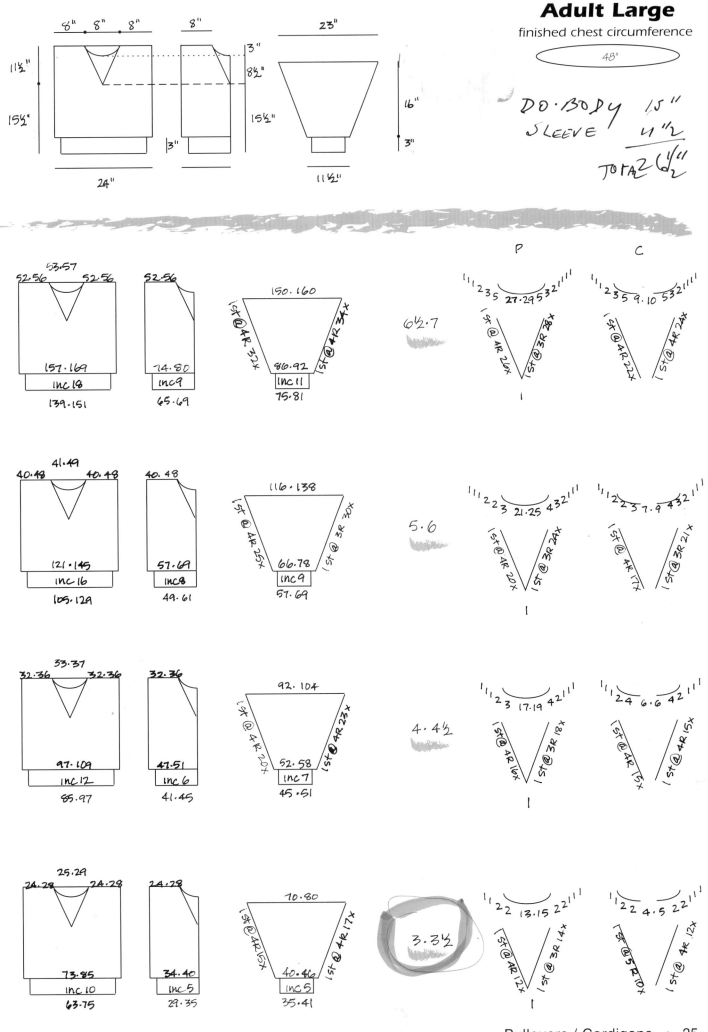

DO·BODY 15"
SLEEVE 4"½
——————
TOTAL 6½"

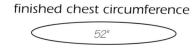

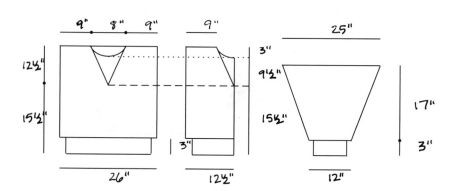

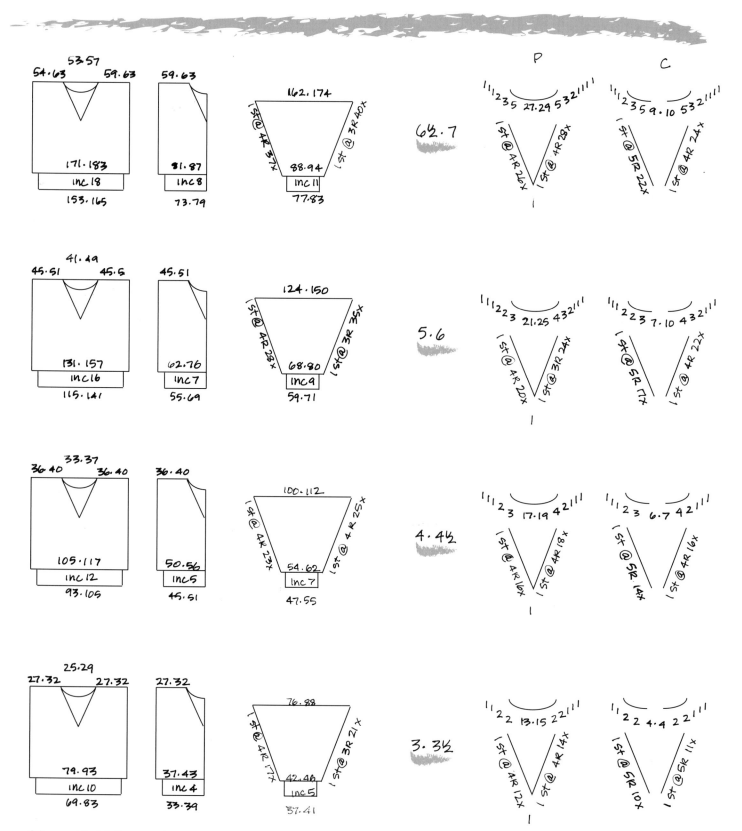

	Child			Adult				
	S • 24"	M • 28"	L • 32"	XS • 36"	S • 40"	M • 44"	L • 48"	XL • 52"

BACK PULLOVER/CARDIGAN

	S • 24"	M • 28"	L • 32"	XS • 36"	S • 40"	M • 44"	L • 48"	XL • 52"
With smaller needles, cast on __ sts.	69•75	81•89	93•101	105•113	115•125	129•139	139•151	153•165
Work 1/1 rib for __ inches,	2	2	2½	2½	2½	3	3	3
increasing __ sts across last row of rib,	10	10	12	14	16	16	18	18
__ sts.	79•85	91•99	105•113	119•127	131•141	145•155	157•169	171•183
Change to larger needles and work in st st until piece meas __ inches.	8	10	13	14	15	15	15½	15½

Choose armhole style.

Straight armhole: Place marker at side edge and cont even.

OR

Curved armhole: Bind off sts at each armhole edge in the foll sequence:

	S • 24"	M • 28"	L • 32"	XS • 36"	S • 40"	M • 44"	L • 48"	XL • 52"
					6 | 6	6 | 7	8 | 10	10 | 11
	| 3	3 | 4	5 | 6	6 | 6	3 | 4	4 | 4	5 | 5	6 | 6
	4 | 3	3 | 2	3 | 3	3 | 3	2 | 2	3 | 3	3 | 3	4 | 4
	2 | 2	2 | 2	2 | 2	2 | 2	2 | 2	2 | 2	2 | 2	2 | 2
	1x3 | 1x2	1x2 | 1x3	1x3 | 1x3	1x3 | 1x3	1x4 | 1x4	1x5 | 1x5	1x5 | 1x5	1x5 | 1x5

Cont even until armhole measures:

	S • 24"	M • 28"	L • 32"	XS • 36"	S • 40"	M • 44"	L • 48"	XL • 52"
for straight armhole __ inches	6	7	8	9	10	11	11½	12½
for curved armhole __ inches.	5½	6½	7½	8	9	10	10½	11½

Place all sts on hold for later finishing.

FRONT PULLOVER

Work as for back, including armhole shaping.

AT SAME TIME, choose neckline style.

V-neck: When work meas __ inches, mark center st. Knit to within 3 sts of center st, k2tog, k1. Place center st on hold, join second ball of yarn, k1, SSK, knit to end. Work each side separately, decreasing 1 st at neck edge:

	S • 24"	M • 28"	L • 32"	XS • 36"	S • 40"	M • 44"	L • 48"	XL • 52"
V-neck: When work meas __ inches	8	10	13	14	15	15	15½	15½
for straight shaped garment every __ row	3•3	3•3	3•3	3•3	3•3	3•3	3•3	4•4
for curved shaped garment every __ row	3•2	3•3	3•3	3•3	3•3	3•3	3•3	4•3
__ times.	16•18	19•21	20•21	21•23	23•24	25•27	26•28	26•28

OR

Round neck: When work measures:

	S • 24"	M • 28"	L • 32"	XS • 36"	S • 40"	M • 44"	L • 48"	XL • 52"
for straight shaped garment __ inches	12	14½	18½	20½	22½	23	24	25
for curved shaped garment __ inches.	11½	14	18	19½	21½	22	23	24
Mark center __ sts.	17•19	19•21	21•23	21•23	23•25	23•25	27•29	27•29

Knit to marker, place center sts on hold, join second ball of yarn and knit to end. Working each side separately, at neck edge every other row, bind off in foll sequence:

	S • 24"	M • 28"	L • 32"	XS • 36"	S • 40"	M • 44"	L • 48"	XL • 52"
						| 5		
		3 | 3	3 | 3	3 | 3	4 | 4	5 | 3	5 | 5	5 | 5
	3 | 4	2 | 3	2 | 2	3 | 3	3 | 3	3 | 2	3 | 3	3 | 3
	2 | 2	2 | 2	2 | 2	2 | 2	2 | 2	2 | 2	2 | 2	2 | 2
	1x3 | 1x3	1x3 | 1x3	1x3 | 1x3	1x3 | 1x3	1x3 | 1x3	1x4 | 1x3	1x3 | 1x4	1x3 | 1x4

Cont even until piece meas same as back. Place sts on hold for later three needle bind-off seaming.

FRONT CARDIGAN

	S • 24"	M • 28"	L • 32"	XS • 36"	S • 40"	M • 44"	L • 48"	XL • 52"
With smaller needles, cast on __ sts.	31•35	37•41	43•47	49•53	55•59	61•67	65•71	73•79
Work 1/1 rib for __ inches,	2	2	2½	2½	2½	3	3	3
increasing __ sts across last row of rib—	4	5	6	7	7	7	9	8
__ sts.	35•39	42•46	49•53	56•60	62•66	68•74	74•80	81•87
Change to larger needles and work in st st until piece meas __ inches.	8	10	13	14	15	15	15½	15½

Work armhole as for back.

AT SAME TIME, choose neckline style.

V-neck: When work meas __ inches, dec at neck edge 1 st:

	S • 24"	M • 28"	L • 32"	XS • 36"	S • 40"	M • 44"	L • 48"	XL • 52"
V-neck: When work meas __ inches	8	10	13	14	15	15	15½	15½
for straight shaped garment every __ row	4•3	4•3	4•4	4•4	4•4	4•4	4•4	5•4
for curved shaped garment every __ row	4•3	4•3	4•3	4•3	4•4	4•3	4•4	4•4
__ times	12•15	16•18	16•18	18•20	20•20	21•24	22•24	22•24

	Child			Adult				
	S • 24"	M • 28"	L • 32"	XS • 36"	S • 40"	M • 44"	L • 48"	XL • 52"

OR

Round neck: When work measures:

for straight shaped garment __ inches

for curved shaped garment __ inches

at neck edge bind off in foll sequence:

	Child			Adult				
	S • 24"	M • 28"	L • 32"	XS • 36"	S • 40"	M • 44"	L • 48"	XL • 52"
straight	12	14½	18½	20½	22½	23	24	25
curved	11½	14	18	19½	21½	22	23	24
		6 | 7	6 | 8	7 | 8	8 | 8	7 | 10	9 | 10	9 | 10
	4 | 6	3 | 3	3 | 3	3 | 4	4 | 4	5 | 5	5 | 5	5 | 5
	3 | 4	2 | 2	2 | 2	2 | 3	3 | 3	3 | 3	3 | 3	3 | 3
	2 | 2	2 | 2	2 | 2	2 | 2	2 | 2	2 | 2	2 | 2	2 | 2
	1x3 | 1x3	1x3 | 1x3	1x3 | 1x3	1x3 | 1x3	1x3 | 1x3	1x4 | 1x4	1x3 | 1x4	1x3 | 1x4

Cont even until piece meas same as back. Place sts on hold for later three needle bind-off seaming.

SLEEVE PULLOVER/CARDIGAN

With smaller needles, cast on __ sts.

Work 1/1 rib for __ inches,

increasing __ sts across last row—

__ sts. Change to larger needles.

Sleeve shaping: Work in st st and inc 1 st at beg and end of every __ row

__ times—

__ sts.

Work until piece meas __ inches.

Straight sleeve cap: bind off all sts.

OR

Curved sleeve cap: bind off on each side in foll sequence:

	Child			Adult				
	S • 24"	M • 28"	L • 32"	XS • 36"	S • 40"	M • 44"	L • 48"	XL • 52"
cast on	49•53	53•57	57•61	63•69	69•73	71•77	75•81	77•83
rib inches	2	2	2	3	3	3	3	3
increasing	7	7	7	9	9	9	11	11
sts	56•60	60•64	64•68	72•78	78•82	80•86	86•92	88•94
every __ row	6•6	5•5	6•5	5•5	5•4	4•4	4•4	4•3
times	11•12	16•17	20•22	23•24	26•29	32•34	32•34	37•40
sts	78•84	92•98	104•112	118•126	130•140	144•154	150•160	162•174
meas inches	10½	12½	15½	17½	18	18½	19	20
	4x1 | 4x2	4x1 | 4x1	5x1 | 6x1	6x1 | 6x1	6x1 | 6x1	6x1 | 7x1	8x1 | 10x1	10x1 | 11x1
	3x3 | 3x2	3x2 | 3x3	3x1 | 3x1	3x2 | 4x1	4x1 | 3x3	4x1 | 4x1	5x1 | 5x1	6x1 | 6x1
	2x2 | 2x2	2x5 | 2x3	2x9 | 2x8	2x3 | 3x2	3x2 | 2x11	3x1 | 3x1	3x1 | 3x1	4x1 | 4x1
	3x3 | 3x2	3x2 | 3x3	3x3 | 3x4	1x6 | 2x3	2x3 | 3x3	2x3 | 2x4	2x3 | 2x4	2x3 | 2x4
		4x1	4x1 | 4x1		2x3 | 1x3	1x4	1x8 | 1x7	1x7 | 1x7	1x7 | 1x7
				3x3 | 2x4	2x4	2x6 | 2x5	2x6 | 2x4	2x6 | 2x3
					3x3	3x3	3x3 | 3x4	3x3 | 3x4	3x3 | 4x4

Bind off remaining __ sts.

	Child			Adult				
	26•28	32•34	34•38	40•42	40•48	48•52	50•54	54•58

FINISHING

Work three needle bind off seaming for shoulders, leaving back neck sts on hold. Set sleeve in armhole. Sew side and sleeve seams. For all the following ribbed borders, use smaller circular or dp needles and pick up sts from right side.

PULLOVER v-neck border: Beg at left shoulder, pick up __ sts along left front neck edge, place marker, knit center st through back of loop, place marker, pick up sts along right front neck edge as for left front, knit across back neck sts— __ sts. Work 1/1 rib for one inch, decreasing 1 st before first marker (SSK) and 1 st after second marker (k 2 tog) every other row. Bind off loosely in pattern.

	Child			Adult				
pick up	42•45	49•53	55•60	62•67	68•74	75•81	79•85	85•92
sts	118•128	138•150	152•164	162•182	184•198	202•218	212•228	224•242

PULLOVER round neck border: Beg at left shoulder, pick up __ sts along left front neck curve, knit across center front sts, pick up sts along right front neck curve as for left front, knit across back neck sts— __ sts. Work 1/1 rib for one inch. Bind off loosely in pattern.

	Child			Adult				
pick up	16•17	21•22	21•22	23•24	24•26	27•29	27•29	27•29
sts	82•90	100•108	100•108	110•118	118•126	128•138	134•144	134•144

	Child			Adult				
	S • 24"	M • 28"	L • 32"	XS • 36"	S • 40"	M • 44"	L • 48"	XL • 52"

FINISHING (cont)

CARDIGAN v-neck border: Mark placement for buttonholes, with first at beg of v-neck shaping, the last ¾ inch from lower edge, and __ others spaced evenly between. Mark on right front for female, and on left front for male.

Beg at lower right front edge, pick up __ sts along center front edge, along right front v-neck pick up:

for straight shaped garment __ sts

for curved shaped garment __ sts

knit across back neck sts, along left front v-neck and left center front edge pick up as for right front— __ sts for straight

__ sts for curved

Work 1/1 rib for one inch, bind off loosely in pattern. *NOTE: The border may be worked in two parts, dividing and seaming at left shoulder.*

AT SAME TIME, when border meas half of total width, work buttonholes at markers. (I like the eyelet buttonhole for bulky yarns, and the one-row buttonhole for worsted and finer yarns.)

	S • 24"	M • 28"	L • 32"	XS • 36"	S • 40"	M • 44"	L • 48"	XL • 52"
	1	2	3	3	3	3	4	4
	52·56	65·70	85·91	91·98	98·105	98·105	101·109	101·109
straight	42·45	49·53	55·59	61·66	68·74	75·80	78·84	85·91
curved	39·42	45·49	52·56	56·60	62·67	69·74	73·78	78·85
straight	221·239	267·289	321·343	347·375	379·407	397·425	411·443	425·457
curved	215·233	259·281	315·337	337·363	367·393	385·413	401·431	411·445

CARDIGAN round neck border: Beg at center front right neck edge, pick up __ sts along right neck curve, knit back neck sts, along left neck curve pick up as for right neck— __ sts. Work 1/1 rib for one inch. Bind off loosely in pattern.

Mark placement for buttonholes, with the first ½ inch from top edge, the last ¾ inch from lower edge, and __ others space evenly between. Mark on right front for female, and on left front for male.

Pick up __ sts along each center front edge (straight)

Pick up __ sts along each center front edge (curved) and work 1/1 rib for one inch. Bind off loosely in pattern.

AT SAME TIME when buttonhole border meas half of total width, work buttonholes at markers. (I like the eyelet buttonhole for bulky yarns, and the one-row buttonhole for worsted and finer yarns.)

Sew on buttons. Block, using the wet towel method.

	S • 24"	M • 28"	L • 32"	XS • 36"	S • 40"	M • 44"	L • 48"	XL • 52"
	20·22	25·27	25·27	28·30	31·33	33·36	36·39	40·43
	73·81	89·97	89·97	99·107	109·115	117·127	125·135	133·143
	3	3	4	5	6	6	6	6
straight	85·91	101·109	127·137	139·151	153·165	157·167	163·175	169·183
curved	81·87	97·105	123·133	133·143	146·157	149·161	156·168	162·175

	Child			Adult				
	S • 24"	M • 28"	L • 32"	XS • 36"	S • 40"	M • 44"	L • 48"	XL • 52"

BACK PULLOVER/CARDIGAN

	S • 24"	M • 28"	L • 32"	XS • 36"	S • 40"	M • 44"	L • 48"	XL • 52"
With smaller needles, cast on __ sts.	53•65	63•77	71•87	79•97	87•107	97•119	105•129	115•141
Work 1/1 rib for __ inches,	2	2	2½	2½	2½	3	3	3
increasing __ sts across last row of rib,	8	8	10	12	14	14	16	16
__ sts.	61•73	71•85	81•97	91•109	101•121	111•133	121•145	131•157
Change to larger needles and work in st st until piece meas __ inches.	8	10	13	14	15	15	15½	15½

Choose armhole style.

Straight armhole: Place marker at side edge and cont even.

OR

Curved armhole: Bind off sts at each armhole edge in the foll sequence (5•6 gauge):

	S • 24"	M • 28"	L • 32"	XS • 36"	S • 40"	M • 44"	L • 48"	XL • 52"
						•7	6•7	7•8
			3•4	3•4	5•6	6•4	4•4	4•6
	3•4	3•4	3•3	3•3	3•4	4•2	2•3	3•4
	2•2	2•2	2•2	2•2	2•2	2•2	2•2	2•2
	1x2•1x3	1x3•1x3	1x2•1x3	1x2•1x3	1x3•1x3	1x3•1x4	1x4•1x5	1x4•1x4

Cont even until armhole measures:

	S • 24"	M • 28"	L • 32"	XS • 36"	S • 40"	M • 44"	L • 48"	XL • 52"
for straight armhole __ inches	6	7	8	9	10	11	11½	12½
for curved armhole __ inches.	5½	6½	7½	8	9	10	10½	11½

Place all sts on hold for later finishing.

FRONT PULLOVER

Work as for back, including armhole shaping.

AT SAME TIME, choose neckline style.

V-neck: When work meas __ inches, mark center st. Knit to within 3 sts of center st, k2tog, k1. Place center st on hold, join second ball of yarn, k1, SSK, knit to end. Work each side separately, decreasing 1 st at neck edge:

	S • 24"	M • 28"	L • 32"	XS • 36"	S • 40"	M • 44"	L • 48"	XL • 52"
(V-neck: When work meas __ inches)	8	10	13	14	15	15	15½	15½
for straight shaped garment every __ row	3•2	3•2	3•3	3•3	3•3	4•3	4•3	4•3
for curved shaped garment every __ row	3•2	3•3	3•3	3•2	3•3	3•3	3•3	3•3
__ times.	12•15	15•18	15•18	16•20	18•22	19•23	20•24	20•24

OR

Round neck: When work measures:

	S • 24"	M • 28"	L • 32"	XS • 36"	S • 40"	M • 44"	L • 48"	XL • 52"
for straight shaped garment __ inches	12	14½	18½	20½	22½	23	24	25
for curved shaped garment __ inches.	11½	14	18	19½	21½	22	23	24
Mark center __ sts.	13•15	15•17	17•19	17•21	17•21	17•21	21•25	21•25

Knit to marker, place center sts on hold, join second ball of yarn and knit to end. Working each side separately, at neck edge every other row, bind off in foll sequence (5•6 gauge):

	S • 24"	M • 28"	L • 32"	XS • 36"	S • 40"	M • 44"	L • 48"	XL • 52"
		•3		•3		3•5	3•4	3•4
	2•3	3•2	2•3	3•2	3•4	3•3	2•3	2•3
	2•2	2•2	2•2	2•2	2•2	2•2	2•2	2•2
	1x2•1x3	1x3•1x3	1x3•1x4	1x3•1x3	1x3•1x3	1x3•1x3	1x3•1x3	1x3•1x3

Cont even until piece meas same as back. Place sts on hold for later three needle bind-off seaming.

FRONT CARDIGAN

	S • 24"	M • 28"	L • 32"	XS • 36"	S • 40"	M • 44"	L • 48"	XL • 52"
With smaller needles, cast on __ sts.	23•29	28•34	33•41	37•47	41•51	47•57	49•61	55•69
Work 1/1 rib for __ inches,	2	2	2½	2½	2½	3	3	3
increasing __ sts across last row of rib—	4	5	5	5	6	6	8	7
__ sts.	27•33	33•39	38•46	42•52	47•57	53•63	57•69	62•76
Change to larger needles and work in st st until piece meas __ inches.	8	10	13	14	15	15	15½	15½

Work armhole as for back.

AT SAME TIME, choose neckline style.

V-neck: When work meas __ inches, dec at neck edge 1 st:

	S • 24"	M • 28"	L • 32"	XS • 36"	S • 40"	M • 44"	L • 48"	XL • 52"
(V-neck: When work meas __ inches)	8	10	13	14	15	15	15½	15½
for straight shaped garment every __ row	4•3	3•3	4•3	4•3	4•3	4•3	4•3	5•4
for curved shaped garment every __ row	4•3	3•3	4•3	4•3	4•3	4•3	4•3	4•3
__ times	9•12	13•15	13•16	13•18	15•19	17•20	17•21	17•22

	Child			Adult				
	S • 24"	M • 28"	L • 32"	XS • 36"	S • 40"	M • 44"	L • 48"	XL • 52"

OR

Round neck: When work measures:

	S • 24"	M • 28"	L • 32"	XS • 36"	S • 40"	M • 44"	L • 48"	XL • 52"
for straight shaped garment __ inches	12	14½	18½	20½	22½	23	24	25
for curved shaped garment __ inches	11½	14	18	19½	21½	22	23	24

at neck edge bind off in foll sequence:

S • 24"	M • 28"	L • 32"	XS • 36"	S • 40"	M • 44"	L • 48"	XL • 52"
3 / 4 2 / 3 2 / 2 1x2 / 1x3	· / 5 5 / 3 3 / 2 2 / 2 1x3 / 1x3	6 / 7 2 / 3 2 / 2 1x3 / 1x4	· / 8 5 / 3 3 / 2 2 / 2 1x3 / 1x3	5 / 7 3 / 4 2 / 3 2 / 2 1x3 / 1x3	6 / 7 3 / 5 3 / 3 2 / 2 1x3 / 1x3	7 / 9 3 / 4 2 / 3 2 / 2 1x3 / 1x3	7 / 10 3 / 4 2 / 3 2 / 2 1x3 / 1x3

Cont even until piece meas same as back. Place sts on hold for later three needle bind-off seaming.

SLEEVE PULLOVER/CARDIGAN

	S • 24"	M • 28"	L • 32"	XS • 36"	S • 40"	M • 44"	L • 48"	XL • 52"
With smaller needles, cast on __ sts.	39•47	41•49	43•53	49•59	53•63	55•65	57•69	59•71
Work 1/1 rib for __ inches,	2	2	2	3	3	3	3	3
increasing __ sts across last row—	7	5	5	7	7	9	9	9
__ sts. Change to larger needles!	46•54	46•54	48•58	56•66	60•70	64•74	66•78	68•80

Choose sleeve shaping.

Straight sleeve cap: Work in st st and inc

	S • 24"	M • 28"	L • 32"	XS • 36"	S • 40"	M • 44"	L • 48"	XL • 52"
1 st at beg and end of every __ row	8•6	6•4	5•4	6•4	5•4	4•3	4•3	4•3
__ times —	7•9	12•15	16•19	17•21	20•25	23•29	25•30	28•35
__ sts.	60•72	70•84	80•96	90•108	100•120	110•132	116•138	124•150
When work meas __ inches, bind off all sts.	10½	12½	15½	17½	18	18½	19	20

OR

Curved sleeve cap:

When work meas __ inches, bind off on each side in foll sequence:

S • 24"	M • 28"	L • 32"	XS • 36"	S • 40"	M • 44"	L • 48"	XL • 52"

4x1 / 4x2
3x1 / 3x1
2x3 / 2x3
3x1 / 3x1
4x1 / 4x1
	3x2 / 4x2
	2x4 / 3x2
	3x3 / 2x2
	    / 3x2
	    / 4x1
		4x1 / 4x1
		3x2 / 3x8
		2x5 / 4x1
		    / 3x1
		    / 4x1
			3x3 / 4x1
			2x2 / 3x2
			1x4 / 2x7
			2x2 / 3x4
			3x3 /
				3x3 / 6x1
				2x9 / 4x1
				3x2 / 3x2
				    / 2x6
				    / 3x4
					5x1 / 6x1
					3x2 / 4x1
					2x4 / 3x2
					1x4 / 2x4
					2x4 / 1x4
					3x2 / 3x4
					    / 4x1
						6x1 / 7x1
						4x1 / 4x1
						2x4 / 3x2
						1x4 / 2x4
						2x4 / 1x4
						4x2 / 3x4
						    / 5x1
							7x1 / 8x1
							4x1 / 6x1
							2x4 / 4x1
							1x4 / 2x4
							3x2 / 1x4
							4x3 / 3x4
							    / 4x2

	S • 24"	M • 28"	L • 32"	XS • 36"	S • 40"	M • 44"	L • 48"	XL • 52"
Bind off remaining __ sts.	20•24	24•28	26•32	30•36	34•40	36•44	40•46	42•50

FINISHING

Work three needle bind off seaming for shoulders, leaving back neck sts on hold. Set sleeve in armhole. Sew side and sleeve seams. For all the following ribbed borders, use smaller circular or dp needles and pick up sts from right side.

PULLOVER v-neck border: Beg at left shoulder, pick up __ sts along left front neck edge, place marker, knit center st through back of loop, place marker, pick up as for sts along right front neck edge, knit across back neck sts— __ sts. Work 1/1 rib for one inch, decreasing 1 st before first marker (SSK) and 1 st after second marker (k 2 tog) every other row. Bind off loosely in pattern.

	S • 24"	M • 28"	L • 32"	XS • 36"	S • 40"	M • 44"	L • 48"	XL • 52"
pick up __ sts	32•39	38•46	43•51	48•57	53•63	58•70	61•73	66•79
__ sts	90•110	108•130	118•140	130•156	144•172	156•188	164•196	174•208

PULLOVER round neck border: Beg at left shoulder, pick up __ sts along left front neck curve, knit across center front sts, pick up as for sts along right front neck curve, knit across back neck sts— __ sts. Work 1/1 rib for one inch. Bind off loosely in pattern.

	S • 24"	M • 28"	L • 32"	XS • 36"	S • 40"	M • 44"	L • 48"	XL • 52"
pick up __ sts	13•16	16•20	16•20	17•20	19•22	21•25	21•25	21•25
__ sts	64•78	78•94	78•94	84•102	92•110	98•118	104•124	104•124

FINISHING (cont)

	Child			Adult				
	S • 24"	M • 28"	L • 32"	XS • 36"	S • 40"	M • 44"	L • 48"	XL • 52"

CARDIGAN v-neck border: Mark placement for buttonholes, with first at beg of v-neck shaping, the last ¾ inch from lower edge, and

__ others spaced evenly between. Mark on right front for female, and on left front for male. Beg at lower right front edge,

pick up __ sts along center front edge, along right front v-neck pick up:

for straight shaped garment __ sts

for curved shaped garment __ sts

knit across back neck sts,

along left front v-neck and left center front edge pick up as for right front— __ sts. for straight

__ sts. for curved

Work 1/1 rib for one inch, bind off loosely in pattern. *NOTE: The border may be worked in two parts, dividing and seaming at left shoulder.*

AT SAME TIME, when border meas half of total width, work buttonholes at markers. (I like the eyelet buttonhole for bulky yarns, and the one-row buttonhole for worsted and finer yarns.)

	Child			Adult				
	S • 24"	M • 28"	L • 32"	XS • 36"	S • 40"	M • 44"	L • 48"	XL • 52"
others spaced evenly between	1	2	3	3	3	3	4	4
pick up sts along center front edge	40·48	50·60	65·78	70·84	75·90	75·90	78·93	78·93
for straight shaped garment sts	32·39	38·45	42·51	47·57	53·63	58·69	60·72	65·78
for curved shaped garment sts	30·36	35·42	40·48	43·52	48·58	53·64	56·67	60·72
sts for straight	169·205	207·247	245·295	267·323	293·351	305·365	317·379	327·391
sts for curved	165·199	201·241	241·289	259·313	283·341	295·355	309·369	317·379

CARDIGAN round neck border: Beg at center front right neck edge, pick up __ sts along right neck curve, knit back neck sts, along left neck curve pick up as for right neck— __ sts. Work 1/1 rib for one inch. Bind off loosely in pattern. Mark placement for buttonholes, with the first ½ inch from top edge, the last ¾ inch from lower edge, and __ others spaced evenly between. Mark on right front for female, and on left front for male. Pick up __ sts along each center front edge (straight) Pick up __ sts along each center front edge (curved) and work 1/1 rib for one inch. Bind off loosely in pattern.

AT SAME TIME, when buttonhole border meas half of total width, work buttonholes at markers. (I like the eyelet buttonhole for bulky yarns, and the one-row buttonhole for worsted and finer yarns.)

Sew on buttons. Block, using the wet towel method.

	Child			Adult				
	S • 24"	M • 28"	L • 32"	XS • 36"	S • 40"	M • 44"	L • 48"	XL • 52"
pick up sts along right neck curve	16·19	20·23	20·23	22·26	24·28	26·31	28·33	31·37
sts	57·69	71·83	71·83	77·93	85·101	91·109	97·115	103·123
others spaced evenly between	3	3	4	5	6	6	6	6
Pick up sts along each center front edge (straight)	65·78	77·93	97·117	107·129	117·141	121·145	125·151	131·157
Pick up sts along each center front edge (curved)	62·75	75·90	95·114	102·123	112·135	115·138	120·144	125·150

4 • 4½ sts per inch

	Child S•24"	Child M•28"	Child L•32"	Adult XS•36"	Adult S•40"	Adult M•44"	Adult L•48"	Adult XL•52"
BACK PULLOVER/CARDIGAN								
With smaller needles, cast on __ sts.	43•49	51•57	57•65	63•73	71•81	79•91	85•97	93•105
Work 1/1 rib for __ inches,	2	2	2½	2½	2½	3	3	3
increasing __ sts across last row of rib,	6	8	8	10	10	10	12	12
__ sts.	49•55	59•65	65•73	73•83	81•91	89•101	97•109	105•117
Change to larger needles and work in st st until piece meas __ inches.	8	10	13	14	15	15	15½	15½

Choose armhole style.

Straight armhole: Place marker at side edge and cont even.

OR

Curved armhole: Bind off sts at each armhole edge in the foll sequence (values shown as 4-gauge / 4½-gauge):

	Child S•24"	Child M•28"	Child L•32"	Adult XS•36"	Adult S•40"	Adult M•44"	Adult L•48"	Adult XL•52"
			3 / 4	3 / 3	3 / 4	4 / 5	6 / 6	6 / 6
	2 / 2	3 / 3	3 / 3	3 / 3	3 / 3	3 / 4	3 / 4	4 / 4
	2 / 2	2 / 2	2 / 2	2 / 2	2 / 2	2 / 2	2 / 2	2 / 2
	1x2 / 1x2	1x2 / 1x3	1x2 / 1x3	1x3 / 1x2	1x2 / 1x3	1x3 / 1x3	1x3 / 1x4	1x4 / 1x4

Cont even until armhole measures:

	Child S•24"	Child M•28"	Child L•32"	Adult XS•36"	Adult S•40"	Adult M•44"	Adult L•48"	Adult XL•52"
for straight armhole __ inches	6	7	8	9	10	11	11½	12½
for curved armhole __ inches.	5½	6½	7½	8	9	10	10½	11½

Place all sts on hold for later finishing.

FRONT PULLOVER

Work as for back, including armhole shaping.

AT SAME TIME, choose neckline style.

V-neck: When work meas __ inches, mark center st. Knit to within 3 sts of center st, k2tog, k1. Place center st on hold, join second ball of yarn, k1, SSK, knit to end. Work each side separately, decreasing 1 st at neck edge:

	Child S•24"	Child M•28"	Child L•32"	Adult XS•36"	Adult S•40"	Adult M•44"	Adult L•48"	Adult XL•52"
V-neck: When work meas __ inches	8	10	13	14	15	15	15½	15½
for straight shaped garment every __ row	3•3	3•3	4•3	4•3	4•3	4•3	4•3	4•3
for curved shaped garment every __ row	3•3	3•2	3•3	3•3	3•3	4•3	3•3	4•3
__ times.	10•11	12•14	12•14	13•15	14•16	15•17	16•18	16•18

OR

Round neck: When work measures:

	Child S•24"	Child M•28"	Child L•32"	Adult XS•36"	Adult S•40"	Adult M•44"	Adult L•48"	Adult XL•52"
for straight shaped garment __ inches	12	14½	18½	20½	22½	23	24	25
for curved shaped garment __ inches.	11½	14	18	19½	21½	22	23	24
Mark center __ sts.	11•13	13•13	13•15	13•15	13•15	15•17	17•19	17•19

Knit to marker, place center sts on hold, join second ball of yarn and knit to end. Working each side separately, at neck edge every other row, bind off in foll sequence (values shown as 4-gauge / 4½-gauge):

	Child S•24"	Child M•28"	Child L•32"	Adult XS•36"	Adult S•40"	Adult M•44"	Adult L•48"	Adult XL•52"
		2 / 3	2 / 2	2 / 2	2 / 3	3 / 4	3 / 4	3 / 4
	2 / 2	2 / 2	2 / 2	2 / 2	2 / 2	2 / 2	2 / 2	2 / 2
	1x3 / 1x3	1x2 / 1x3	1x2 / 1x3	1x2 / 1x3	1x3 / 1x3	1x3 / 1x3	1x3 / 1x3	1x3 / 1x3

Cont even until piece meas same as back. Place sts on hold for later three needle bind-off seaming.

FRONT CARDIGAN

	Child S•24"	Child M•28"	Child L•32"	Adult XS•36"	Adult S•40"	Adult M•44"	Adult L•48"	Adult XL•52"
With smaller needles, cast on __ sts.	17•21	22•25	25•29	30•34	35•39	37•43	41•45	45•51
Work 1/1 rib for __ inches,	2	2	2½	2½	2½	3	3	3
increasing __ sts across last row of rib—	4	4	5	4	4	5	6	5
__ sts.	21•25	26•29	30•34	34•38	39•43	42•48	47•51	50•56

Change to larger needles and work in st st until piece meas __ inches.

Work armhole as for back.

AT SAME TIME, choose neckline style.

V-neck: When work meas __ inches, dec at neck edge 1 st:

	Child S•24"	Child M•28"	Child L•32"	Adult XS•36"	Adult S•40"	Adult M•44"	Adult L•48"	Adult XL•52"
V-neck: When work meas __ inches	8	10	13	14	15	15	15½	15½
for straight shaped garment every __ row	5•4	4•3	4•4	5•4	4•4	5•4	4•4	5•4
for curved shaped garment every __ row	4•3	4•3	4•3	4•4	4•3	4•4	4•4	4•4
__ times	7•9	9•11	10•12	11•12	13•14	13•15	15•15	14•16

	Child			Adult				
	S • 24"	M • 28"	L • 32"	XS • 36"	S • 40"	M • 44"	L • 48"	XL • 52"

OR

Round neck: When work measures:

		Child			Adult				
for straight shaped garment __ inches		12	14½	18½	20½	22½	23	24	25
for curved shaped garment __ inches		11½	14	18	19½	21½	22	23	24

at neck edge bind off in foll sequence:

S		M		L		XS		S		M		L		XL	
	3	3	3	4	5	4	4	5	5	5	6	6	6	6	7
2	2	2	3	2	2	2	3	3	4	3	4	4	4	3	4
2	2	2	2	2	2	2	2	2	2	2	2	2	2	2	2
1x3	1x2	1x2	1x3	1x2	1x3	1x3	1x3	1x3	1x3	1x3	1x3	1x3	1x3	1x3	1x3

Cont even until piece meas same as back. Place sts on hold for later three needle bind-off seaming.

SLEEVE PULLOVER/CARDIGAN

	S • 24"	M • 28"	L • 32"	XS • 36"	S • 40"	M • 44"	L • 48"	XL • 52"
With smaller needles, cast on __ sts.	31·35	33·37	35·39	39·43	41·47	43·49	45·51	47·55
Work 1/1 rib for __ inches,	2	2	2	3	3	3	3	3
increasing __ sts across last row—	5	5	5	5	5	7	7	7
__ sts. Change to larger needles!	36·40	38·42	40·44	44·48	46·52	50·56	52·58	54·62

Sleeve shaping.
Work in st st and inc

	S • 24"	M • 28"	L • 32"	XS • 36"	S • 40"	M • 44"	L • 48"	XL • 52"
1 st at beg and end of every __ row	8·7	7·5	6·5	6·5	5·4	4·4	4·4	4·4
__ times—	6·7	9·11	12·14	14·17	17·19	19·22	20·23	23·25
__ sts.	48·54	56·64	64·72	72·82	80·90	88·100	92·104	100·112

Straight sleep cap:

	S • 24"	M • 28"	L • 32"	XS • 36"	S • 40"	M • 44"	L • 48"	XL • 52"
When work meas __ inches, bind off all sts.	10½	12½	15½	17½	18	18½	19	20

OR

Curved sleeve cap:

	S • 24"	M • 28"	L • 32"	XS • 36"	S • 40"	M • 44"	L • 48"	XL • 52"
When work meas __ inches, bind off on each side in foll sequence:	10½	12½	15½	17½	18	18½	19	20

S		M		L		XS		S		M		L		XL	
3x2	3x6	4x1	4x1	3x2	4x1	3x2	3x2	3x2	3x3	4x1	5x1	6x1	6x1	6x1	6x1
2x2		3x1	3x2	2x6	3x2	2x3	2x9	2x9	2x6	3x1	4x1	3x1	4x1	4x1	4x1
3x2		2x3	2x2	3x1	2x4	1x3	3x1	3x1	3x3	2x11	3x1	2x3	3x1	2x3	2x9
		3x2	3x1		3x2	2x3					2x9	1x4	2x9	1x3	3x3
			4x1			3x1					3x1	2x3	4x1	2x3	
												3x2		4x2	

	S • 24"	M • 28"	L • 32"	XS • 36"	S • 40"	M • 44"	L • 48"	XL • 52"
Bind off remaining __ sts.	16·18	18·22	22·24	24·28	26·30	30·34	30·34	34·38

FINISHING

Work three needle bind off seaming for shoulders, leaving back neck sts on hold. Set sleeve in armhole. Sew side and sleeve seams. For all the following ribbed borders, use smaller circular or dp needles and pick up sts from right side.

PULLOVER v-neck border: Beg at left shoulder, pick up __ sts along left front neck edge, place marker, knit center st through back of loop, place marker, pick up __ sts along right front neck edge, knit across back neck sts— __ sts.

	S • 24"	M • 28"	L • 32"	XS • 36"	S • 40"	M • 44"	L • 48"	XL • 52"
pick up __ sts	26·29	30·34	34·38	38·43	42·47	46·52	48·54	52·59
__ sts.	74·82	86·98	94·106	104·118	114·128	124·140	130·146	138·156

Work 1/1 rib for one inch, decreasing 1 st before first marker (SSK) and 1 st after second marker (k 2 tog) every other row. Bind off loosely in pattern.

PULLOVER round neck border: Beg at left shoulder, pick up __ sts along left front neck curve, knit across center front sts, pick up __ sts along right front neck curve, knit across back neck sts— __ sts.

	S • 24"	M • 28"	L • 32"	XS • 36"	S • 40"	M • 44"	L • 48"	XL • 52"
pick up __ sts	10·11	12·15	12·15	14·15	15·17	16·17	17·19	17·19
__ sts.	52·58	62·72	62·72	68·76	72·82	78·88	84·94	84·94

Work 1/1 rib for one inch. Bind off loosely in pattern.

	Child			Adult				
4 • 4½ sts per inch	S • 24"	M • 28"	L • 32"	XS • 36"	S • 40"	M • 44"	L • 48"	XL • 52"

FINISHING (cont)

CARDIGAN v-neck border: Mark placement for buttonholes, with first at beg of v-neck shaping, the last ¾ inch from lower edge, and
__ others spaced evenly between. Mark on right front for female, and on left front for male.

__ others	1	2	3	4	4	4	4	4

Beg at lower right front edge,
pick up __ sts along center front edge,

pick up	32·36	40·45	52·59	56·63	60·68	60·68	62·70	62·70

along right front v-neck pick up:

for straight shaped garment __ sts	26·29	30·34	34·38	38·42	42·47	42·52	48·54	52·58
for curved shaped garment __ sts	24·27	28·31	32·36	34·39	38·43	42·48	45·50	48·54

knit across back neck sts,
along left front v-neck and left center front edge
pick up as for right front— __ sts for straight
__ sts for curved

__ sts for straight	137·153	165·183	197·223	215·241	233·263	241·275	253·285	261·293
__ sts for curved	133·149	161·181	193·219	207·235	225·255	235·267	247·277	253·285

Work 1/1 rib for one inch, bind off loosely in pattern.
NOTE: The border may be worked in two parts, dividing and seaming at left shoulder.
AT SAME TIME, when border meas half of total width, work buttonholes at markers. (I like the eyelet buttonhole for bulky yarns, and the one-row buttonhole for worsted and finer yarns.)

CARDIGAN round neck border: Beg at center front right neck edge, pick up __ sts along right neck curve, knit back neck sts, along left neck curve pick up as for right neck— __ sts. Work 1/1 rib for one inch. Bind off loosely in pattern.

pick up __ sts along right	13·14	16·18	16·18	18·19	19·21	20·23	22·25	25·28
pick up as for right neck— __ sts	47·51	57·65	57·65	63·69	67·75	71·81	77·87	83·93

Mark placement for buttonholes, with the first ½ inch from top edge, the last ¾ inch from lower edge, and __ others spaced evenly between. Mark on right front for female, and on left front for male.

__ others	3	3	4	5	6	6	6	6

Pick up __ sts along each center front edge (straight)
Pick up __ sts along each center front edge (curved)

(straight)	51·59	61·69	77·87	87·97	95·105	97·109	101·113	105·117
(curved)	50·56	60·67	76·85	82·92	90·101	92·103	96·108	100·112

and work 1/1 rib for one inch. Bind off loosely in pattern.
AT SAME TIME, when buttonhole border meas half of total width, work buttonholes at markers. (I like the eyelet buttonhole for bulky yarns, and the one-row buttonhole for worsted and finer yarns.)

Sew on buttons. Block, using the wet towel method.

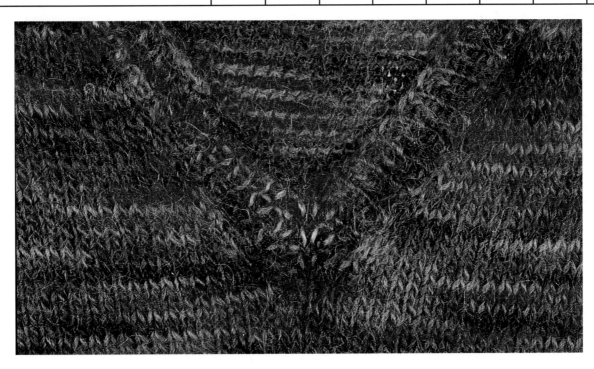

🌀 3 • 3½ sts per inch

	Child			Adult				
	S • 24"	M • 28"	L • 32"	XS • 36"	S • 40"	M • 44"	L • 48"	XL • 52"

BACK PULLOVER/CARDIGAN

With smaller needles, cast on 63 sts.
Work 1/1 rib for 3 inches,
increasing 10 sts across last row of rib,
73 sts.
Change to larger needles and work in st st until
piece meas 15 inches.
Choose armhole style.

Straight armhole: Place marker at side edge and cont even.
OR
Curved armhole: Bind off sts at each armhole edge in the foll sequence:

	33•39	37•45	43•51	47•57	53•63	59•71	63•75	69•83
	2	2	2½	2½	2½	3	3	3
	4	6	6	8	8	8	10	10
	37•43	43•51	49•57	55•65	61•71	67•79	73•85	79•93
	8	10	13	14	15	15	15½	15½

				2	3	4	4	5	4	6
						3	3	5	3	4
	2	2	2	2	2	2	2	3	2	3	2
	2	2	2	2	2	2	2	2	2	2	2
	1x3	1x3	1x3	1x2	1x2	1x2	1x2	1x3	1x2	1x3	1x3	1x3	1x2	1x3	1x3	1x3

Cont even until armhole measures
for straight armhole 11 inches. 11½
for curved armhole 10 inches.
Place all sts on hold for later finishing.

	6	7	8	9	10	11	11½	12½
	5½	6½	7½	8	9	10	10½	11½

FRONT PULLOVER

Work as for back, including armhole shaping.
AT SAME TIME, choose neckline style.
V-neck: When work meas __ inches, mark center st.
Knit to within 3 sts of center st, k2tog, k1. Place center st on hold, join second ball of yarn, k1, SSK, knit to end. Work each side separately, decreasing 1 st at neck edge:
for straight shaped garment every __ row

	8	10	13	14	15	15	15½	15½
	3•3	3•3	4•3	4•3	4•3	4•13	4•3	4•4

for curved shaped garment every __ row
__ times.

	3•2	3•3	3•3	3•3	3•3	4•3	3•3	4•3
	8•9	9•10	9•11	10•11	11•13	11•13	12•14	12•14

OR
Round neck: When work measures:
for straight shaped garment 24 inches.
for curved shaped garment 23 inches.
Mark center 13 sts. Knit to marker, place center sts on hold, join second ball of yarn and knit to end. Working each side separately, at neck edge every other row, bind off in foll sequence:

	12	14½	18½	20½	22½	23	24	25
	11½	14	18	19½	21½	22	23	24
	7•9	9•11	9•11	9•11	11•13	11•13	13•15	13•15

				2	2	2	2	2	2	2	2	2
	2	2	2	2	2	2	2	2	2	2	2	2
	1x3	1x3	1x3	1x3	1x3	1x2	1x2	1x2	1x2	1x3	1x2	1x3	1x2	1x3	1x2	1x3

Cont even until piece meas same as back. Place sts on hold for later three needle bind-off seaming.

FRONT CARDIGAN

With smaller needles, cast on __ sts.
Work 1/1 rib for __ inches,
increasing __ sts across last row of rib—
__ sts.
Change to larger needles and work in st st until piece meas __ inches.
Work armhole as for back.
AT SAME TIME, choose neckline style.
V-neck: When work meas __ inches, dec at neck edge 1 st:

	13•17	16•19	19•22	23•27	25•29	27•33	29•35	33•39
	2	2	2½	2½	2½	3	3	3
	3	4	4	3	4	4	5	4
	16•20	20•23	23•26	26•30	29•33	31•37	34•40	37•43
	8	10	13	14	15	15	15½	15½
	8	10	13	14	15	15	15½	15½

for straight shaped garment every __ row

	4•3	4•4	4•4	4•4	4•4	5•4	5•4	5•5

for curved shaped garment every __ row
__ times

	4•3	4•4	4•3	4•4	4•3	5•4	4•3	5•4
	6•8	8•8	8•9	9•9	10•11	9•11	10•12	10•11

OR

Round neck: When work measures:
  for straight shaped garment ___ inches
  for curved shaped garment ___ inches
at neck edge bind off in foll sequence:

Cont even until piece meas same as back. Place sts on hold for later three needle bind-off seaming.

	Child			Adult				
	S • 24"	M • 28"	L • 32"	XS • 36"	S • 40"	M • 44"	L • 48"	XL • 52"
straight shaped	12	14½	18½	20½	22½	23	24	25
curved shaped	11½	14	18	19½	21½	22	23	24
			| 3	3 | 3	4 | 4	3 | 4	4 | 5	4 | 4
	2 | 3	3 | 3	3 | 2	2 | 2	2 | 2	2 | 2	2 | 2	2 | 2
	2 | 2	2 | 2	2 | 2	2 | 2	2 | 2	2 | 2	2 | 2	2 | 2
	1x2 | 1x3	1x3 | 1x3	1x3 | 1x2	1x2 | 1x2	1x2 | 1x2	1x2 | 1x3	1x2 | 1x3	1x2 | 1x3

SLEEVE PULLOVER/CARDIGAN

With smaller needles, cast on _35_ sts.
Work 1/1 rib for _3_ inches,
increasing _5_ sts across last row—
_40_ sts. Change to larger needles!
Sleeve shaping.
Work in st st and inc
1 st at beg and end of every _4_ row
__ times —
__ sts.
Straight sleeve cap:
When work meas __ inches, bind off all sts.
OR
Curved sleeve cap:
When work meas __ inches, bind off on each side in foll sequence:

Bind off remaining _24_ sts.

	Child			Adult				
	S • 24"	M • 28"	L • 32"	XS • 36"	S • 40"	M • 44"	L • 48"	XL • 52"
cast on	23·27	25·29	27·31	29·33	31·37	33·39	35·41	47·55
rib inches	2	2	2	3	3	3	3	3
increasing	3	3	3	5	5	5	5	7
sts	26·30	28·32	30·34	34·38	36·42	38·44	40·46	54·62
inc every 4 row	7·6	6·5	6·5	6·5	5·4	4·4	4·4	4·3
times	5·6	7·9	9·11	10·13	12·14	14·17	15·17	17·21
sts	36·42	42·50	48·56	54·64	60·70	66·78	70·80	76·88
straight cap	10½	12½	15½	17½	18	18½	19	20
curved cap	10½	12½	15½	17½	18	18½	19	20
	3x1 | 3x1	3x1 | 3x4	3x1 | 4x1	3x1 | 3x2	3x1 | 3x2	4x1 | 4x2	4x1 | 5x1	4x1 | 6x1
	2x3 | 2x2	2x2 | 4x1	2x5 | 3x1	2x2 | 2x6	2x7 | 2x4	2x6 | 2x4	3x1 | 3x1	3x1 | 4x1
	3x1 | 3x1	2x2 |	| 2x3	1x2 | 3x1	3x1 | 3x3	3x2 | 3x3	2x5 | 2x3	2x6 | 2x3
	| 4x1	4x1 |	| 3x2	2x3 |			3x2 | 3x4	3x2 | 3x4
				3x1 |				
bind off remaining	12·14	14·18	16·18	18·22	20·24	22·28	24·28	26·32

FINISHING

Work three needle bind off seaming for shoulders, leaving back neck sts on hold. Set sleeve in armhole. Sew side and sleeve seams. For all the following ribbed borders, use smaller circular or dp needles and pick up sts from right side.
PULLOVER v-neck border: Beg at left shoulder, pick up ___ sts along left front neck edge, place marker, knit center st through back of loop, place marker, pick up ___ sts along right front neck edge, knit across back neck sts— ___ sts.
Work 1/1 rib for one inch, decreasing 1 st before first marker (SSK) and 1 st after second marker (k 2 tog) every other row. Bind off loosely in pattern.

PULLOVER round neck border: Beg at left shoulder, pick up _12_ sts along left front neck curve, knit across center front sts, pick up ___ sts along right front neck curve, knit across back neck sts — ___ sts.
Work 1/1 rib for one inch. Bind off loosely in pattern.

	Child			Adult				
	S • 24"	M • 28"	L • 32"	XS • 36"	S • 40"	M • 44"	L • 48"	XL • 52"
v-neck pick up	19·23	23·27	26·30	29·33	32·37	35·41	36·42	39·46
v-neck total	56·66	66·76	72·84	80·90	88·102	94·110	98·114	104·122
round neck pick up	8·9	10·11	10·11	11·12	11·13	12·14	12·14	12·14
round neck total	40·46	48·54	48·54	52·58	56·66	58·68	62·72	62·72

	Child			Adult				
	S • 24"	M • 28"	L • 32"	XS • 36"	S • 40"	M • 44"	L • 48"	XL • 52"

FINISHING (cont)

CARDIGAN v-neck border: Mark placement for buttonholes, with first at beg of v-neck shaping, the last ¾ inch from lower edge, and __ others spaced evenly between. Mark on right front for female, and on left front for male. Beg at lower right front edge, pick up __ sts along center front edge, along right front v-neck pick up:
for straight shaped garment __ sts
for curved shaped garment __ sts
knit across back neck sts, along left front v-neck and left center front edge pick up as for right front — __ sts for straight
__ sts for curved
Work 1/1 rib for one inch, bind off loosely in pattern. *NOTE: The border may be worked in two parts, dividing and seaming at left shoulder.*
AT SAME TIME, when border meas half of total width, work buttonholes at markers. (I like the eyelet buttonhole for bulky yarns, and the one-row buttonhole for worsted and finer yarns.)

	S • 24"	M • 28"	L • 32"	XS • 36"	S • 40"	M • 44"	L • 48"	XL • 52"
others	1	2	3	3	3	3	4	4
pick up center front	24·28	30·35	39·46	42·49	45·53	45·53	47·54	47·54
straight shaped	19·22	23·27	25·30	28·33	32·37	35·41	36·42	39·45
curved shaped	18·21	21·24	24·28	26·30	29·34	32·37	34·39	36·42
sts for straight	103·119	125·145	147·175	161·187	177·207	183·215	191·221	197·227
sts for curved	101·117	121·139	145·171	157·181	171·201	177·207	187·215	191·221

CARDIGAN round neck border: Beg at center front right neck edge, pick up __ sts along right neck curve, knit back neck sts, along left neck curve pick up as for right neck— __ sts. Work 1/1 rib for one inch. Bind off loosely in pattern.
Mark placement for buttonholes, with the first ½ inch from top edge, the last ¾ inch from lower edge, and __ others spaced evenly between. Mark on right front for female, and on left front for male.
Pick up __ sts along each center front edge (straight)
Pick up __ sts along each center front edge (curved) and work 1/1 rib for one inch. Bind off loosely in pattern.
AT SAME TIME, when buttonhole border meas half of total width, work buttonholes at markers. (I like the eyelet buttonhole for bulky yarns, and the one-row buttonhole for worsted and finer yarns.)

Sew on buttons. Block, using the wet towel method.

	S • 24"	M • 28"	L • 32"	XS • 36"	S • 40"	M • 44"	L • 48"	XL • 52"
pick up along right neck curve	9·11	12·14	12·14	13·15	14·16	15·18	17·19	19·22
pick up as for right neck	35·41	43·49	43·49	47·53	51·59	53·63	59·67	63·73
others	3	3	4	5	6	6	6	6
each center front edge (straight)	39·45	47·55	59·69	65·75	71·83	73·85	75·87	79·91
each center front edge (curved)	37·44	45·52	57·66	61·72	67·79	69·80	72·84	75·87

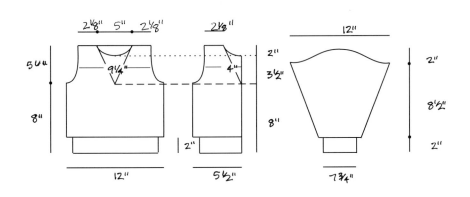

Child's Small

finished chest circumference

24"

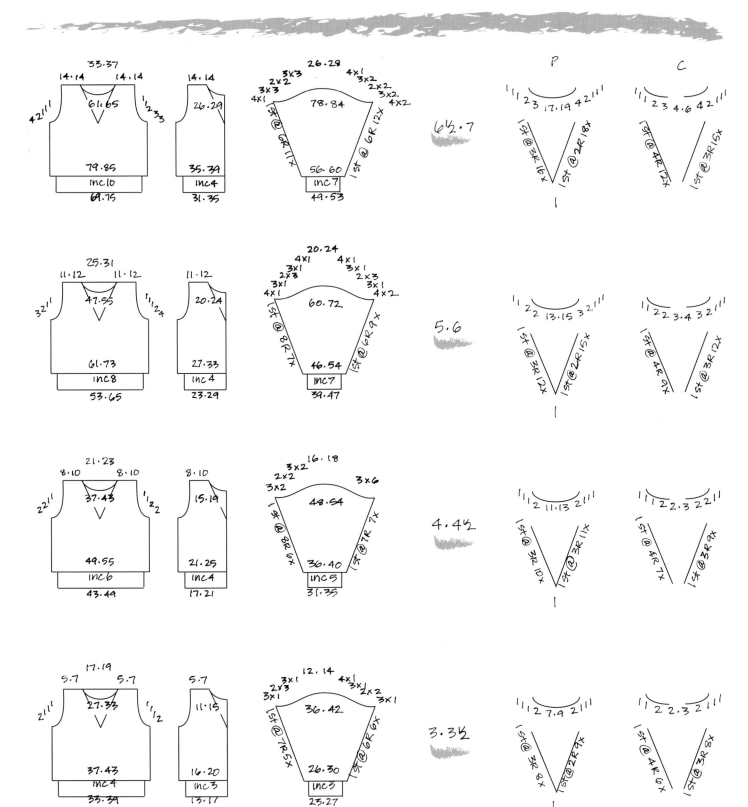

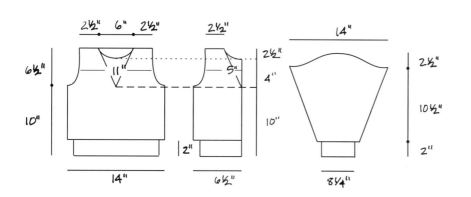

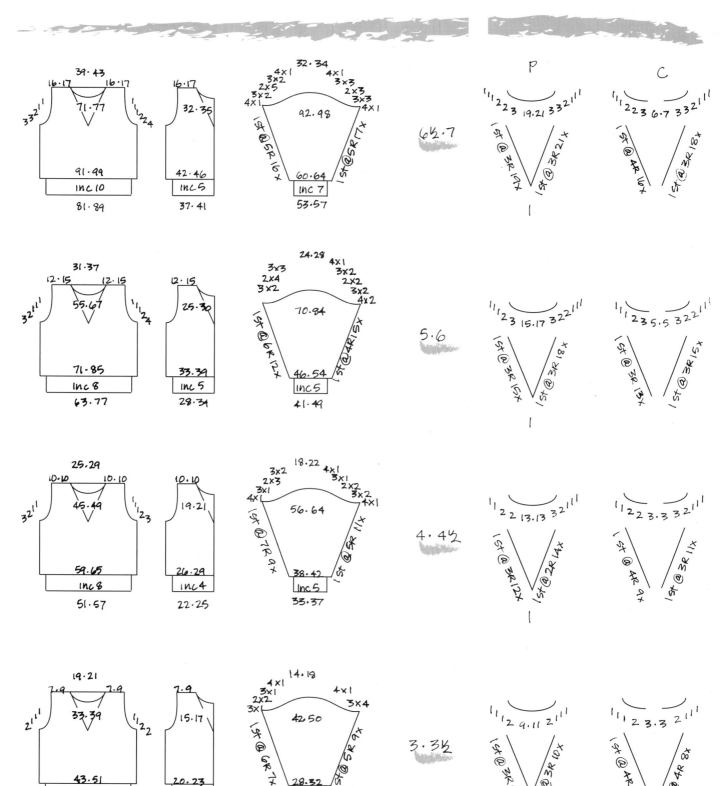

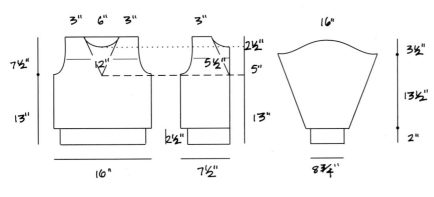

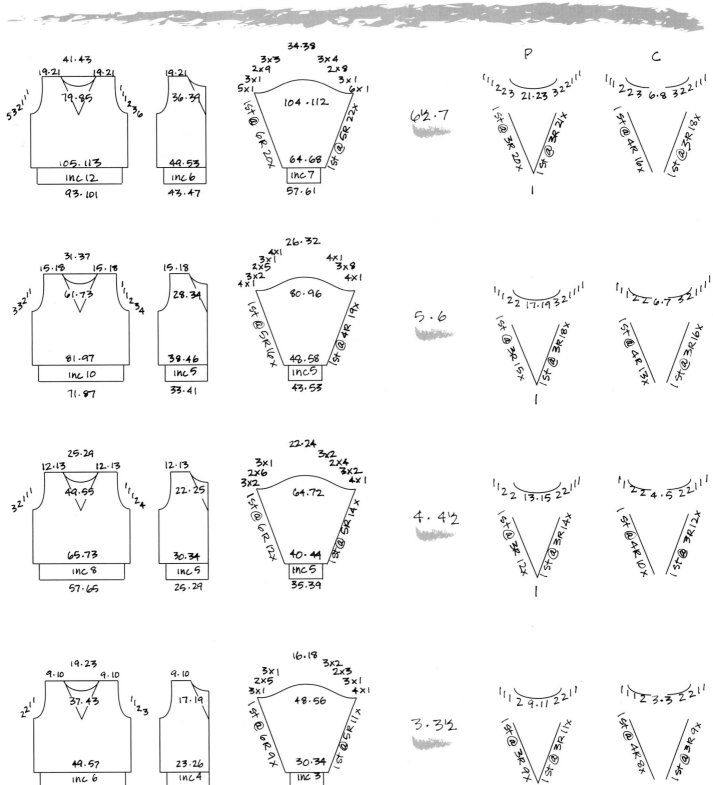

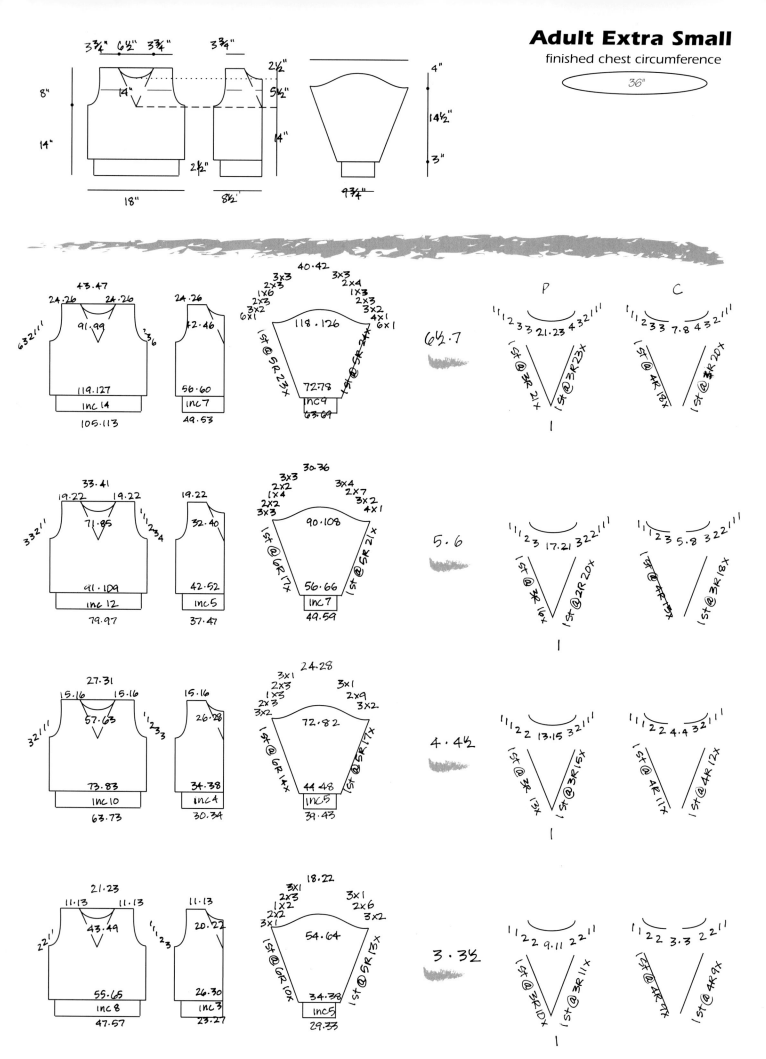

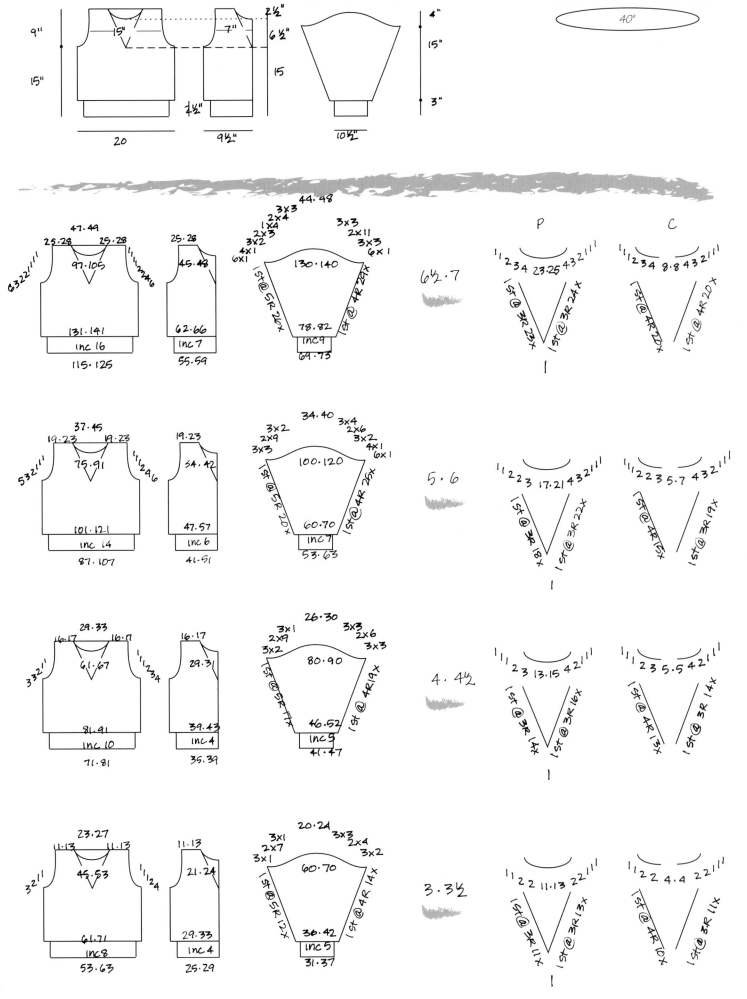

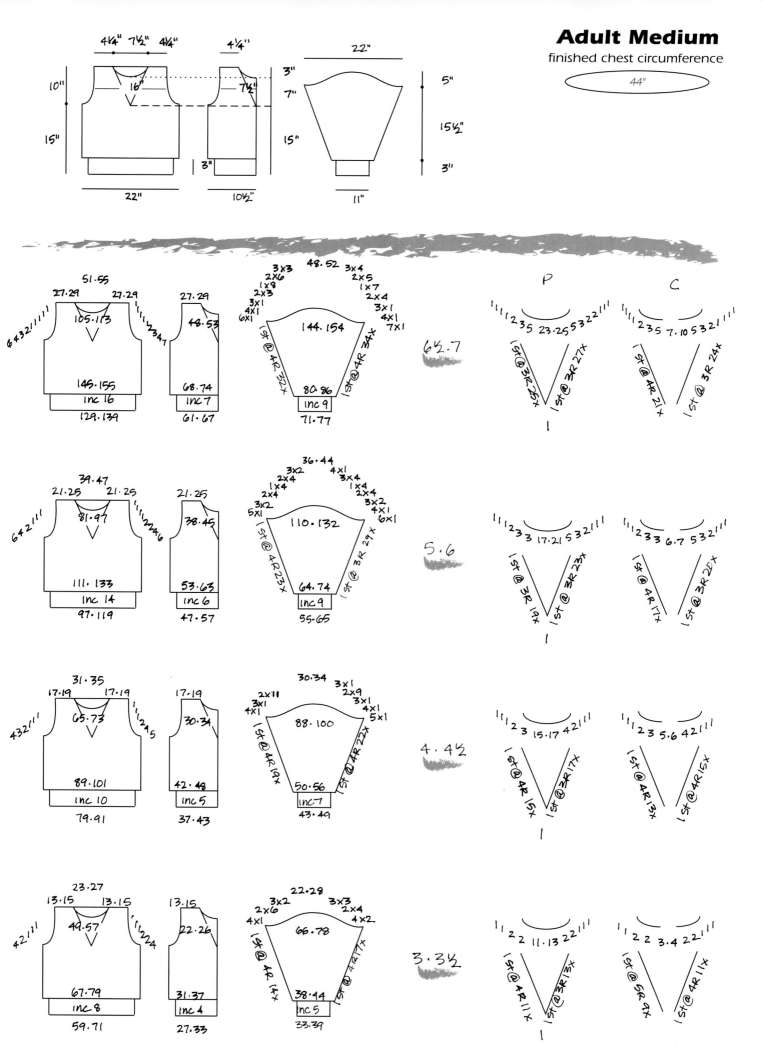

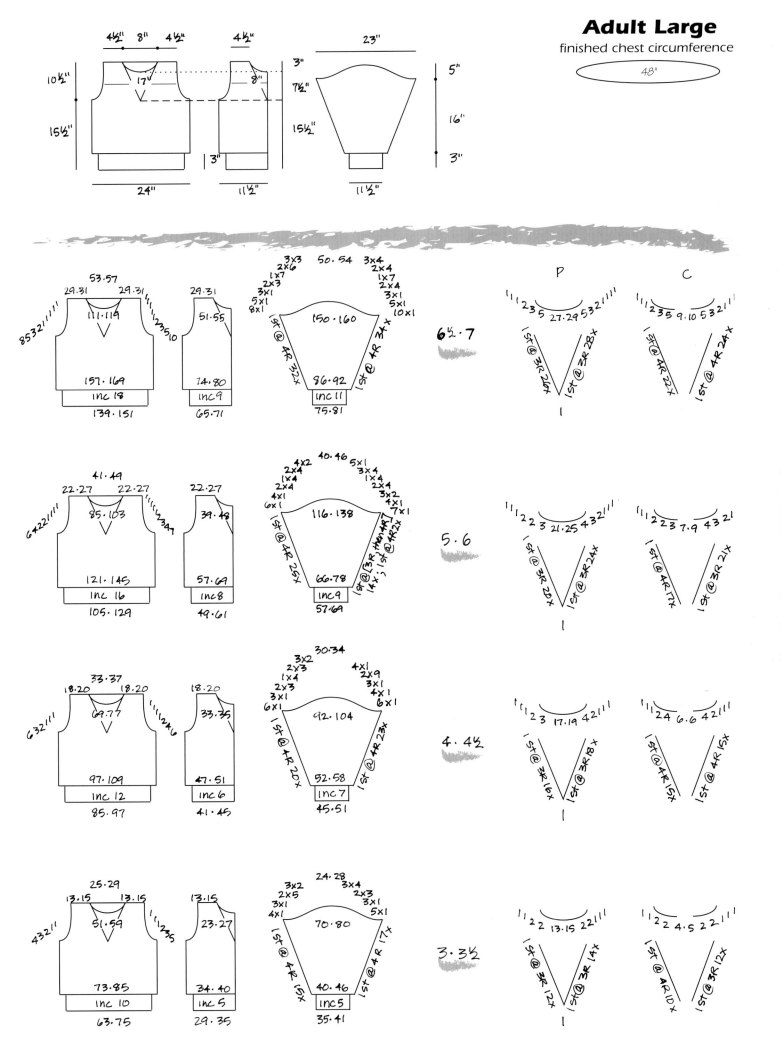

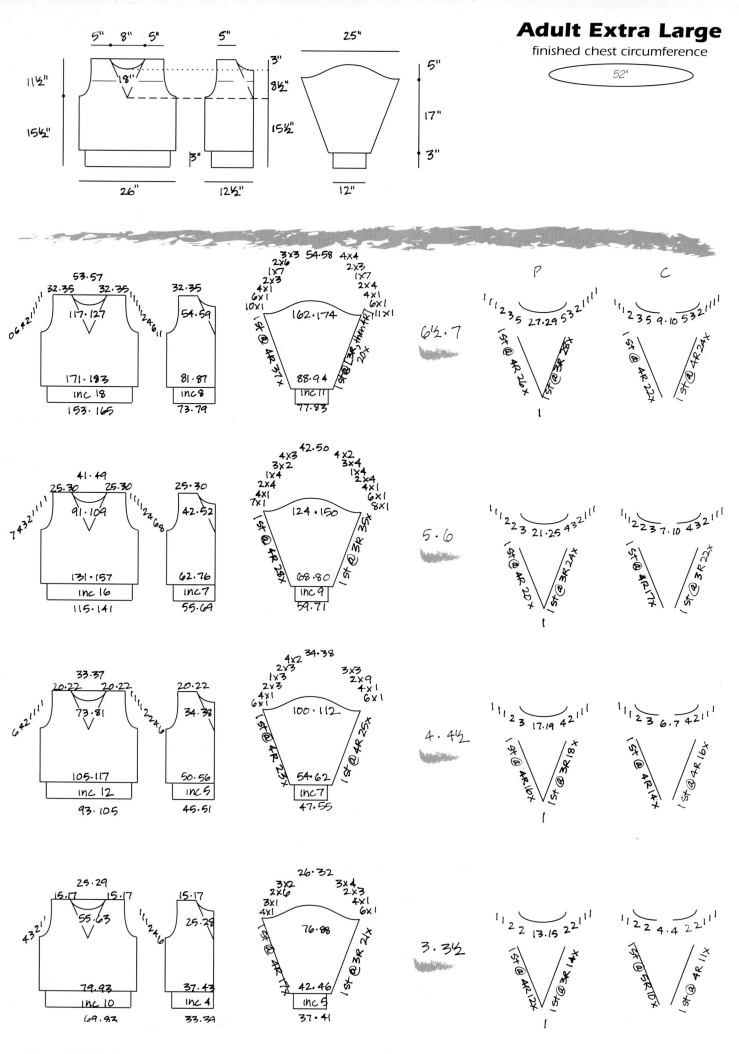

Tunics

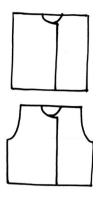

Choose:

- short or medium tunic with round or v-neck, or easy lapel
- straight or curved armholes

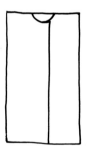
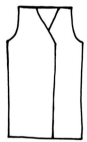
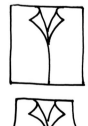

Short Tunic	Child			Adult				
	S • 24"	M • 28"	L • 32"	XS • 36"	S • 40"	M • 44"	L • 48"	XL • 52"
6½ • 7 sts per inch yardage	300	450	600	750	950	1100	1300	1500
Cotton Fine	2	3	3	4	5	5	6	7
Nature Spun (F)	1	2	2	3	3	4	5	5
Wild foote	2	2	3	4	5	6	6	7
5 • 6 sts per inch yardage	250	350	450	600	700	850	1000	1150
Cotton Fleece	2	2	2	3	3	4	5	6
Kaleidoscope	3	4	5	6	7	8	10	11
Nature Spun (S)	2	2	3	4	4	5	6	7
Top of the Lamb (S)	1	1	2	2	2	3	3	4
4 • 4½ sts per inch yardage	200	300	400	500	600	750	850	1000
Country Classics (W)	1	2	3	3	4	4	5	6
Handpaint Originals	3	4	5	6	7	9	10	12
Lamb's Pride (W)	1	2	3	3	4	4	5	6
Lamb's Pride Superwash (W)	1	2	2	3	3	4	5	5
Nature Spun (W)	1	2	2	3	3	4	4	5
Prairie Silk	3	4	5	6	7	9	10	12
Top of the Lamb (W)	1	2	3	3	4	4	5	6
3 • 3½ sts per inch yardage	150	250	300	350	450	550	650	750
Country Classics (B)	2	2	3	3	4	5	6	6
Lamb's Pride (B)	2	2	3	3	4	5	6	7
Lamb's Pride Superwash (B)	2	3	3	4	5	5	6	7

(Yardage and skein estimates are approximations only.)

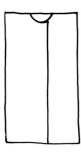

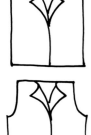

Medium Tunic	Child			Adult				
	S • 24"	M • 28"	L • 32"	XS • 36"	S • 40"	M • 44"	L • 48"	XL • 52"
6½ • 7 sts per inch yardage	550	850	1100	1300	1500	1700	1900	2100
Cotton Fine	3	4	5	6	7	8	9	10
Nature Spun (F)	2	3	4	5	5	6	7	7
Wildfoote	3	4	6	7	7	8	9	10
5 • 6 sts per inch yardage	450	650	850	1000	1150	1300	1450	1600
Cotton Fleece	3	4	4	5	6	7	7	8
Kaleidoscope	5	7	8	10	11	13	14	15
Nature Spun (S)	3	4	5	6	7	8	8	9
Top of the Lamb (S)	2	2	3	3	4	4	5	5
4 • 4½ sts per inch yardage	350	550	750	900	1000	1150	1250	1400
Country Classics (W)	2	3	4	5	6	7	7	8
Handpaint Originals	4	7	9	11	12	14	15	16
Lamb's Pride (W)	2	3	4	5	6	7	7	8
Lamb's Pride Superwash (W)	2	3	4	5	5	6	7	7
Nature Spun (W)	2	3	4	4	5	5	6	6
Prairie Silk	4	7	9	11	12	14	15	16
Top of the Lamb (W)	2	3	4	5	6	7	7	8
3 • 3½ sts per inch yardage	250	450	550	650	750	850	950	1050
Country Classics (B)	2	4	5	6	6	7	8	9
Lamb's Pride (B)	2	4	5	6	6	7	8	9
Lamb's Pride Superwash (B)	3	5	5	6	7	8	9	10

(Yardage and skein estimates are approximations only.)

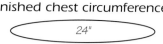
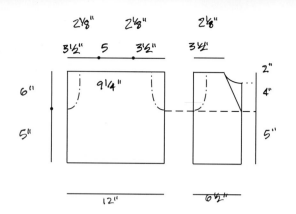

2⅛"   2⅛"   2⅛"

3½" 5 3½"   3½"

6"   9¼"

5"

2"

4"

5"

12"   6½"

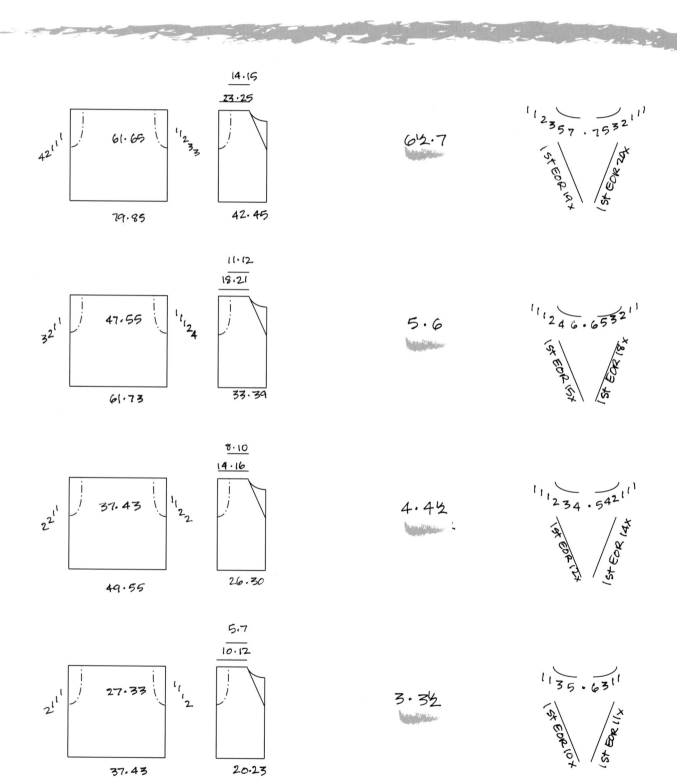

14.15

23.25

42||| 61.65 |||2₃₃

79.85

6½.7

¹|₁₂₃₅₇ · ₇₅₃₂|¹¹
1st EOR 19x   1st EOR 20x

11.12

18.21

32||| 47.55 |||₁₂₄

61.73

5·6

¹|₁₂₄₆ · ₆₅₃₂|¹¹
1st EOR 15x   1st EOR 18x

8·10

14·16

22||| 37.43 |||₂₂

49.55

4·4½

¹|₁₂₃₄ · ₅₄₂|¹¹
1st EOR 17x   1st EOR 14x

5·7

10·12

2||| 27.33 |||₂

37.43

3·3½

¹|₁₃₅ · ₆₃|¹¹
1st EOR 10x   1st EOR 11x

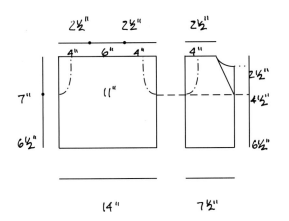

2½"   2½"   2½"

4" 6" 4"   4"

7"   11"   2½"

                                4½"

6½"   6½"

14"   7½"

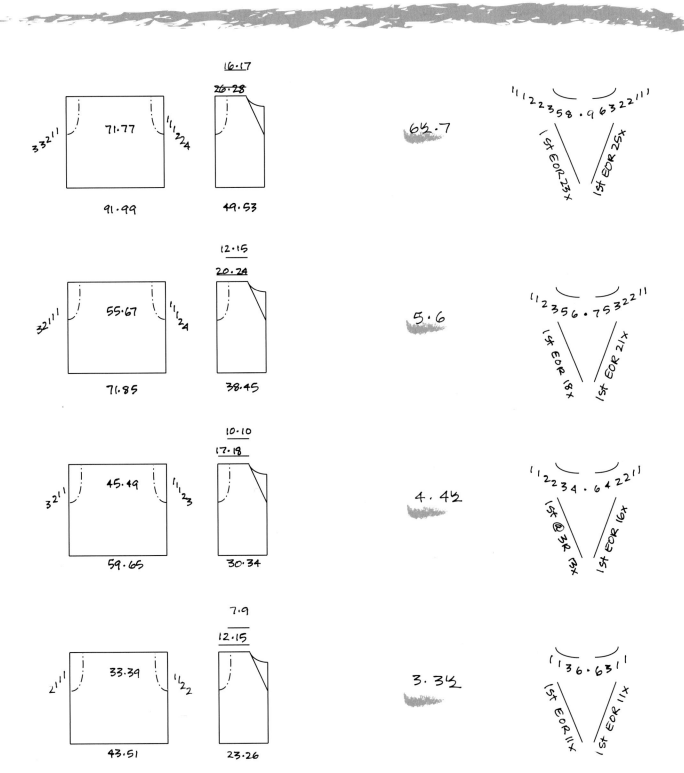

16·17

26·28

33²¹¹   71·77   ¹¹₂₂₄

91·99   49·53

6½·7

¹¹₁₂₂₃₅₈ · ₉₆₃₂₂¹¹
1st EOR 23x   1st EOR 26x

12·15

20·24

32¹¹¹   55·67   ¹¹₂₂₄

71·85   38·45

5·6

¹¹₂₃₅₆ · ₇₅₃₂₂¹¹
1st EOR 18x   1st EOR 21x

10·10

17·18

32¹¹   45·49   ¹¹₂₃

59·65   30·34

4·4½

¹¹₂₂₃₄ · ₆₄₂₂¹¹
1st @ 3R 13x   1st EOR 16x

7·9

12·15

2¹¹¹   33·39   ¹¹₂₂

43·51   23·26

3·3½

¹¹₃₆ · ₆₃¹¹
1st EOR 11x   1st EOR 11x

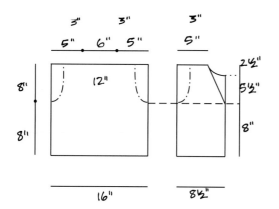

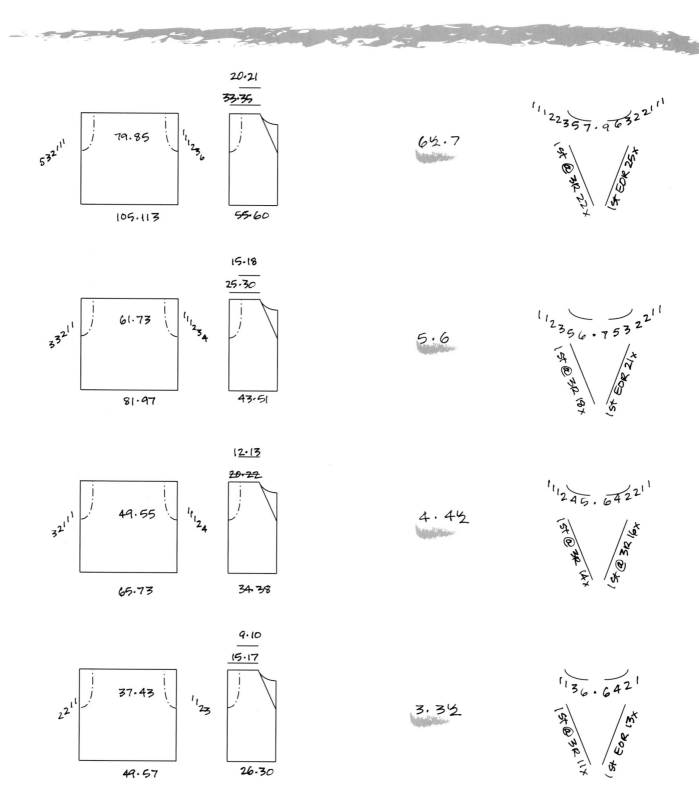

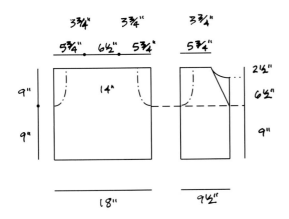

3¾" 3¾" 3¾"

5¾" • 6½" • 5¾" 5¾"

9" 14" 2½" 6½" 9"

9"

18" 9½"

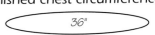

24·27 / 38·41

91·99

63²¹¹ ¹¹²³6

119·127 62·67

6½·7

¹¹²²²³58·963²²²¹¹
1st @ 3R 24x 1st @ 3R 26x

19·23 / 29·35

71·85

33²¹¹ ¹¹²³4

91·109 48·57

5·6

¹¹²³57·853²²¹¹
1st @ 3R 14x 1st EOR 22x

15·17 / 23·27

57·63

32¹¹¹ ¹¹²³3

73·83 38·43

4·4½

¹¹²46·642²¹¹
1st @ 3R 15x 1st @ 3R 16x

11·13 / 17·21

43·49

22¹¹ ¹¹²³

55·65 29·33

3·3½

¹¹²35·53²¹
1st @ 3R 12x 1st @ 3R 12x

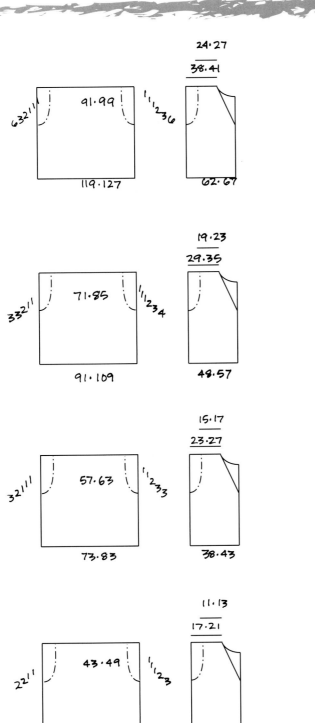

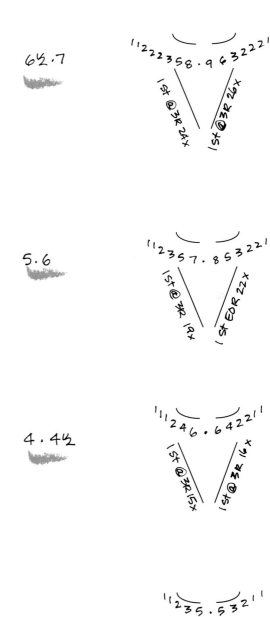

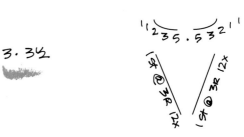

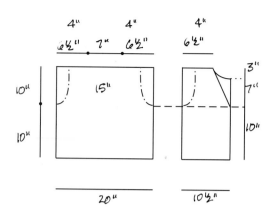

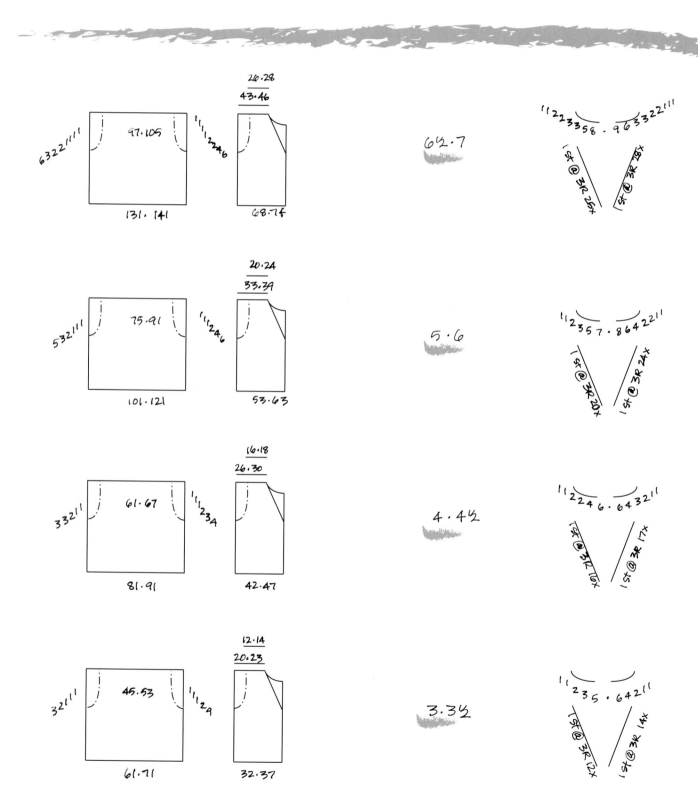

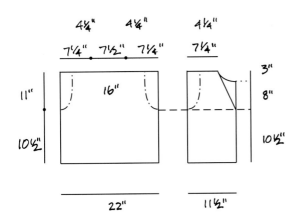

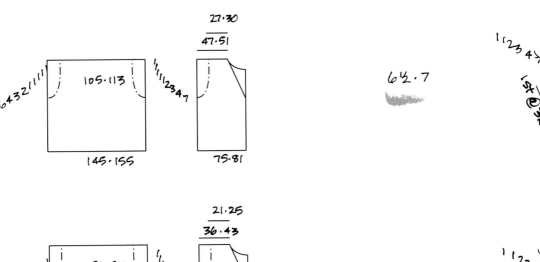

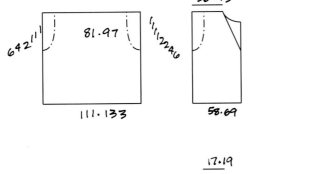

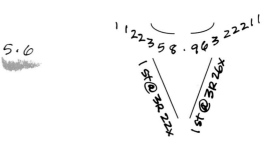

6½ · 7

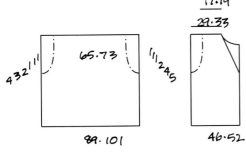

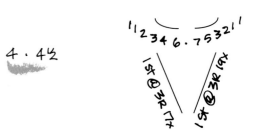

5 · 6

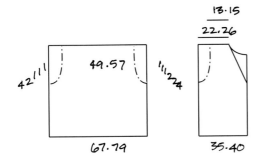

4 · 4½

3 · 3½

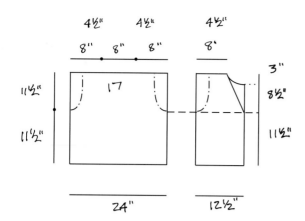

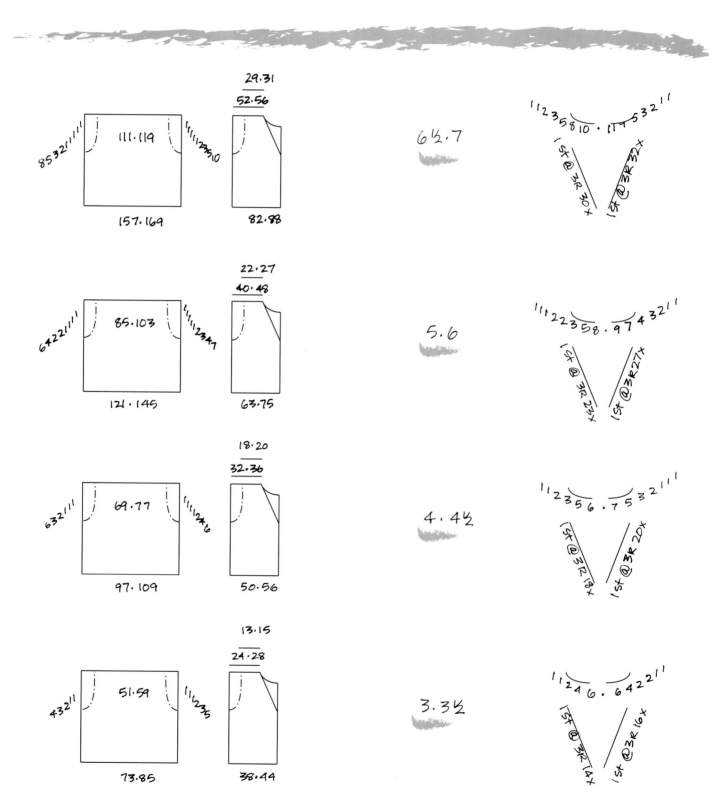

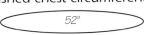

52"

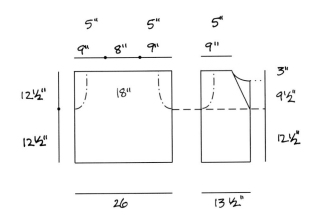

5"   5"   5"
9"   8"   9"   9"

12½"   18"   3"
                                           9½"
12½"   12½"

26   13½"

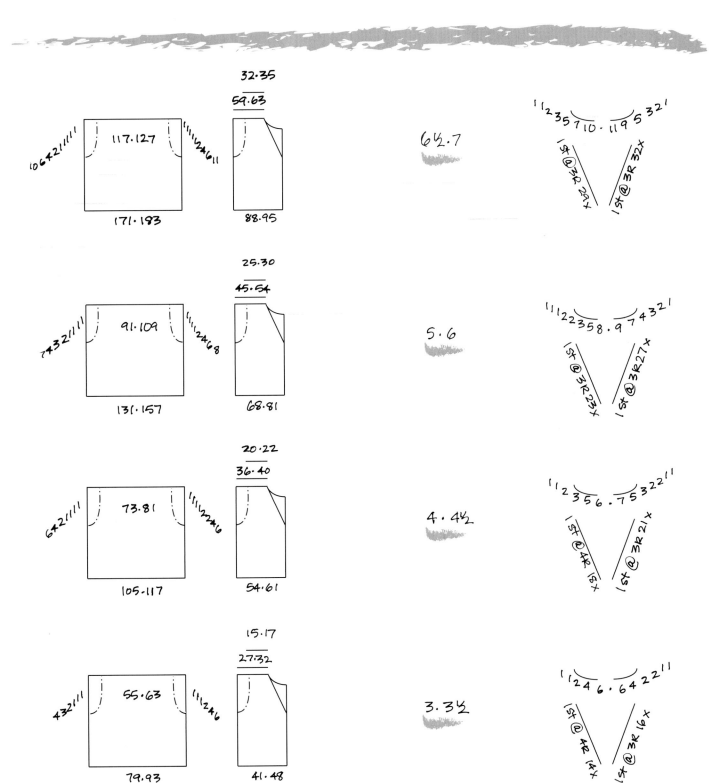

32·35
59·63

117·127   6½·7

106 4 2 ¹¹ ¹   ¹¹¹¹ 2 4 6 ¹¹

171·183   88·95

25·30
45·54

91·109   5·6

7 4 3 2 ¹¹ ¹   ¹¹ ¹ 2 4 6 8

131·157   68·81

20·22
36·40

73·81   4·4½

6 4 2 ¹¹ ¹   ¹¹ ¹ ¹ 2 2 4 6

105·117   54·61

15·17
27·32

55·63   3·3½

4 3 2 ¹¹ ¹   ¹¹ ¹ 2 4 6

79·93   41·48

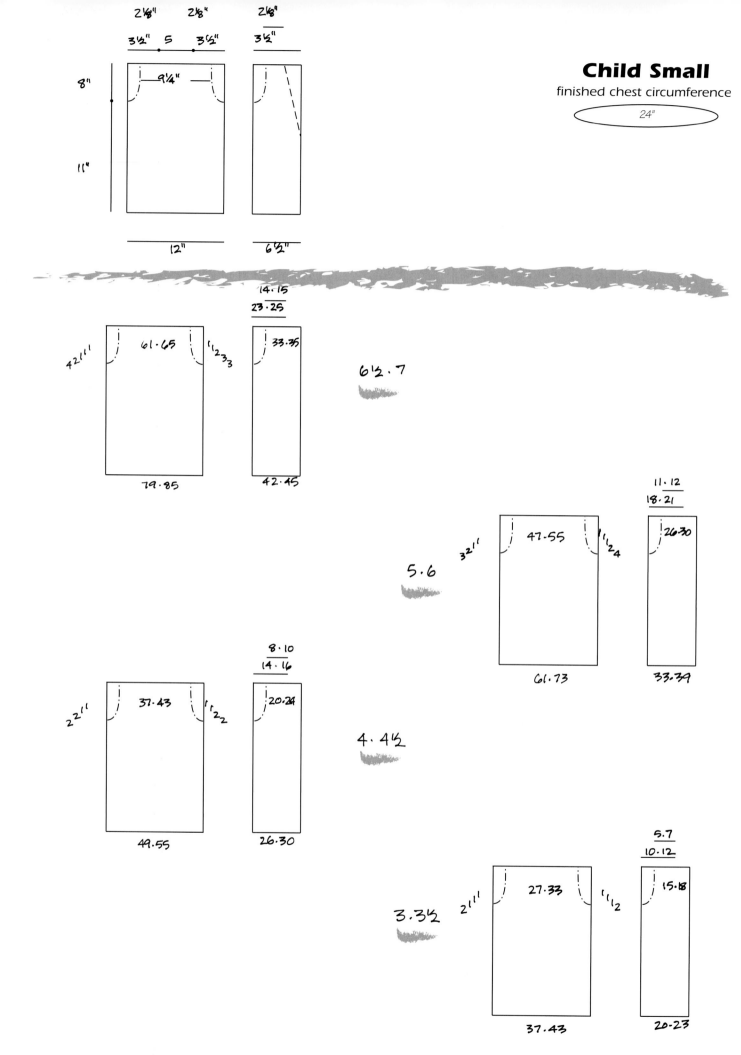

Child Small

finished chest circumference

24"

2⅛"   2⅛"   2⅛"

3½"   5   3½"   3½"

8"

9¼"

11"

12"   6½"

14·15

23·25

42"   61·65   ⁱⁱ₂₃₃   33·35   6½·7

79·85   42·45

11·12

18·21

32"   47·55   ⁱⁱ₂₄   26·30

5·6

61·73   33·39

8·10

14·16

22"   37·43   ⁱⁱ₂₂   20·24

49·55   26·30

4·4½

5·7

10·12

21"   27·33   ⁱⁱ₂   15·18

3·3½

37·43   20·23

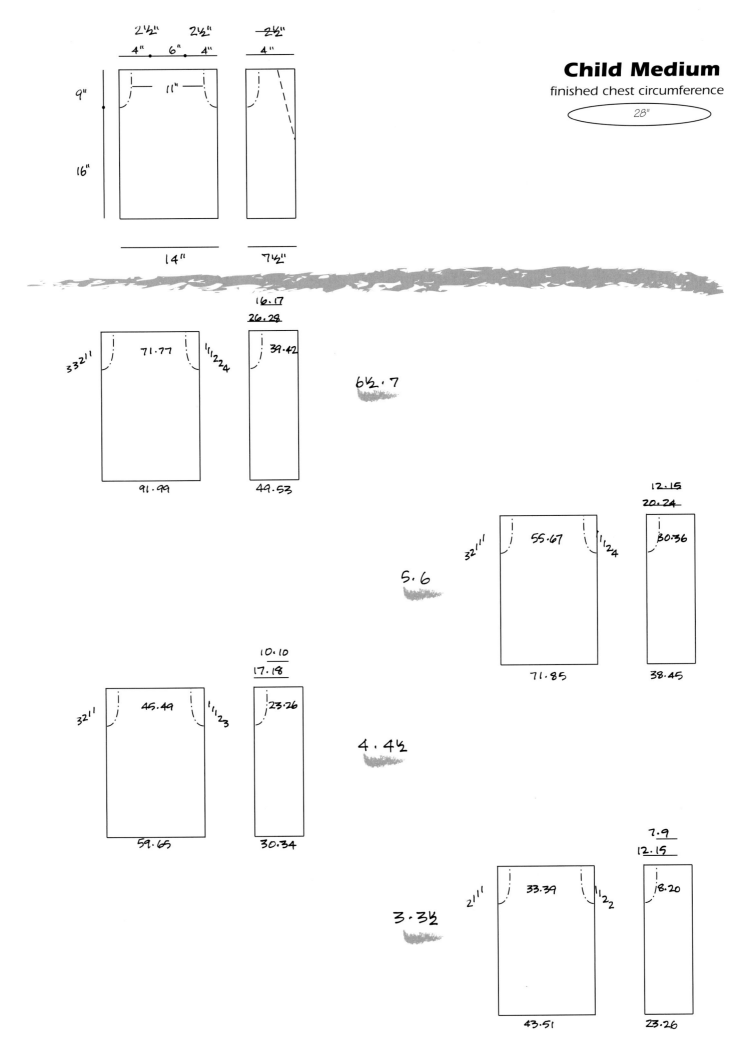

Child Medium
finished chest circumference

28"

2½"   2½"   2½"
4"   6"   4"   4"

9"

11"

16"

14"   7½"

16.17
26.28

33 21"   71.77   11 2 24   39.42

6½.7

91.99   49.53

12.15
20.24

32 21"   55.67   11 2 4   30.36

5.6

71.85   38.45

10.10
17.18

32 21"   45.49   11 2 3   23.26

4.4½

59.65   30.34

7.9
12.15

2 21"   33.39   11 2 2   18.20

3.3½

43.51   23.26

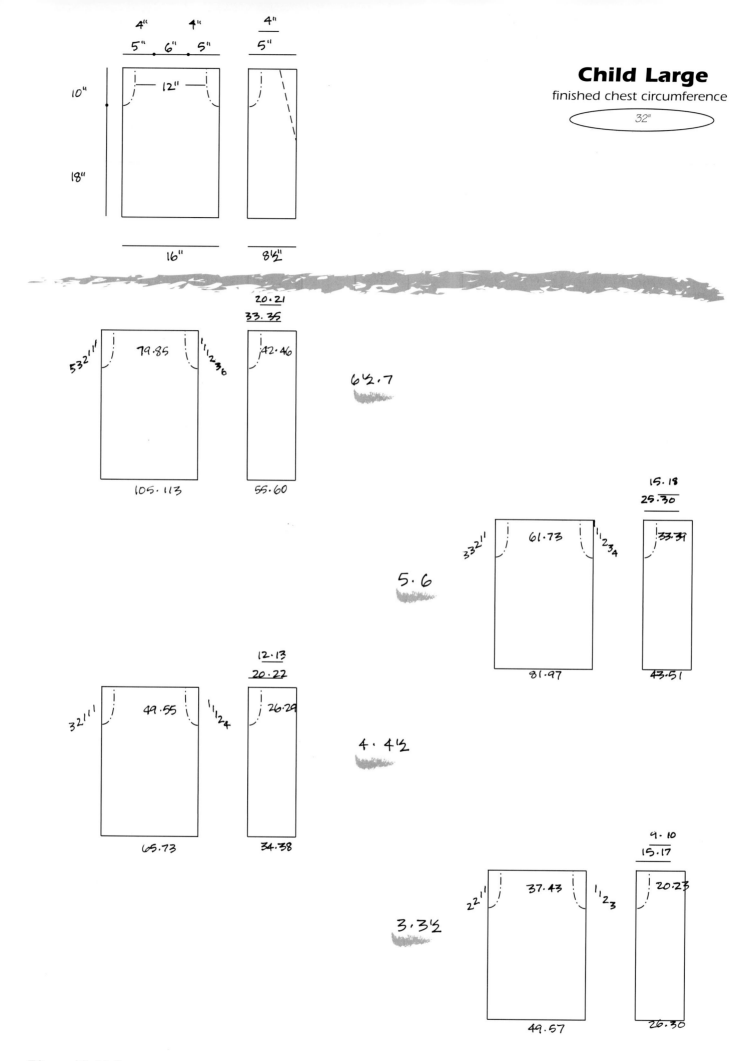

Child Large

finished chest circumference

32"

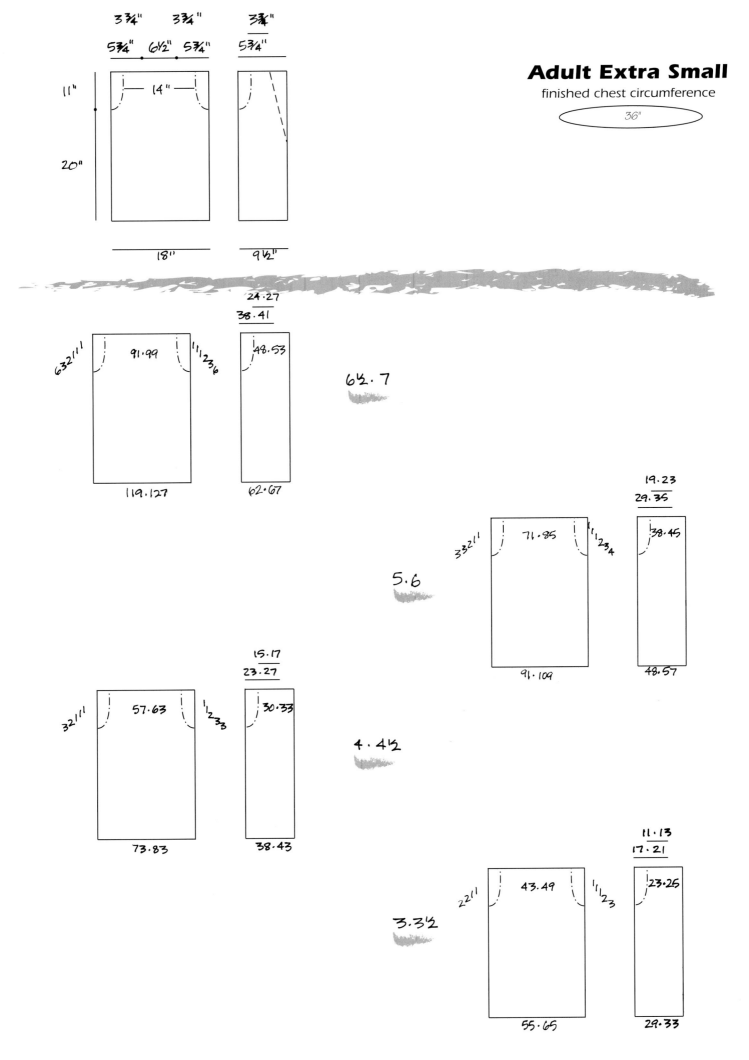

3¾"   3¾"   3¾"

5¾" 6½" 5¾"   5¾"

11"   ┌─ 14" ─┐

20"

18"   9½"

24·27

38·41

63²⁽ᴵᴵ   91·99   ᴵᴵ₂₃₆   48·53

6½· 7

119·127   62·67

33²⁽ᴵᴵ   76·85   ᴵᴵ₂₃₄   38·45

5·6

19·23

29·35

91·109   48·57

32²⁽ᴵᴵ   57·63   ᴵᴵ₂₃₃   30·33

4· 4½

15·17

23·27

73·83   38·43

22⁽ᴵ   43·49   ᴵᴵ₂₃   23·25

3·3½

11·13

17·21

55·65   29·33

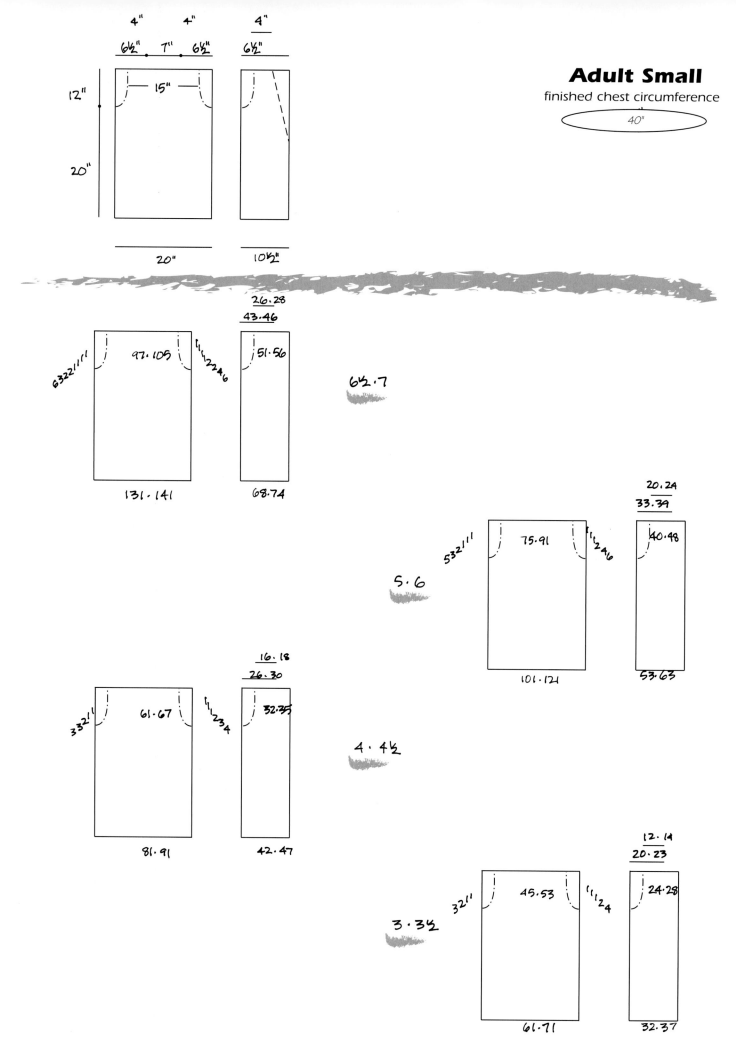

4"   4"   4"

6½"   7"   6½"   6½"

12"   15"

20"

20"   10½"

26·28
43·46

6322¹¹   97·105   ¹¹₂₂₄₆   51·56

6½·7

131·141   68·74

20·24
33·39

53²¹¹   75·91   ¹¹₂₄₆   40·48

5·6

101·121   53·63

16·18
26·30

33²¹¹   61·67   ¹¹₂₃₄   32·35

4·4½

81·91   42·47

12·14
20·23

32¹¹   45·53   ¹¹₂₄   24·28

3·3½

61·71   32·37

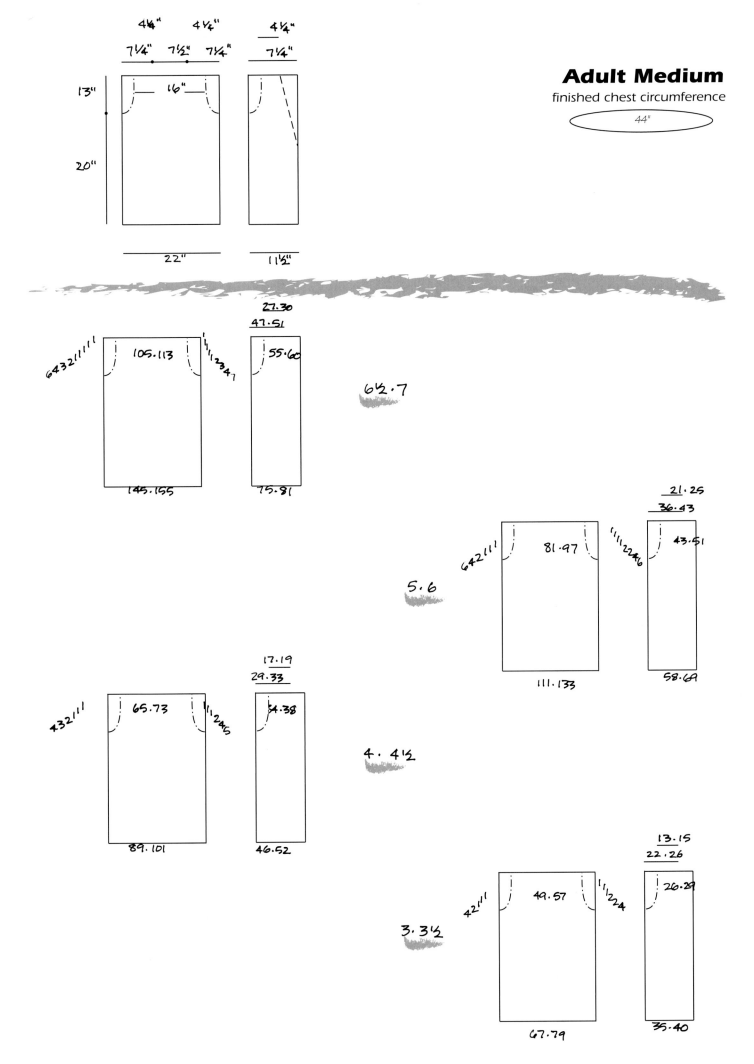

Adult Medium
finished chest circumference

44"

4¼" 4¼" 4¼"

7¼" 7½" 7¼" 7¼"

13" 16"

20"

22" 11½"

27.30
47.51

6432''''' 105.113 '''1234'7 55.60

6½·7

145.155 75.81

21.25
36.43

642''' 81.97 '''122*6 43.51

5·6

111.133 58.69

17.19
29.33

432''' 65.73 ''1245 54.38

4·4½

89.101 46.52

13.15
22·26

42''' 49.57 '''1224 26.29

3·3½

67·79 35.40

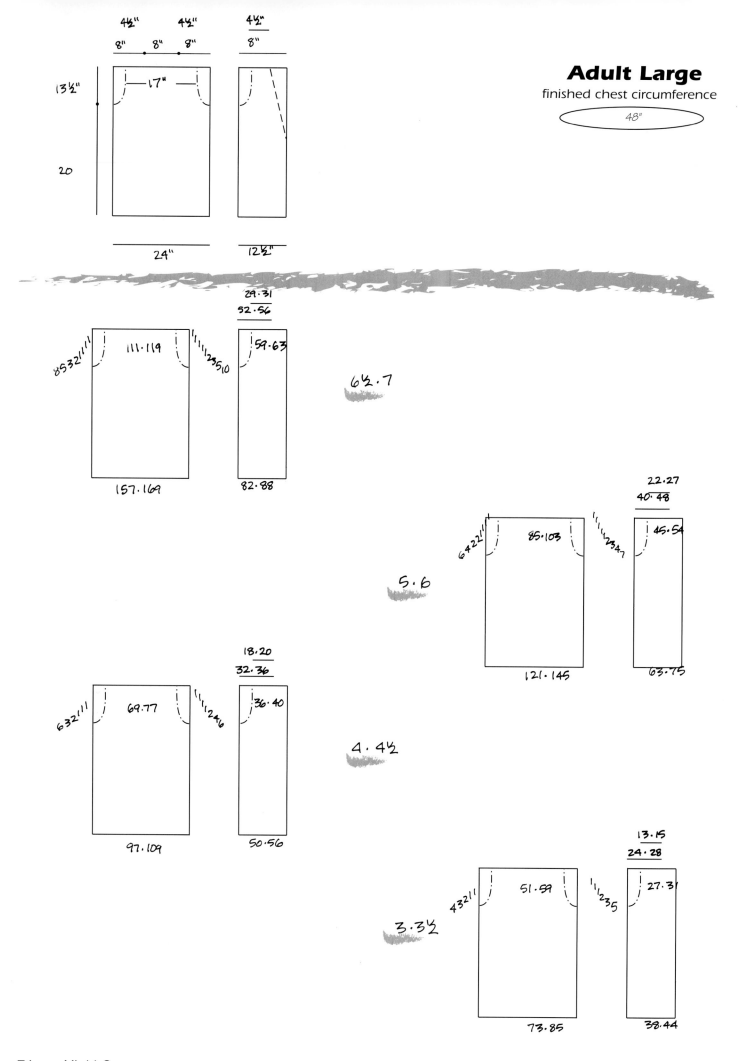

4½" 4½" 4½"

8" 8" 8"   8"

13½"

17"

20

24" 12½"

29·31
52·56

8532" 111·119 1235₁₀ 59·63

6½·7

157·169 82·88

22·27
40·48

6422" 85·103 12347 45·54

5·6

121·145 63·75

18·20
32·36

632" 69·77 12₄6 36·40

4·4½

97·109 50·56

13·15
24·28

432" 51·59 1235 27·31

3·3½

73·85 38·44

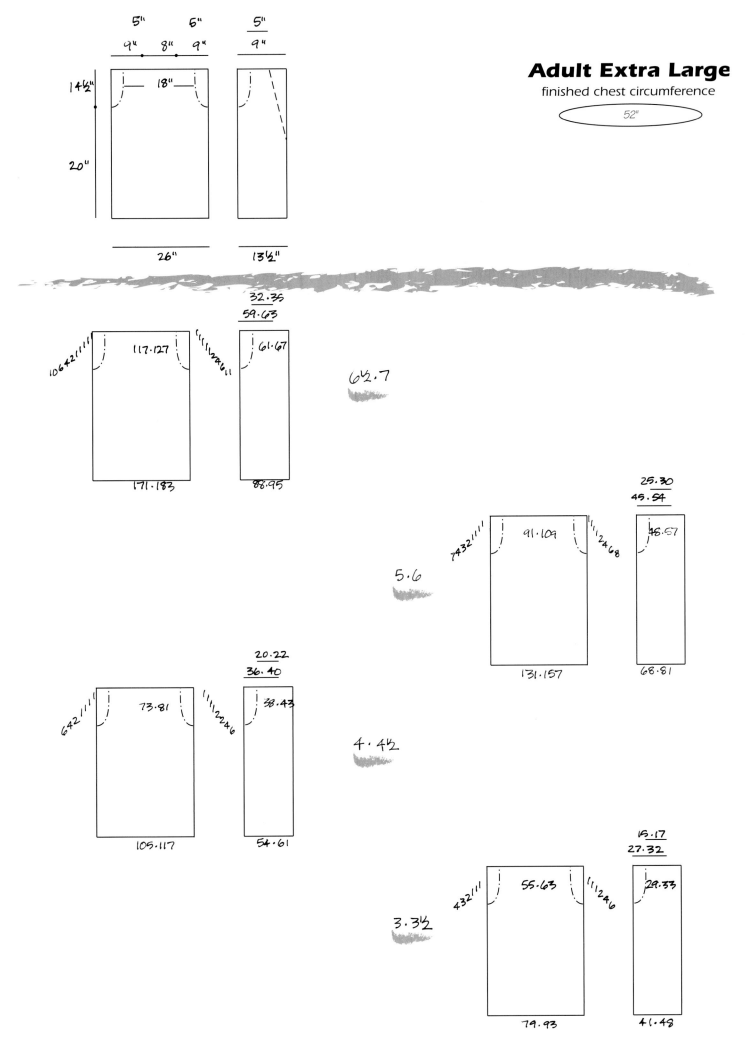

6½ • 7 sts per inch

	Child			Adult				
	S • 24"	M • 28"	L • 32"	XS • 36"	S • 40"	M • 44"	L • 48"	XL • 52"

BACK TUNIC ▪ Short/Medium

With needles for gauge, cast on __ sts. Choose seed or garter stitch and work until piece measures for

	S • 24"	M • 28"	L • 32"	XS • 36"	S • 40"	M • 44"	L • 48"	XL • 52"
cast on sts	79•85	91•99	105•113	119•127	131•141	145•155	157•169	171•183
short tunic: __ inches	5	6½	8	9	10	10½	11½	12½
medium tunic: __ inches	11	16	18	20	20	20	20	20

Choose armhole style.
Straight armhole: Place marker at side edge and cont even.
OR
Curved armhole: Bind off sts at each armhole edge in foll sequence:

	S • 24"		M • 28"		L • 32"		XS • 36"		S • 40"		M • 44"		L • 48"		XL • 52"	
									6	6	6	7	8	10	10	11
		3	3	4	5	6	6	6	3	4	4	4	5	5	6	6
	4	3	3	2	3	3	3	3	2	2	2	2	3	3	4	4
	2	2	2	2	2	2	2	2	2	2	2	2	2	2	2	2
	1x3	1x2	1x2	1x3	1x3	1x3	1x3	1x3	1x4	1x4	1x5	1x5	1x5	1x5	1x5	1x5

When armhole measures for

	S • 24"	M • 28"	L • 32"	XS • 36"	S • 40"	M • 44"	L • 48"	XL • 52"
short tunic __ inches	6	7	8	9	10	11	11½	12½
medium tunic __ inches,	8	9	10	11	12	13	13½	14½

work shoulder sts for

	S • 24"	M • 28"	L • 32"	XS • 36"	S • 40"	M • 44"	L • 48"	XL • 52"
straight armhole __ sts	23•25	26•28	33•35	38•41	43•46	47•51	52•56	59•63
curved armhole __ sts,	14•15	16•17	20•21	24•27	26•28	27•30	29•31	32•35

bind off center __ sts for neck, work to end. Place shoulder sts on hold for later finishing.

	S • 24"	M • 28"	L • 32"	XS • 36"	S • 40"	M • 44"	L • 48"	XL • 52"
	33•35	39•43	39•43	43•45	45•49	51•53	53•57	53•57

FRONT TUNIC ▪ Short/Medium

Cast on __ sts.
Work as for back, including armhole shaping.
AT SAME TIME, choose neckline style.
Lapel collar (as shown on medium tunic schematic)
Cont even until work meas same as back.
Bind off __ sts on neck edge, work to end.
OR

	S • 24"	M • 28"	L • 32"	XS • 36"	S • 40"	M • 44"	L • 48"	XL • 52"
cast on sts	42•45	49•53	55•60	62•67	68•74	75•81	82•88	88•95
lapel bind off sts	19•20	23•25	22•25	24•26	25•28	28•30	30•32	29•32

V-neck: When work measures for

	S • 24"	M • 28"	L • 32"	XS • 36"	S • 40"	M • 44"	L • 48"	XL • 52"
short tunic __ inches	5	6½	8	9	10	10½	11½	12½
medium tunic __ inches	11	16	18	20	20	20	20	20
dec at neck edge 1 st every __ row	2•2	2•2	3•2	3•3	3•3	3•3	3•3	3•3
__ times. Cont even until piece meas same as back.	19•20	23•25	22•25	24•26	25•28	28•30	30•32	29•32

OR
Round neck: When work measures for

	S • 24"	M • 28"	L • 32"	XS • 36"	S • 40"	M • 44"	L • 48"	XL • 52"
short tunic __ inches	9	11	13½	15½	17	18½	20	22
medium tunic __ inches,	15	20½	23½	26½	27	28	28½	29½

bind off at neck edge in foll sequence:

	S • 24"		M • 28"		L • 32"		XS • 36"		S • 40"		M • 44"		L • 48"		XL • 52"	
											10	10	10	11	10	11
	7	7	8	9	7	9	8	9	8	9	7	8	8	9	7	9
	5	5	5	6	5	6	5	6	5	6	4	5	5	5	5	5
	3	3	3	3	3	3	3	3	3x2	3x2	3	3	3	3	3	3
	2	2	2x2	2x2	2x2	2x2	2x3	2x3	2x2	2x2	2	2	2	2	2	2
	1x2	1x3	1x3	1x3	1x3	1x3	1x3	1x3	1x2	1x2	1x2	1x3	1x2	1x2	1x2	1x2

Cont even until work meas same as back. Place rem shoulder sts on hold for later three needle bind off seaming.

FINISHING

Work three needle bind off seam for shoulders.
Sew side seams.
Single crochet edge:
With crochet hook approximately same size as knitting needles used, beg at lower center edge of right front. Work approx 2 sc for every 3 rows, and 1 sc for each st. For turning corners, work 3 sc into 1 st at square corners, and 2 sc into "soft" corner at v-neck shaping.
Single crochet around armhole edges, beg at side seam.
Block, using the wet towel method.

5 • 6 sts per inch

	Child			Adult				
	S • 24"	M • 28"	L • 32"	XS • 36"	S • 40"	M • 44"	L • 48"	XL • 52"

BACK TUNIC ▪ Short/Medium

With needles for guage, cast on __ sts. Choose seed or garter stitch and work until piece measures for

	S • 24"	M • 28"	L • 32"	XS • 36"	S • 40"	M • 44"	L • 48"	XL • 52"
cast on sts	61·73	71·85	81·97	91·109	101·121	111·133	121·145	131·157
short tunic: __ inches	5	6½	8	9	10	10½	11½	12½
medium tunic: __ inches	11	16	18	20	20	20	20	20

Choose armhole style.

Straight armhole: Place marker at side edge and cont even.

OR

Curved armhole: Bind off sts at each armhole edge in foll sequence:

	S • 24"	M • 28"	L • 32"	XS • 36"	S • 40"	M • 44"	L • 48"	XL • 52"
						| 6		10 | 11
			3 | 4	3 | 4	5 | 6	6 | 4	6 | 7	6 | 6
	3 | 4	3 | 4	3 | 3	3 | 3	3 | 4	4 | 2	4 | 4	4 | 4
	2 | 2	2 | 2	2 | 2	2 | 2	2 | 2	2 | 2	2 | 2	2 | 2
	1x2 | 1x3	1x3 | 1x3	1x2 | 1x3	1x2 | 1x3	1x2 | 1x3	1x3 | 1x4	1x4 | 1x5	1x5 | 1x5

When armhole measures for

	S • 24"	M • 28"	L • 32"	XS • 36"	S • 40"	M • 44"	L • 48"	XL • 52"
short tunic __ inches	6	7	8	9	10	11	11½	12½
medium tunic __ inches,	8	9	10	11	12	13	13½	14½

work shoulder sts for

	S • 24"	M • 28"	L • 32"	XS • 36"	S • 40"	M • 44"	L • 48"	XL • 52"
straight armhole __ sts	18·21	20·24	25·30	29·35	33·39	36·43	40·48	45·54
curved armhole __ sts,	11·12	12·15	15·18	19·23	20·24	21·25	22·27	25·30
bind off center __ sts for neck	25·31	31·37	31·37	33·39	35·43	39·47	41·49	41·49

work to end. Place shoulder sts on hold for later finishing.

FRONT TUNIC ▪ Short/Medium

Cast on __ sts.

	S • 24"	M • 28"	L • 32"	XS • 36"	S • 40"	M • 44"	L • 48"	XL • 52"
cast on sts	33·39	38·45	43·51	48·57	53·63	58·69	63·75	68·81

Work as for back, including armhole shaping.

AT SAME TIME, choose neckline style.

Lapel collar (as shown on medium tunic schematic)
Cont even until work meas same as back.
Bind off __ sts on neck edge, work to end.

	S • 24"	M • 28"	L • 32"	XS • 36"	S • 40"	M • 44"	L • 48"	XL • 52"
bind off sts	15·18	18·21	18·21	19·22	20·24	22·26	23·27	23·27

OR

V-neck: When work measures for

	S • 24"	M • 28"	L • 32"	XS • 36"	S • 40"	M • 44"	L • 48"	XL • 52"
short tunic __ inches	5	6½	8	9	10	10½	11½	12½
medium tunic __ inches	11	16	18	20	20	20	20	20

dec at neck edge 1 st every __ row __ times. Cont even until piece meas same as back.

OR

Round neck: When work measures for

	S • 24"	M • 28"	L • 32"	XS • 36"	S • 40"	M • 44"	L • 48"	XL • 52"
short tunic __ inches	9	11	13½	15½	17	18½	20	22
medium tunic __ inches,	15	20½	23½	26½	27	28	28½	29½

bind off at neck edge in foll sequence:

	S • 24"	M • 28"	L • 32"	XS • 36"	S • 40"	M • 44"	L • 48"	XL • 52"
							| 9	| 9
	| 6	6 | 7	6 | 7	6 | 7	7 | 8	7 | 8	8 | 7	8 | 7
	6 | 5	5 | 5	5 | 5	5 | 5	5 | 5	5 | 6	5 | 4	5 | 4
	4 | 3	3 | 3	3 | 3	3 | 3	3 | 3	3 | 4	3 | 3	3 | 3
	2 | 2	2 | 2x2	2 | 2x2	2 | 2x2	2 | 2x2	2x2 | 2x3	2x2 | 2	2x2 | 2
	1x3 | 1x2	1x2 | 1x2	1x2 | 1x2	1x2 | 1x2	1x2 | 1x2	1x2 | 1x2	1x3 | 1x2	1x3 | 1x2

Cont even until work meas same as back. Place rem shoulder sts on hold for later three needle bind off seaming.

FINISHING

Work three needle bind off seam for shoulders.
Sew side seams.
Single crochet edge:
With crochet hook approximately same size as knitting needles used, beg at lower center edge of right front. Work approx 2 sc for every 3 rows, and 1 sc for each st. For turning corners, work 3 sc into 1 st at square corners, and 2 sc into "soft" corner at v-neck shaping.
Single crochet around armhole edges, beg at side seam.
Block, using the wet towel method.

	Child			Adult				
4 • 4½ sts per inch	S • 24"	M • 28"	L • 32"	XS • 36"	S • 40"	M • 44"	L • 48"	XL • 52"

BACK TUNIC ▪ Short/Medium

With needles for gauge, cast on __ sts. Choose seed or garter stitch and work until piece measures for

	S	M	L	XS	S	M	L	XL
cast on	49·55	59·65	65·73	73·83	81·91	89·101	97·109	105·117
short tunic: __ inches	5	6½	8	9	10	10½	11½	12½
medium tunic: __ inches	11	16	18	20	20	20	20	20

Choose armhole style.

Straight armhole: Place marker at side edge and cont even.

OR

Curved armhole: Bind off sts at each armhole edge in foll sequence:

(each size shown as left / right)

step	S	M	L	XS	S	M	L	XL
	· / ·	· / ·	· / ·	· / 3	3 / 4	4 / 5	6 / 6	6 / 6
	2 / 2	3 / 3	3 / 4	3 / 3	3 / 3	3 / 4	3 / 4	4 / 2
	2 / 2	2 / 2	2 / 2	2 / 2	2 / 2	2 / 2	2 / 2	2 / 2
	1x2 / 1x2	1x2 / 1x3	1x3 / 1x3	1x3 / 1x2	1x2 / 1x3	1x3 / 1x3	1x3 / 1x4	1x4 / 1x4

When armhole measures for

	S	M	L	XS	S	M	L	XL
short tunic __ inches	6	7	8	9	10	11	11½	12½
medium tunic __ inches,	8	9	10	11	12	13	13½	14½

work shoulder sts for

	S	M	L	XS	S	M	L	XL
straight armhole __ sts	14·16	17·18	20·22	23·27	26·30	29·33	32·36	36·40
curved armhole __ sts,	8·10	10·10	12·13	15·17	16·18	17·19	18·20	20·22
bind off center __ sts for neck	21·23	25·29	25·29	27·29	29·31	31·35	33·37	33·37

work to end. Place shoulder sts on hold for later finishing.

FRONT TUNIC ▪ Short/Medium

Cast on __ sts.
Work as for back, including armhole shaping.

	S	M	L	XS	S	M	L	XL
cast on	26·30	30·34	34·38	38·43	42·47	46·52	50·56	54·61

AT SAME TIME, choose neckline style.

Lapel collar (as shown on medium tunic schematic)
Cont even until work meas same as back.
Bind off __ sts on neck edge, work to end.

	S	M	L	XS	S	M	L	XL
bind off	12·14	13·16	14·16	15·16	16·17	17·19	18·20	18·21

OR

V-neck: When work measures for

	S	M	L	XS	S	M	L	XL
short tunic __ inches	5	6½	8	9	10	10½	11½	12½
medium tunic __ inches	11	16	18	20	20	20	20	20

dec at neck edge 1 st every __ row __ times. Cont even until piece meas same as back.

OR

Round neck: When work measures for

	S	M	L	XS	S	M	L	XL
short tunic __ inches	9	11	13½	15½	17	18½	20	22
medium tunic __ inches,	15	20½	23½	26½	27	28	28½	29½

bind off at neck edge in foll sequence:

(each size shown as left / right)

step	S	M	L	XS	S	M	L	XL
	· / ·	· / ·	· / ·	· / ·	· / 6	· / ·	· / ·	· / 6
	4 / 5	4 / 6	5 / 6	6 / 6	6 / 6	6 / 7	6 / 7	6 / 7
	3 / 4	3 / 4	4 / 4	4 / 4	6 / 4	4 / 5	5 / 5	5 / 5
	2 / 2	2x2 / 2x2	2 / 2x2	2 / 2x2	2x2 / 2	2 / 2	2 / 2	2 / 2x2
	1x3 / 1x3	1x2 / 1x2	1x3 / 1x2	1x3 / 1x2	1x2 / 1x2	1x2 / 1x2	1x2 / 1x3	1x2 / 1x2

Cont even until work meas same as back. Place rem shoulder sts on hold for later three needle bind off seaming.

FINISHING

Work three needle bind off seam for shoulders.
Sew side seams.

Single crochet edge:
With crochet hook approximately same size as knitting needles used, beg at lower center edge of right front. Work approx 2 sc for every 3 rows, and 1 sc for each st. For turning corners, work 3 sc into 1 st at square corners, and 2 sc into "soft" corner at v-neck shaping.
Single crochet around armhole edges, beg at side seam.
Block, using the wet towel method.

	Child			**Adult**				
	S • 24"	M • 28"	L • 32"	XS • 36"	S • 40"	M • 44"	L • 48"	XL • 52"

BACK TUNIC ▪ Short/Medium

With needles for gauge, cast on ___ sts. Choose seed or garter stitch and work until piece measures for

	S • 24"	M • 28"	L • 32"	XS • 36"	S • 40"	M • 44"	L • 48"	XL • 52"
cast on	37·43	43·51	49·57	55·65	61·71	67·79	73·85	79·93
short tunic: ___ inches	5	6½	8	9	10	10½	11½	12½
medium tunic: ___ inches	11	16	18	20	20	20	20	20

Choose armhole style.
Straight armhole: Place marker at side edge and cont even.
OR
Curved armhole: Bind off sts at each armhole edge in foll sequence:

	S • 24"	M • 28"	L • 32"	XS • 36"	S • 40"	M • 44"	L • 48"	XL • 52"
			| 2	2 | 3	2 | 3	4 | 4	4 | 5	4 | 6
	2 | 2	2 | 2	2 | 2	2 | 2	3 | 4	4 | 2	3 | 3	3 | 4
	1x3 | 1x3	1x3 | 1x2	1x2 | 1x2	1x2 | 1x3	1x3 | 1x3	2 | 2	2 | 2	2 | 2
						1x3 | 1x3	1x2 | 1x3	1x3 | 1x3

When armhole measures for

	S • 24"	M • 28"	L • 32"	XS • 36"	S • 40"	M • 44"	L • 48"	XL • 52"
short tunic ___ inches	6	7	8	9	10	11	11½	12½
medium tunic ___ inches,	8	9	10	11	12	13	13½	14½

work shoulder sts for

	S • 24"	M • 28"	L • 32"	XS • 36"	S • 40"	M • 44"	L • 48"	XL • 52"
straight armhole ___ sts	10·12	12·15	15·17	17·21	20·23	22·26	24·28	27·32
curved armhole ___ sts,	5·7	7·9	9·10	11·13	12·14	13·15	13·15	15·17
bind off center ___ sts for neck	17·19	19·21	19·23	21·23	21·25	23·27	25·29	25·29

work to end. Place shoulder sts on hold for later finishing.

FRONT TUNIC ▪ Short/Medium

Cast on ___ sts.
Work as for back, including armhole shaping.
AT SAME TIME, choose neckline style.
Lapel collar (as shown on medium tunic schematic)
Cont even until work meas same as back.
Bind off ___ sts on neck edge, work to end.
OR

	S • 24"	M • 28"	L • 32"	XS • 36"	S • 40"	M • 44"	L • 48"	XL • 52"
Cast on	20·23	23·26	26·30	29·33	32·37	35·40	38·44	41·48
Bind off sts on neck edge	10·11	11·11	11·13	12·12	12·14	13·14	14·16	14·16

V-neck: When work measures for

	S • 24"	M • 28"	L • 32"	XS • 36"	S • 40"	M • 44"	L • 48"	XL • 52"
short tunic ___ inches	5	6½	8	9	10	10½	11½	12½
medium tunic ___ inches	11	16	18	20	20	20	20	20

dec at neck edge 1 st every ___ row ___ times. Cont even until piece meas same as back.
OR
Round neck: When work measures for

	S • 24"	M • 28"	L • 32"	XS • 36"	S • 40"	M • 44"	L • 48"	XL • 52"
short tunic ___ inches	9	11	13½	15½	17	18½	20	22
medium tunic ___ inches,	15	20½	23½	26½	27	28	28½	29½

bind off at neck edge in foll sequence:

	S • 24"	M • 28"	L • 32"	XS • 36"	S • 40"	M • 44"	L • 48"	XL • 52"
			| 6	| 6	5 | 5	5 | 6	6 | 6	6 | 6
	5 | 6	6 | 6	6 | 4	5 | 3	3 | 3	3 | 4	4 | 4	4 | 4
	3 | 3	3 | 3	3 | 2	3 | 2	2 | 2	2 | 2	2 | 2x2	2 | 2x2
	1x2 | 1x2	1x2 | 1x2	1x2 | 1	1x2 | 1x2	1x2 | 1x2	1x2 | 1x2	1x2 | 1x2	1x2 | 1x2

Cont even until work meas same as back. Place rem shoulder sts on hold for later three needle bind off seaming.

FINISHING

Work three needle bind off seam for shoulders.
Sew side seams.
Single crochet edge:
With crochet hook approximately same size as knitting needles used, beg at lower center edge of right front. Work approx 2 sc for every 3 rows, and 1 sc for each st. For turning corners, work 3 sc into 1 st at square corners, and 2 sc into "soft" corner at v-neck shaping.
Single crochet around armhole edges, beg at side seam.
Block, using the wet towel method.

Choose:

- long tunice with deep v-neck and
  curved armholes

Long Tunic	Adult				
	XS • 36"	S • 40"	M • 44"	L • 48"	XL • 52"
6½ • 7 sts per inch yardage	1800	2100	2300	2500	2800
Cotton Fine	9	10	11	12	13
Nature Spun (F)	6	7	8	9	10
Wild foote	9	10	11	12	14
5 • 6 sts per inch yardage	1400	1600	1800	1900	2100
Cotton Fleece	7	8	9	9	10
Kaleidoscope	14	8	9	9	10
Nature Spun (S)	8	9	10	11	12
Top of the Lamb (S)	4	5	6	6	6
4 • 4½ sts per inch yardage	1200	1400	1500	1600	1800
Country Classics (W)	7	8	8	9	10
Handpaint Originals	14	16	18	19	21
Lamb's Pride (W)	7	8	8	9	10
Lamb's Pride Superwash (W)	6	7	8	8	9
Nature Spun (W)	5	6	7	7	8
Prairie Silk	14	16	18	19	21
Top of the Lamb (W)	7	8	8	9	10
3 • 3½ sts per inch yardage	900	1000	1100	1200	1400
Country Classics (B)	8	8	9	10	12
Lamb's Pride (B)	8	8	9	10	12
Lamb's Pride Superwash (B)	9	10	10	11	13

(Yardage and skein estimates are approximations only.)

finished chest circumference

36"

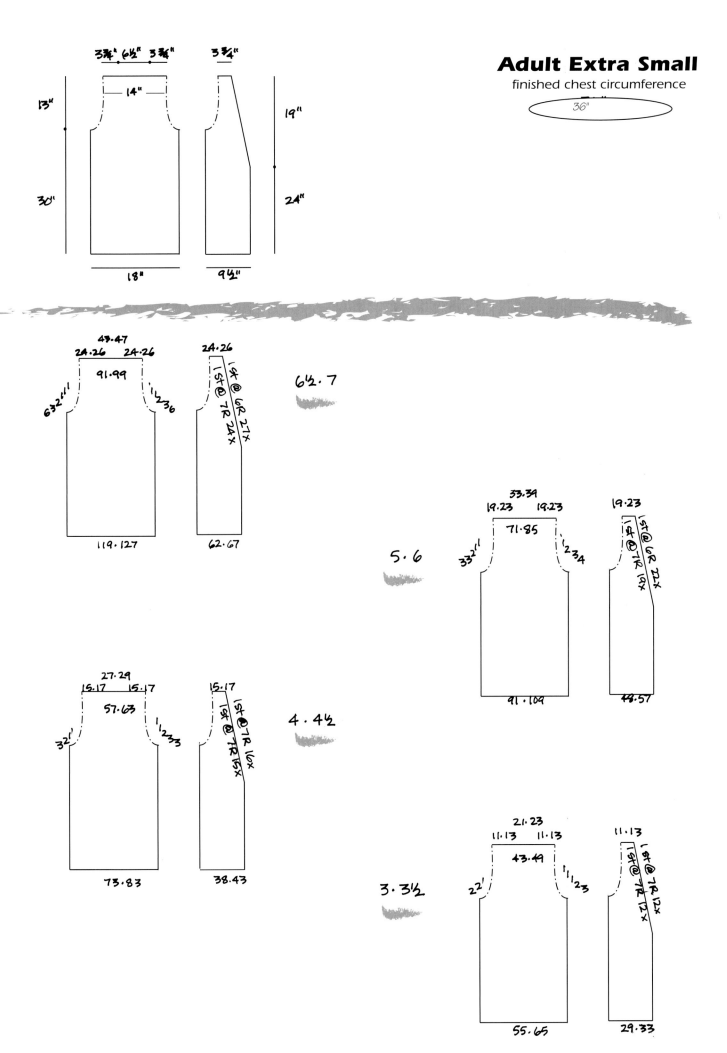

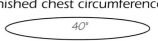

40"

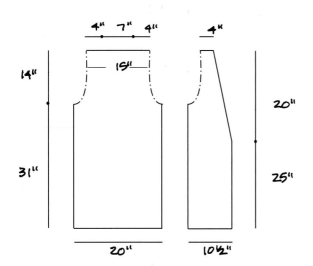

4" 7" 4"

4"

15"

14"

20"

31"

25"

20"

10½"

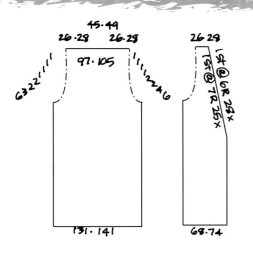

45·49
26·28   26·28

26·28

97·105

6322¹¹

111224 6

1 st @ 6R 24x
1st @ 7R 25x

6½·7

131·141

68·74

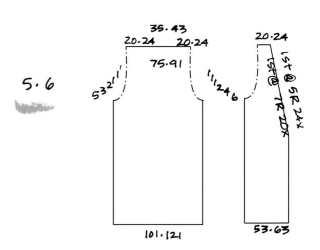

35·43
20·24   20·24

20·24

75·91

532¹¹

111246

1 st @ 5R 24x
1 st @ 7R 20x

5·6

101·121

53·63

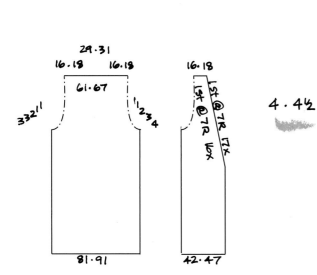

29·31
16·18   16·18

16·18

61·67

332¹¹

11234

1 st @ 7R 17x
1st @ 7R 16x

4·4½

81·91

42·47

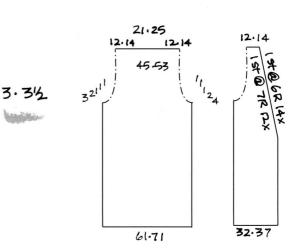

21·25
12·14   12·14

12·14

45·53

32¹¹

11124

1 st @ 6R 14x
1 st @ 7R 12x

3·3½

61·71

32·37

82 • Vicki Square

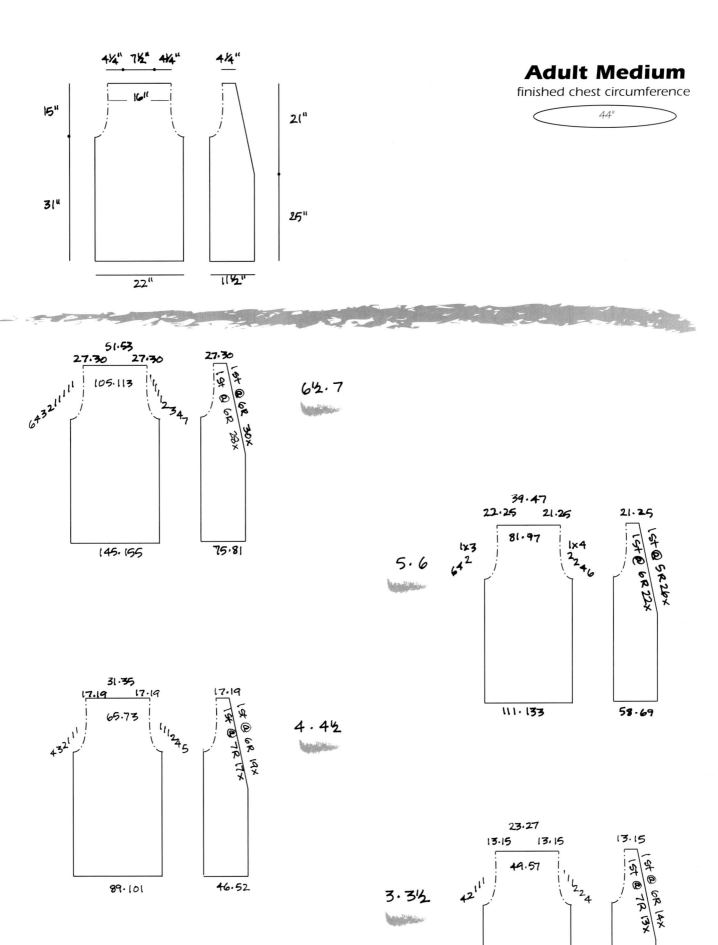

4¼" 7½" 4¼"   4¼"

16"

15"

31"

21"

25"

22"   11½"

51.53
27.30   27.30   27.30

105.113   1st @ 6R 30x
6432¹¹¹¹   1st @ 6R 29x
¹²³⁴7

6½.7

145.155   75.81

39.47
22.25   21.25   21.25

1x3   81.97   1x4
6¹²   2246   1st @ 5R 26x
1st @ 6R 22x

5.6

111.133   58.69

31.35
17.19   17.19   17.19

65.73   1st @ 6R 19x
432¹¹¹   ¹¹₂₄5   1st @ 7R 17x

4.4½

89.101   46.52

23.27
13.15   13.15   13.15

49.57   1st @ 6R 14x
42¹¹¹   ¹²₂₄   1st @ 7R 13x

3.3½

67.79   35.40

48"

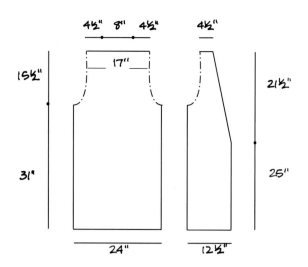

4½" 8" 4½" 4½"

17"

15½"

21½"

31"

25"

24" 12½"

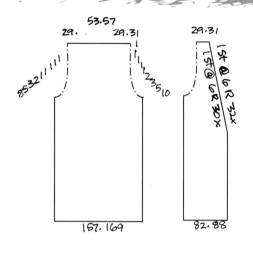

53.57
29. 29.31 29.31

8532/////
/////23510

6½ . 7

1st @ 6R 32x
1st @ 6R 30x

157.169 82.88

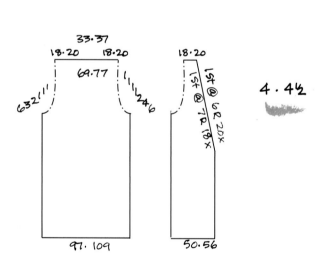

33.37
18.20 18.20 18.20

69.77

632//
//2446

4 . 4½

1st @ 6R 20x
1st @ 7R 18x

97.109 50.56

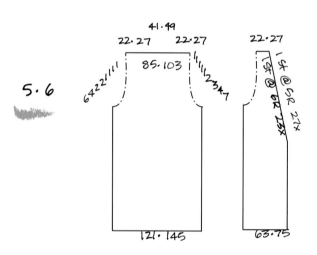

41.49
22.27 22.27 22.27

85.103

6422///
///2347

5 . 6

1st @ 5R 27x
1st @ 6R 25x

121.145 63.75

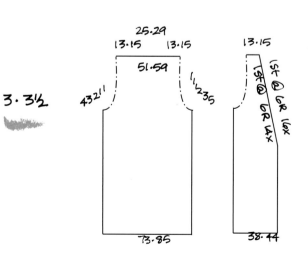

25.29
13.15 13.15 13.15

51.59

432//
//235

3 . 3½

1st @ 6R 16x
1st @ 6R 14x

73.85 38.44

52"

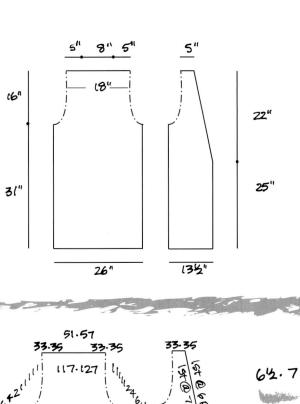

5"   8"   5"   5"

18"

6"

31"

22"

25"

26"   13½"

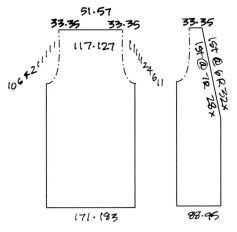

51·57

33·35   33·35   33·35

117·127

106 42''''

1111 24 6 11

171·183   88·95

1 st @ 6R 32x
1 st @ 7R 28x

6½·7

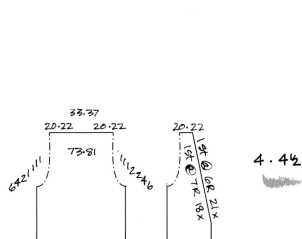

33·37

20·22   20·22   20·22

73·81

64 2''''

1111 2 2 4 6

105·117   54·61

1 st @ 6R 21x
1 st @ 7R 18x

4·4½

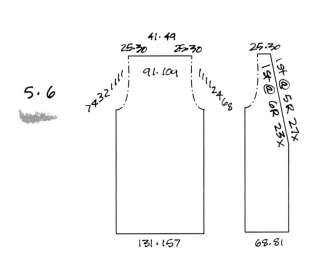

41·49

25·30   25·30   25·30

91·109

74 32''''

1111 24 68

131·157   68·81

1 st @ 5R 27x
1 st @ 6R 23x

5·6

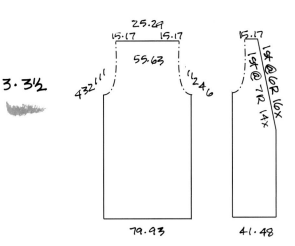

25·29

15·17   15·17   15·17

55·63

4 32''''

1111 24 6

79·93   41·48

1 st @ 6R 16x
1 st @ 7R 14x

3·3½

	Adult				
	XS • 36"	S • 40"	M • 44"	L • 48"	XL • 52"

BACK LONG TUNIC

With needles for gauge, cast on __ sts.
Work in seed stitch until piece measures for long tunic: __ inches (this armhole is meant to be deep)
Curved armhole: Bind off sts at each armhole edge in foll sequence:

	XS • 36"	S • 40"	M • 44"	L • 48"	XL • 52"
cast on	119·127	131·141	145·155	157·169	171·183
inches	30	31	31	31	31
			6 | 7	8 | 10	10 | 11
	6 | 6	6 | 6	4 | 4	5 | 5	6 | 6
	3 | 3	3 | 4	3 | 3	3 | 3	4 | 4
	2 | 2	2x2 | 2x2	2 | 2	2 | 2	2 | 2
	1x3 | 1x3	1x4 | 1x4	1x5 | 1x5	1x5 | 1x5	1x5 | 1x5

When armhole meas __ inches, work __ sts for shoulder, bind off center __ sts for neck, work to end. Place shoulder sts on hold for later finishing.

	XS • 36"	S • 40"	M • 44"	L • 48"	XL • 52"
armhole meas	13	14	15	15½	16
shoulder	24·26	26·28	27·30	29·31	33·35
neck	43·47	45·49	51·53	53·57	51·57

FRONT LONG TUNIC

Cast on __ sts. Work in seed stitch until piece meas __ inches.
Shape deep V-neck: dec at neck edge 1 st every __ row, __ times.
AT SAME TIME, when piece meas __ inches from beg, work armhole as for back. Cont even until work meas same as back. Place shoulder sts on hold for later finishing.

	XS • 36"	S • 40"	M • 44"	L • 48"	XL • 52"
cast on	62·67	68·74	75·81	82·88	88·95
inches	24	25	25	25	25
dec every	7·6	7·6	6·6	6·6	7·6
times	24·27	25·28	28·30	30·32	28·32
meas	30	31	31	31	31

FINISHING

Work 3 needle bind off seam for shoulders.
NOTE: Be sure to gauge for garter stitch. It may be different than gauge for seed stitch on the same size needles. The sample pictured is knit seed stitch in Prairie Silk at 5 sts / inch and the garter stitch border is Prairie Silk at 4 sts / inch. Turn to the appropriate page matching your garter stitch gauge to follow finishing instructions, or change needle size to achieve gauge to match seed stitch.
Garter stitch border: Beg at lower center edge of right front, pick up approx __ sts along center front edge, __ sts on neck edge, __ sts on back neck, and same number of sts on left front as for right front.
(This requires a long circular needle, or the border may be knit in 2 parts, dividing and seaming at left shoulder.)
Knit 2 rows, bind off on row 3 (WS row).
Armhole border: Pick up approx __ sts evenly along front and back armholes. Knit 2 rows, bind off on row 3 (WS row).

Sew side seams. Block, using the wet towel method.

	XS • 36"	S • 40"	M • 44"	L • 48"	XL • 52"
center front	156·168	162·175	162·175	162·175	162·175
neck edge	125·135	131·142	139·149	142·153	145·156
back neck	43·47	45·49	51·53	53·57	51·57
armhole border	174·188	190·204	206·224	218·236	220·238

	Adult				
	XS • 36"	S • 40"	M • 44"	L • 48"	XL • 52"

BACK LONG TUNIC

With needles for gauge, cast on __ sts.
Work in seed stitch until piece measures for
long tunic: __ inches (this armhole is meant
to be deep)

Curved armhole: Bind off sts at each armhole edge
in foll sequence:

	XS • 36"	S • 40"	M • 44"	L • 48"	XL • 52"
cast on	91·109	101·121	111·133	121·145	131·157
long tunic inches	30	31	31	31	31

Bind off sequence:

XS	S	M	L	XL
			7	7 | 8
3 | 4	5 | 6	6 | 6	6 | 4	4 | 6
3 | 3	3 | 4	4 | 4	4 | 3	3 | 4
2 | 2	2 | 2	2 | 2x2	2x2 | 2	2 | 2
1x2 | 1x3	1x3 | 1x3	1x3 | 1x4	1x4 | 1x5	1x4 | 1x4

When armhole meas __ inches,
work __ sts for shoulder,
bind off center __ sts for neck, work to end. Place
shoulder sts on hold for later finishing.

	XS • 36"	S • 40"	M • 44"	L • 48"	XL • 52"
armhole meas inches	13	14	15	15½	16
sts for shoulder	19·23	20·24	21·25	22·27	25·30
center sts for neck	33·39	35·43	39·47	41·49	41·49

FRONT LONG TUNIC

Cast on __ sts. Work in seed stitch until piece meas
__ inches.
Shape deep V-neck: dec at neck edge 1 st every __
row, __ times.
AT SAME TIME, when piece meas __ inches from beg, work
armhole as for back. Cont even until work meas same as back.
Place shoulder sts on hold for later finishing.

	XS • 36"	S • 40"	M • 44"	L • 48"	XL • 52"
cast on	48·57	53·63	58·69	63·75	68·81
inches	24	25	25	25	25
dec every __ row	7·6	7·5	6·5	6·5	6·5
__ times	19·22	20·24	22·26	23·27	23·27
when piece meas inches	30	31	31	31	31

FINISHING

Work 3 needle bind off seam for shoulders.
*NOTE: Be sure to gauge for garter stitch. It may be different
than gauge for seed stitch on the same size needles. The
sample pictured is knit seed stitch in Prairie Silk at 5 sts / inch
and the garter stitch border is Prairie Silk at 4 sts/inch. Turn to
the appropriate page matching your garter stitch gauge to follow
finishing instructions, or change needle size to achieve gauge
to match seed stitch.*
Garter stitch border: Beg at lower center edge of right front,
pick up approx __ sts along center front edge,
__ sts on neck edge,
__ sts on back neck, and
same number of sts on left front as for right front.
(This requires a long circular needle, or the border may be knit
in 2 parts, dividing and seaming at left shoulder.)
Knit 2 rows, bind off on row 3 (WS row).
Armhole border: Pick up approx __ sts evenly along front
and back armholes. Knit 2 rows, bind off on row 3 (WS row).

Sew side seams. Block, using the wet towel method.

	XS • 36"	S • 40"	M • 44"	L • 48"	XL • 52"
center front edge	120·144	125·150	125·150	125·150	125·150
neck edge	96·115	101·121	107·128	109·131	112·134
back neck	33·39	35·43	39·47	41·49	41·49
armhole border	134·162	146·176	164·198	164·198	170·204

4 • 4½ sts per inch

	XS • 36"	S • 40"	M • 44"	L • 48"	XL • 52"

BACK LONG TUNIC

With needles for gauge, cast on __ sts.
Work in seed stitch until piece measures for
long tunic: __ inches (this armhole is meant
to be deep)

	XS • 36"	S • 40"	M • 44"	L • 48"	XL • 52"
Cast on sts	73•83	81•91	89•101	97•109	105•117
inches	30	31	31	31	31

Curved armhole: Bind off sts at each armhole edge
in foll sequence:

	XS • 36"		S • 40"		M • 44"		L • 48"		XL • 52"	
		3	3	4	4	5	6	6	6	6
	3	3	3	3	3	4	3	4	4	4
	2	2	2	2	2	2	2	2	2	2x2
	1x3	1x2	1x2	1x3	1x3	1x3	1x3	1x4	1x4	1x4

When armhole meas __ inches,
work __ sts for shoulder,
bind off center __ sts for neck, work to end. Place
shoulder sts on hold for later finishing.

	XS • 36"	S • 40"	M • 44"	L • 48"	XL • 52"
armhole meas inches	13	14	15	15½	16
work sts for shoulder	15•17	16•18	17•19	18•20	20•22
bind off center sts	27•29	29•31	31•35	33•37	33•37

FRONT LONG TUNIC

Cast on __ sts. Work in seed stitch until piece meas
__ inches.
Shape deep V-neck: dec at neck edge 1 st every __
row, __ times.
AT SAME TIME, when piece meas __ inches from beg, work
armhole as for back. Cont even until work meas same as back.
Place shoulder sts on hold for later finishing.

	XS • 36"	S • 40"	M • 44"	L • 48"	XL • 52"
Cast on sts	38•43	42•47	46•52	50•56	54•61
inches	24	25	25	25	25
dec every __ row	7•7	7•7	7•6	7•6	7•6
__ times	15•16	16•17	17•19	18•20	18•21
meas inches from beg	30	31	31	31	31

FINISHING

Work 3 needle bind off seam for shoulders.
*NOTE: Be sure to gauge for garter stitch. It may be different
than gauge for seed stitch on the same size needles. The
sample pictured is knit seed stitch in Prairie Silk at 5 sts / inch
and the garter stitch border is Prairie Silk at 4 sts / inch. Turn to
the appropriate page matching your garter stitch gauge to follow
finishing instructions, or change needle size to achieve gauge
to match seed stitch.*
Garter stitch border: Beg at lower center edge of right front,
pick up approx __ sts along center front edge,
__ sts on neck edge,
__ sts on back neck, and
same number of sts on left front as for right front.
(This requires a long circular needle, or the border may be knit
in 2 parts, dividing and seaming at left shoulder.)
Knit 2 rows, bind off on row 3 (WS row).
Armhole border: Pick up approx __ sts evenly along front
and back armholes. Knit 2 rows, bind off on row 3 (WS row).

Sew side seams. Block, using the wet towel method.

	XS • 36"	S • 40"	M • 44"	L • 48"	XL • 52"
pick up center front edge	96•108	100•112	100•112	100•112	100•112
sts on neck edge	77•86	81•91	85•96	87•98	89•100
sts on back neck	27•29	29•31	31•35	33•37	33•37
Armhole border	108•120	118•132	128•142	136•150	136•152

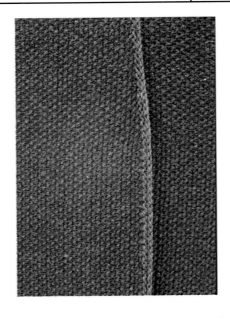

3 • 3½ sts per inch

BACK LONG TUNIC

With needles for gauge, cast on __ sts.
Work in seed stitch until piece measures for
long tunic: __ inches (this armhole is meant
to be deep)
Curved armhole: Bind off sts at each armhole edge
in foll sequence:

When armhole meas __ inches,
work __ sts for shoulder,
bind off center __ sts for neck, work to end. Place
shoulder sts on hold for later finishing.

	Adult				
	XS • 36"	**S • 40"**	**M • 44"**	**L • 48"**	**XL • 52"**
Cast on	55·65	61·71	67·79	73·85	79·93
inches	30	31	31	31	31
armhole seq	2 | 3 2 | 2 1x2 | 1x3	3 | 4 2 | 2 1x3 | 1x3	4 4 | 2 2 | 2 1x3 | 1x3	4 | 5 3 | 3 2 | 2 1x2 | 1x3	4 | 6 3 | 4 2 | 2 1x3 | 1x3
armhole meas	13	14	15	15½	16
shoulder sts	11·13	12·14	13·15	13·15	15·17
neck sts	21·23	21·25	23·27	25·29	25·29

FRONT LONG TUNIC

Cast on __ sts. Work in seed stitch until piece meas
__ inches.
Shape deep V-neck: dec at neck edge 1 st every __
row, __ times.
AT SAME TIME, when piece meas __ inches from beg, work
armhole as for back. Cont even until work meas same as back.
Place shoulder sts on hold for later finishing.

	XS • 36"	S • 40"	M • 44"	L • 48"	XL • 52"
Cast on	29·33	32·37	35·40	38·44	41·48
inches	24	25	25	25	25
every row	7·7	7·6	7·6	6·6	7·6
times	12·12	12·14	13·14	14·16	14·16
piece meas	30	31	31	31	31

FINISHING

Work 3 needle bind off seam for shoulders.
*NOTE: Be sure to gauge for garter stitch. It may be different
than gauge for seed stitch on the same size needles. The
sample pictured is knit seed stitch in Prairie Silk at 5 sts / inch
and the garter stitch border is Prairie Silk at 4 sts / inch. Turn to
the appropriate page matching your garter stitch gauge to follow
finishing instructions, or change needle size to achieve gauge
to match seed stitch.*
Garter stitch border: Beg at lower center edge of right front,
pick up approx __ sts along center front edge,
__ sts on neck edge,
__ sts on back neck, and
same number of sts on left front as for right front.
(This requires a long circular needle, or the border may be knit
in 2 parts, dividing and seaming at left shoulder.)
Knit 2 rows, bind off on row 3 (WS row).
Armhole border: Pick up approx __ sts evenly along front
and back armholes. Knit 2 rows, bind off on row 3 (WS row).

Sew side seams. Block, using the wet towel method.

	XS • 36"	S • 40"	M • 44"	L • 48"	XL • 52"
center front edge	72·84	75·87	75·87	75·87	75·87
neck edge	57·67	60·71	64·74	65·76	67·78
back neck	21·23	21·25	23·27	25·29	25·29
armhole border	80·94	86·100	96·110	100·118	98·114

Jackets

	Child			Adult				
	S • 24"	M • 28"	L • 32"	XS • 36"	S • 40"	M • 44"	L • 48"	XL • 52"
5 • 6 sts per inch yardage	750	1000	1300	1600	1900	2100	2300	2500
Cotton Fleece	4	5	7	8	9	10	11	12
Kaleidoscope	4	11	13	15	18	20	22	24
Nature Spun (S)								
Top of the Lamb (S)								
4 • 4½ sts per inch yardage	650	850	1100	1400	1650	1800	1950	2150
Country Classics (W)	4	5	6	8	9	10	11	12
Handpaint Originals	8	10	13	16	19	21	23	25
Lamb's Pride (W)	4	5	6	8	9	10	11	12
Lamb's Pride Superwash (W)	4	5	6	7	9	9	10	11
Nature Spun (W)	3	4	5	6	7	8	8	9
Prairie Silk	8	10	13	16	19	21	23	25
Top of the Lamb (W)	4	5	6	8	9	10	11	12
3 • 3½ sts per inch yardage	500	650	850	1050	1250	1350	1450	1650
Country Classics (B)	4	6	7	9	10	11	12	14
Lamb's Pride (B)	4	6	7	9	10	11	12	14
Lamb's Pride Superwash (B	5	6	8	10	12	13	14	15

(Yardage and skein estimates are approximations only.)

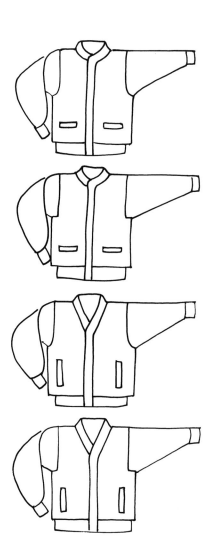

Choose:

- round or v-neck
- notched or curved armholes with straight or shaped sleeve cap
- horizontal or vertical pockets

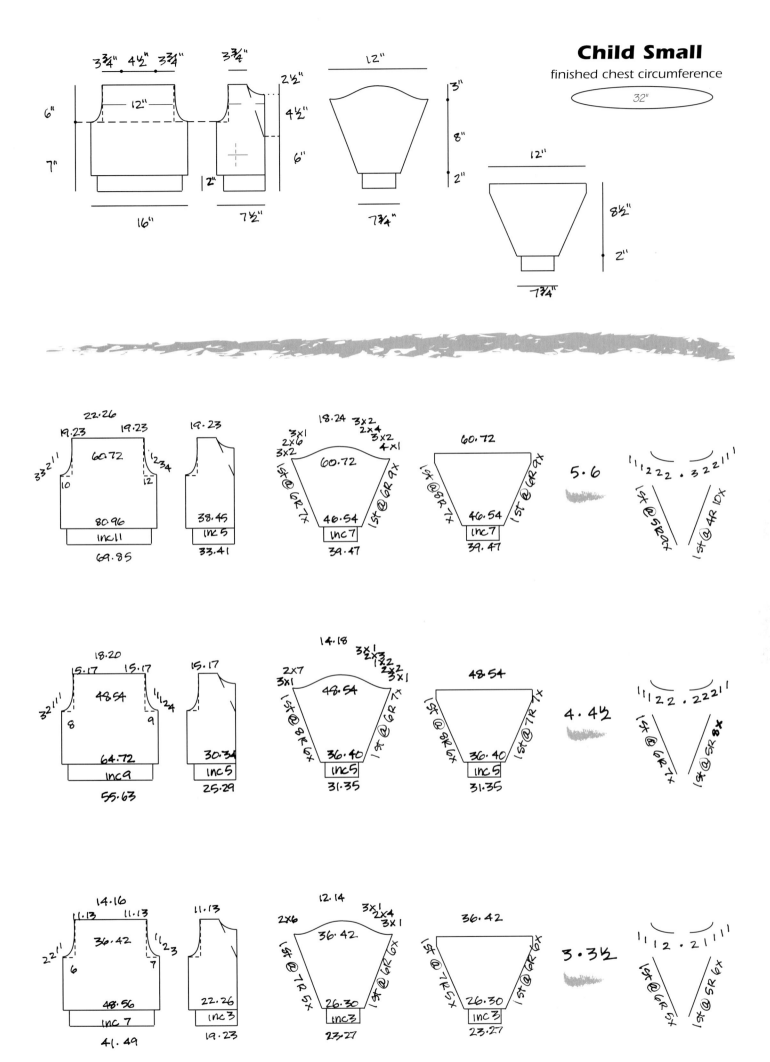

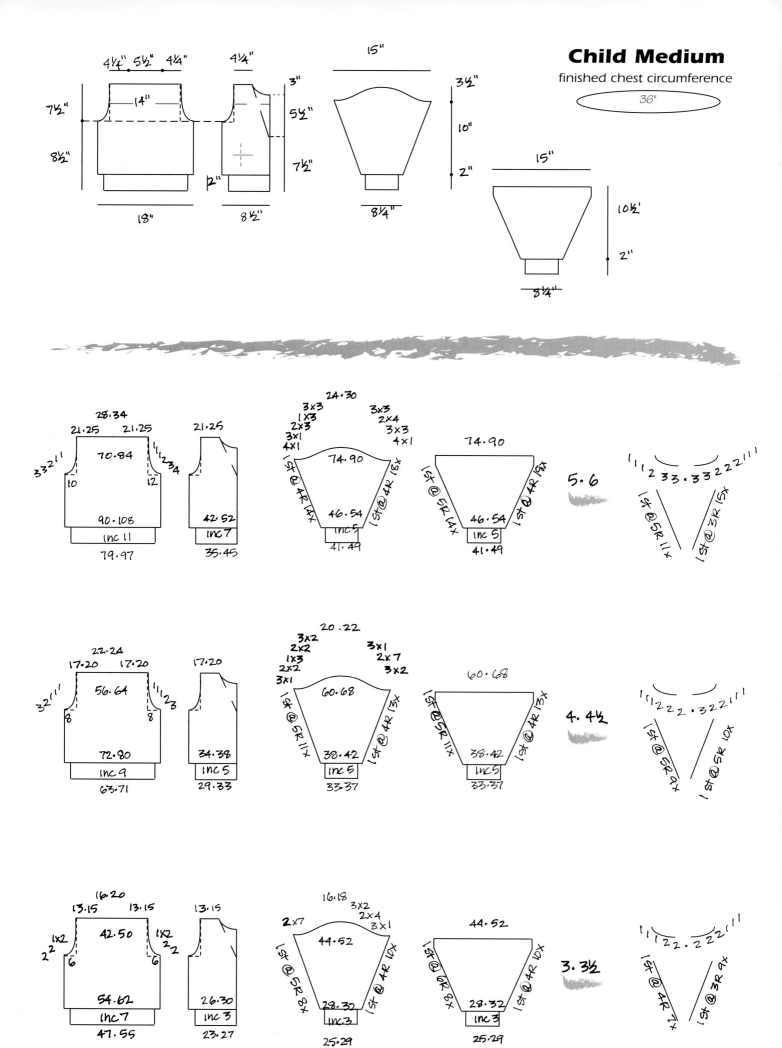

Child Medium

finished chest circumference

36"

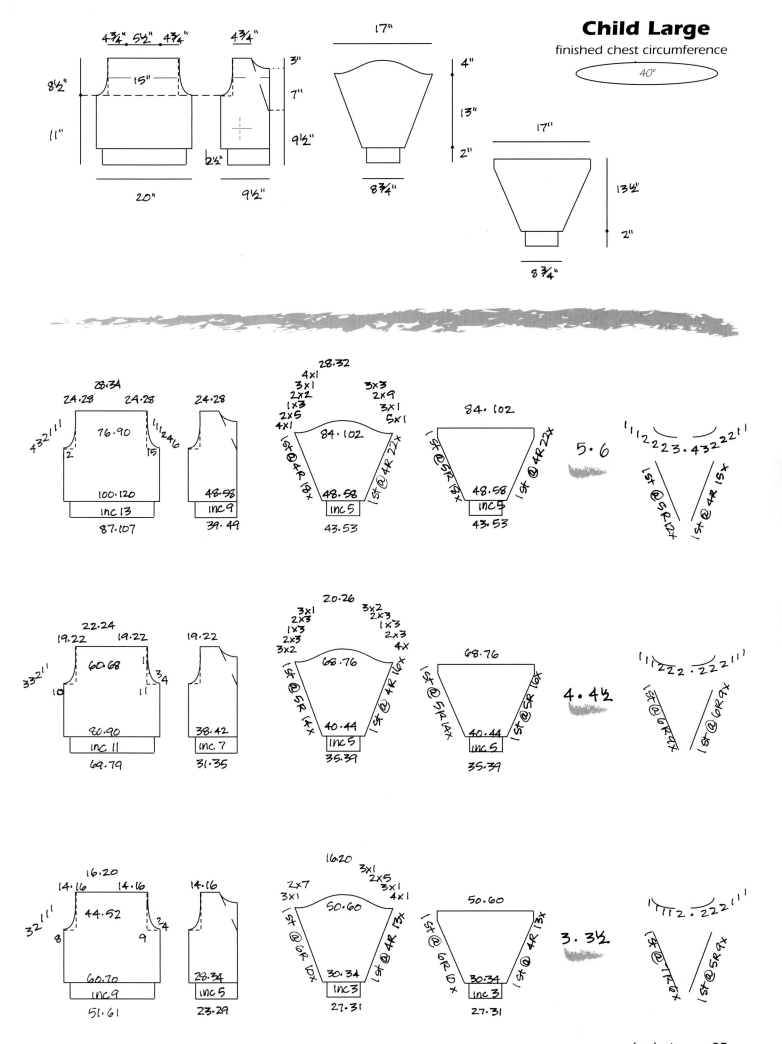

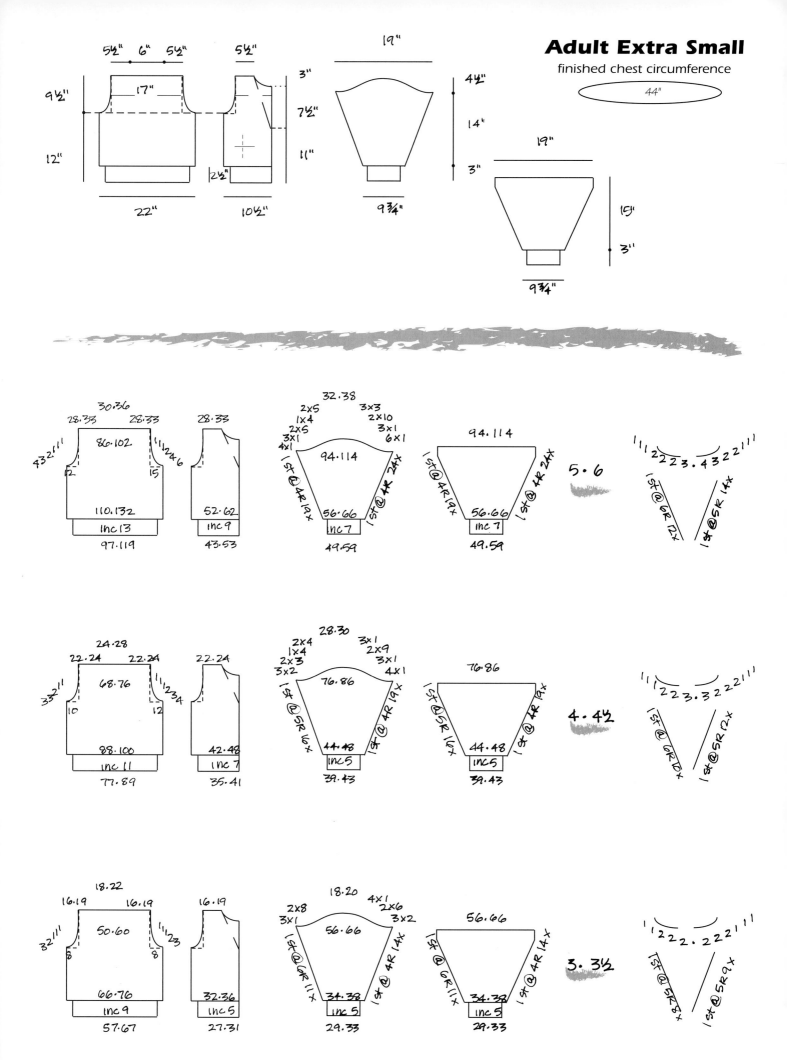

5¼" 6" 5¼"   5½"   19"

9½"   17"   3"

7½"

12"   11"

2½"

22"   10½"   9¾"

4½"

14"

3"

19"

15"

3"

9¾"

30.36
28.33   28.33   28.33

86.102

43 2   11   11 2 4 6

12   15

110.132   52.62

inc13   inc9

97.119   43.53

32.38
2x5   3x3
1x4   2x10
2x5   3x1
3x1   6x1
4x1

94.114

1st @ 4R 19x   1st @ 4R 24x

56.66   49.59

inc7

94.114

1st @ 4R 19x   1st @ 4R 24x

56.66   49.59

inc7

5.6

1 1 2 2 3.4 3 2 2 1 1

1st @ 6R 12x   1st @ 5R 14x

24.28
22.24   22.24   22.24

68.76

33 2   11   11 2 3 4

10   12

88.100   42.48

inc11   inc7

77.89   35.41

28.30
2x4   3x1
1x4   2x9
2x3   3x1
3x2   4x1

76.86

1st @ 5R 16x   1st @ 4R 19x

44.48   39.43

inc5

76.86

1st @ 5R 16x   1st @ 4R 19x

44.48   39.43

inc5

4.4½

1 1 2 2 3.3 2 2 1 1

1st @ 6R 12x   1st @ 5R 12x

18.22
16.19   16.19   16.19

50.60

33 2   11   11 2 3

8   8

66.76   32.36

inc9   inc5

57.67   27.31

18.20
2x8   4x1
3x1   2x6
3x2

56.66

1st @ 6R 11x   1st @ 4R 14x

34.38   29.33

inc5

56.66

1st @ 6R 11x   1st @ 4R 14x

34.38   29.33

inc5

3.3½

1 2 2 2.2 2 2 1 1

1st @ 5R 8x   1st @ 5R 9x

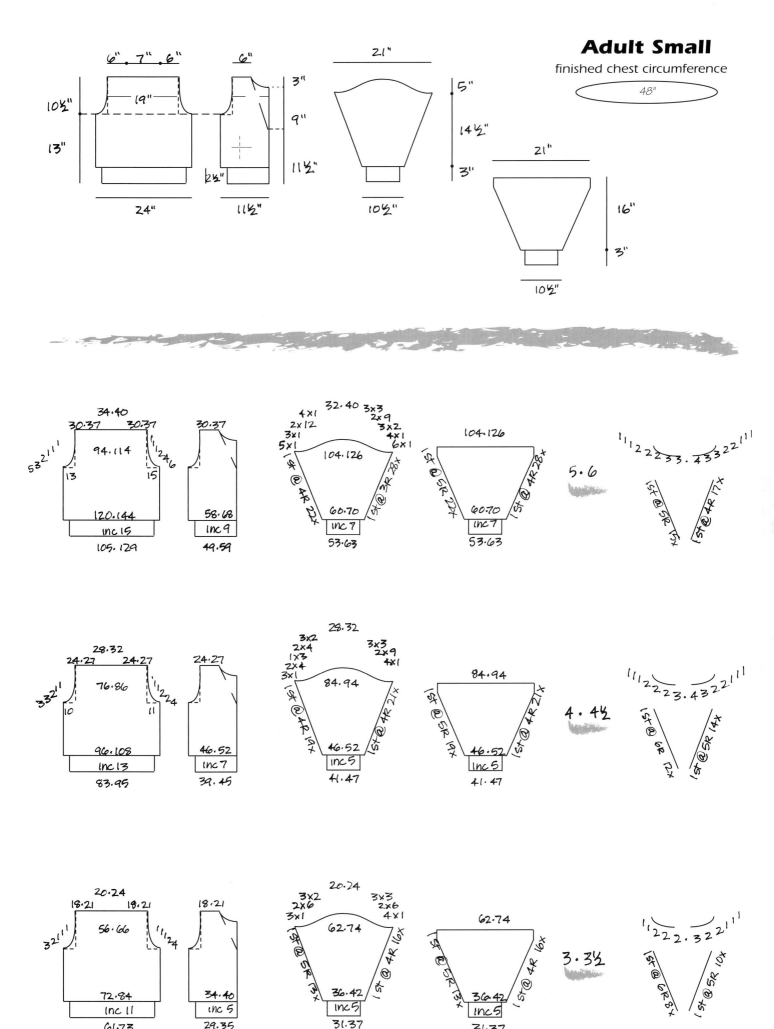

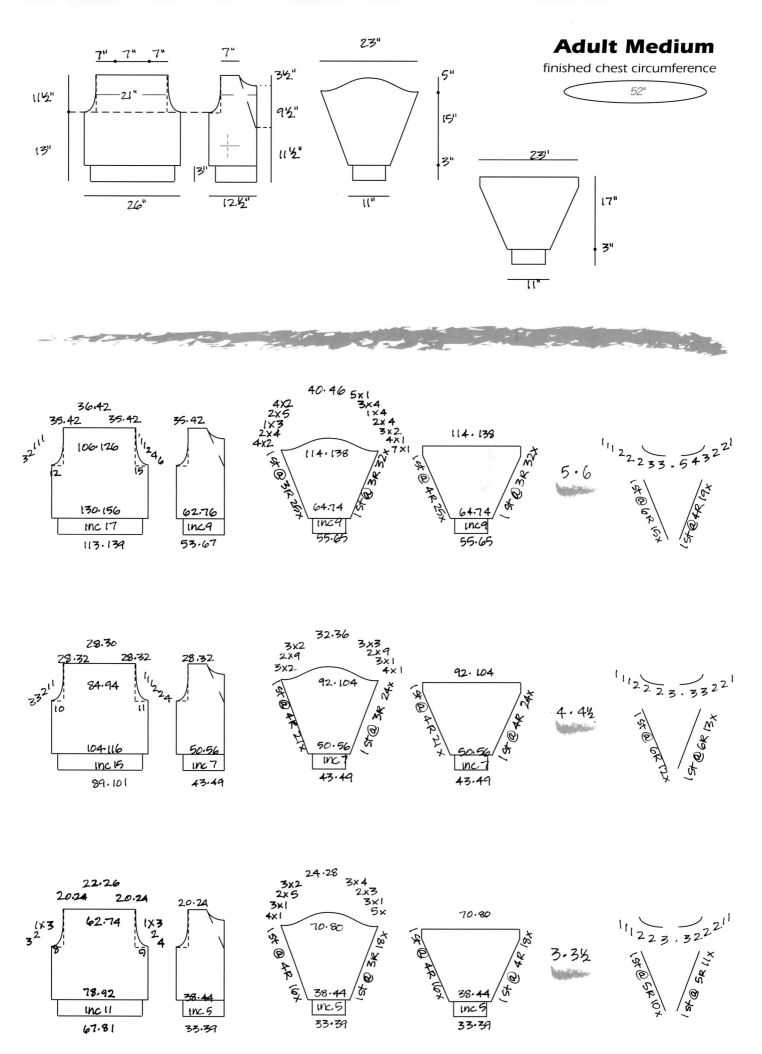

52"

7" 7" 7"   7"

21"

3½"

9½"

11½"

1½"

13"

2   3"

26"   12½"

23"

5"

15"

3"

11"

23"

17"

3"

11"

36·42
35·42   35·42   35·42

32"1"   1½2·4·6

106·126

2   5

130·156
inc 17
113·139

62·76
inc 9
53·67

40·46 5×1
4×2   3×4
2×5   1×4
1×3   2×4
2×4   3×2
4×2   4×1
         7×1
114·138

1st @ 3R 26×   1st @ 3R 32×

64·74
inc 9
55·65

114·138

1st @ 4R 25×

64·74
inc 9
55·65

5·6

1   1 2 2 2 3 3 · 5 4 3 2 2 1

1st @ 6R 16×   1st @ 4R 19×

28·30
28·32   28·32   28·32

32"1"   1½2·4

84·94

10   11

104·116
inc 15
89·101

50·56
inc 7
43·49

32·36
3×2   3×3
2×9   2×9
3×2   3×1
         4×1
92·104

1st @ 4R 21×   1st @ 3R 24×

50·56
inc 7
43·49

92·104

1st @ 4R 21×

50·56
inc 7
43·49

4·4½

1 1 2 2 2 3 · 3 3 2 2 1

1st @ 6R 12×   1st @ 6R 13×

22·26
20·24   20·24   20·24

1×3   1×3
3²   62·74   2 4

8   9

78·92
inc 11
67·81

38·44
inc 5
33·39

24·28
3×2   3×4
2×5   2×3
3×1   3×1
4×1   5×
70·80

1st @ 4R 16×   1st @ 3R 18×

38·44
inc 5
33·39

70·80

1st @ 4R 16×

38·44
inc 5
33·39

3·3½

1 1 2 2 3 · 3 2 2 1

1st @ 5R 10×   1st @ 5R 11×

98 • Vicki Square

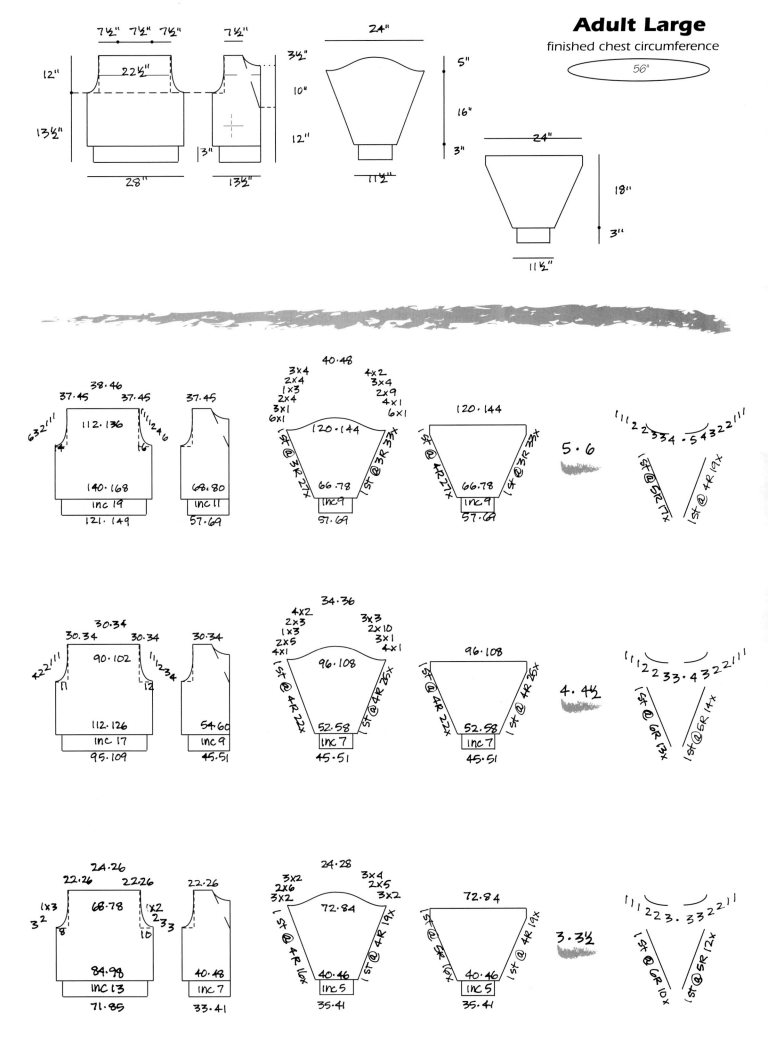

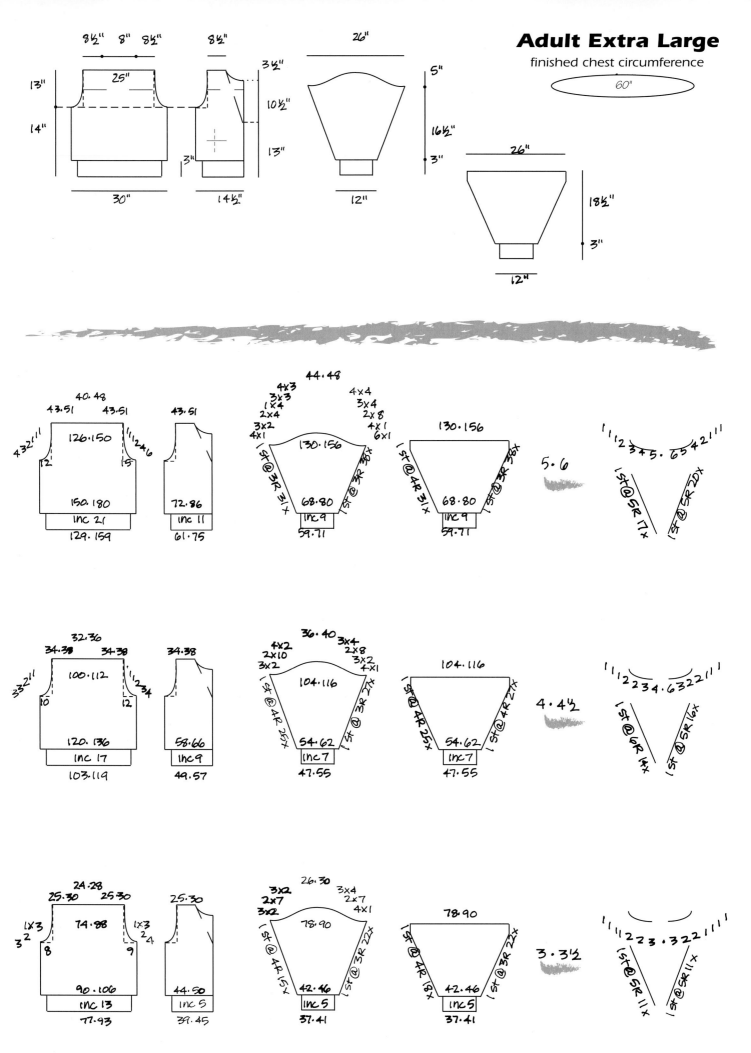

	Child			Adult				
	S • 32"	M • 36"	L • 40"	XS • 44"	S • 48"	M • 52"	L • 56"	XL • 60"

BACK JACKET

	S • 32"	M • 36"	L • 40"	XS • 44"	S • 48"	M • 52"	L • 56"	XL • 60"
With smaller needles, cast on __ sts.	69•85	79•97	87•107	97•119	105•129	113•139	121•149	129•159
Work 1/1 rib for __ inches,	2	2	2½	2½	2½	3	3	3
increasing __ sts across last row of rib,	11	11	13	13	15	17	19	21
__ sts.	80•96	90•108	100•120	110•132	120•144	130•156	140•168	150•180
Change to larger needles and work in st st until piece meas __ inches.	7	8 1/2	11	12	13	13	13½	14

Choose armhole style.

Notched armhole: Bind off __ sts at beg of next 2 rows. Cont even.

	S • 32"	M • 36"	L • 40"	XS • 44"	S • 48"	M • 52"	L • 56"	XL • 60"
	10•12	10•12	12•15	12•15	13•15	12•15	14•16	12•15

OR

Curved armhole: Bind off sts at each armhole edge in foll sequence (left / right):

	S • 32"	M • 36"	L • 40"	XS • 44"	S • 48"	M • 52"	L • 56"	XL • 60"
	3 / 4	3 / 4	4 / 6	4 / 6	5 / 6	4 / 6	6 / 6	4 / 6
	3 / 3	3 / 3	3 / 4	3 / 4	3 / 4	3 / 4	3 / 4	3 / 4
	2 / 2	2 / 2	2 / 2	2 / 2	2 / 2	2 / 2	2 / 2	2 / 2
	1x2 / 1x3	1x2 / 1x3	1x3 / 1x3	1x3 / 1x3	1x3 / 1x3	1x3 / 1x3	1x3 / 1x4	1x3 / 1x3

	S • 32"	M • 36"	L • 40"	XS • 44"	S • 48"	M • 52"	L • 56"	XL • 60"
Cont even until armhole meas __ inches.	6	7½	8½	9½	10½	11½	12	13
Work __ sts for shoulder,	19•23	21•25	24•28	28•33	30•37	35•42	37•45	43•51
bind off center __ sts for neck, work to end. Place shoulder sts on hold for later three needle bind-off seaming.	22•26	28•34	28•34	30•36	34•40	36•42	38•46	40•48

FRONT JACKET

Choose pocket design, and make pocket linings now.

	S • 32"	M • 36"	L • 40"	XS • 44"	S • 48"	M • 52"	L • 56"	XL • 60"
Horizontal pockets: With larger needles cast on __ sts.	18•21	20•24	22•27	25•30	30•36	30•36	30•36	30•36
Work st st for __ inches, place all sts on hold.	2	3	4	4½	5½	5½	5½	5½

OR

	S • 32"	M • 36"	L • 40"	XS • 44"	S • 48"	M • 52"	L • 56"	XL • 60"
Vertical pockets: With larger needles cast on __ sts.	20•24	25•30	25•30	30•36	35•42	35•42	35•42	35•42
Work st st for __ inches. Bind off all sts.	4	5	6	6½	7	7	7	7
FRONT: With smaller needles, cast on __ sts.	33•41	35•45	39•49	43•53	49•59	53•67	57•69	61•75
Work 1/1 rib for __ inches,	2	2	2½	2½	2½	3	3	3
increasing __ sts across last row of rib—	5	7	9	9	9	9	11	11
__ sts. Change to larger needles and work in st st.	38•45	42•52	48•58	52•62	58•68	62•76	68•80	72•86
Horizontal pockets: When piece meas __ inches,	4	5	6½	7	8	8½	8½	8½
from center front knit __ sts,	10•12	11•13	12•15	15•18	17•21	17•21	20•24	22•27
place next __ sts on hold. Place right side of pocket lining against wrong side of front, knit all lining sts from holder, knit remaining __ sts to side edge.	18•21	20•24	22•27	25•30	30•36	30•36	30•36	30•36
(Reverse this sequence for left front). Cont working st st until piece meas same as back to armhole.	10•12	11•15	14•16	12•14	11•11	15•19	18•20	20•23

OR

	S • 32"	M • 36"	L • 40"	XS • 44"	S • 48"	M • 52"	L • 56"	XL • 60"
Vertical pockets: When piece meas __ inches,	3	3	3½	3½	3½	4	4	4
from center front knit __ sts,	20•24	25•30	25•30	30•36	35•42	35•42	35•42	35•42
place rem __ sts on hold.	18•21	17•22	23•28	22•26	23•26	27•34	33•38	37•44
Work even for __ inches, place sts on hold. Take rem sts at side edge from holder and work even	3	4	5	5 1/2	6	6	6	6
for __ inches. Reverse sequence for left front.	3	4	5	5 1/2	6	6	6	6

Cont now working on all sts until piece meas same as back to armhole. Work armhole as for back.

AT SAME TIME, choose neckline style.

	S • 32"	M • 36"	L • 40"	XS • 44"	S • 48"	M • 52"	L • 56"	XL • 60"
V-neck: When work meas __ inches,	6	7½	9½	11	11½	11½	12	13
dec at neck edge 1 st every __ row	5•4	5•3	5•4	6•5	5•4	6•4	5•4	5•5
__ times. Cont even until piece meas same as back.	9•10	11•15	12•15	12•14	15•17	16•19	17•19	17•20

OR

Round neck: When work meas __ inches, at neck edge bind off in foll sequence:

	S • 32"	M • 36"	L • 40"	XS • 44"	S • 48"	M • 52"	L • 56"	XL • 60"
	10½	13	16½	18½	20½	21	22	23½
			/ 4	/ 4	/ 3	3 / 5	/ 5	5 / 6
		3 / 3	3 / 3	3 / 3	3 / 3x3	3 / 3	3x2 / 3	3 / 4
	2x3 / 2x2	2 / 2x3	2x3 / 2x3	2x3 / 2x2	2x3 / 2x2	2x3 / 2x2	2x2 / 2x2	2 / 2
	1x3 / 1x3	1x3 / 1x3	1x3 / 1x2	1x3 / 1x3	1x3 / 1x3	1x3 / 1x3	1x3 / 1x3	1x3 / 1x3

Cont even until piece meas same as back. Place sts on hold for later three needle bind-off seaming.

	Child			Adult				
	S • 32"	M • 36"	L • 40"	XS • 44"	S • 48"	M • 52"	L • 56"	XL • 60"

SLEEVE

	S • 32"	M • 36"	L • 40"	XS • 44"	S • 48"	M • 52"	L • 56"	XL • 60"
With smaller needles, cast on __ sts.	39•47	41•49	43•53	49•59	53•63	55•65	57•69	59•71
Work 1/1 rib for __ inches,	2	2	2	3	3	3	3	3
increasing __ sts across last row —	7	5	5	7	7	9	9	9
__ sts.	46•54	46•54	48•58	56•66	60•70	64•74	66•78	68•80

Sleeve shaping:
Inc 1 stitch at beg and end of every

	S • 32"	M • 36"	L • 40"	XS • 44"	S • 48"	M • 52"	L • 56"	XL • 60"
__ row for *straight* sleeve cap	8•6	5•4	5•4	4•4	5•4	4•3	4•3	4•3
__ row for *curved* sleeve cap:	6•6	4•4	4•4	4•4	4•3	3•3	3•3	3•3
__ times —	7•9	14•18	18•22	19•24	22•28	25•32	27•33	31•38
__ sts.	60•72	74•90	84•102	94•114	104•126	114•138	120•144	130•156

When work meas

	S • 32"	M • 36"	L • 40"	XS • 44"	S • 48"	M • 52"	L • 56"	XL • 60"
__ inches for *straight* sleeve cap: bind off all sts.	10½	12½	15½	18	19	20	21	21½
__ inches for *curved* sleeve cap: bind off on each side in foll sequence:	10	12	15	17	17½	18	19	19½

Curved sleeve cap bind-off sequences (each size has two sub-columns):

	S • 32"		M • 36"		L • 40"		XS • 44"		S • 48"		M • 52"		L • 56"		XL • 60"	
	3x2	4x1	4x1	4x1	4x1	5x1	4x1	6x1	5x1	6x1	4x2	7x1	6x1	6x1	4x1	6x1
	2x6	3x2	3x1	3x3	2x5	3x1	3x1	3x1	3x1	4x1	3x1	4x1	3x1	4x1	3x2	4x1
	3x1	2x4	2x3	2x4	1x3	2x9	2x5	2x10	2x12	3x2	2x4	3x2	2x4	2x9	2x4	2x8
		3x2	3x2	1x3	2x2	3x3	1x4	3x3	4x1	2x9	1x3	2x4	1x3	3x4	1x4	3x4
				3x3	3x1		2x5			3x3	2x5	1x4	2x4	4x2	3x3	4x4
					4x1						4x2	3x4	3x4			4x3
												5x1				

	S • 32"	M • 36"	L • 40"	XS • 44"	S • 48"	M • 52"	L • 56"	XL • 60"
Bind off remaining __ sts.	18•24	24•30	28•32	32•38	32•40	40•46	40•48	44•48

FINISHING

Work three needle bind off seaming for shoulders. Set sleeve in armhole. (For straight sleeve cap and notched armhole see instructions and diagram for Coat with Shawl Collar.) Sew side and sleeve seams. For following borders use smaller needles and pick up sts from right side.

V-neck border: Mark placement for buttonholes, with first at beg of v-neck shaping, the last ¾ inch from lower edge, and __ others spaced evenly between. Mark on right front for female, and on left front for male. Beg at lower right front edge, pick up __ sts along center front edge, __ sts along right front v-neck, __ sts across back neck, pick up sts along left front v-neck, and left center front edge as for right — __ sts. Work 1/1 rib for __ inches, bind off loosely in pattern. *(This requires a long circular needle, or the border may be worked in two parts, dividing and seaming at left shoulder seam)*
AT SAME TIME, when buttonhole border meas half of total width, work one row buttonholes at markers.

	S • 32"	M • 36"	L • 40"	XS • 44"	S • 48"	M • 52"	L • 56"	XL • 60"
__ others spaced evenly between	1	1	2	3	3	3	3	3
__ sts along center front edge,	30•36	38•45	48•57	55•66	58•69	58•69	60•72	65•78
__ sts along right front v-neck,	36•43	44•53	51•61	54•65	62•74	67•80	70•83	72•86
__ sts across back neck	22•26	28•34	28•34	30•36	34•40	36•42	38•46	40•48
__ sts.	154•184	192•230	226•270	248•298	274•326	286•340	298•356	314•376
Work 1/1 rib for __ inches	1¼	1¼	1½	1¾	2	2	2	2

Round neck border: Pick up __ sts along right front neck curve, __ sts across back neck, and along left front neck curve as for right. Work 1/1 rib for __ inches. Bind off loosely in pattern. Mark placement for buttonholes, with the first ¾ inch from top edge, the last ¾ inch from lower edge, and __ others spaced evenly between. Mark on right front for female, and on left front for male. Pick up __ sts on each front edge, and work 1/1 rib for __ inches. Bind off loosely in pattern.
AT SAME TIME, when buttonhole border meas half of total width, work one row buttonholes at markers. Sew on buttons.
Block garment using the wet towel method.

	S • 32"	M • 36"	L • 40"	XS • 44"	S • 48"	M • 52"	L • 56"	XL • 60"
Pick up __ sts along right front neck curve,	13•16	17•21	18•22	19•23	23•28	23•29	25•30	28•33
__ sts across back neck	22•26	28•34	28•34	30•36	34•40	36•42	38•46	40•48
(along left front neck curve)	48•58	62•76	64•78	68•82	80•94	82•100	88•106	96•114
__ inches	1	1	1	1¼	1¼	1¼	1½	1½
__ others spaced evenly between	2	3	4	5	5	5	5	5
Pick up __ sts on each front edge	58•69	70•84	88•105	98•117	108•129	110•132	115•138	123•147
for __ inches	1	1	1	1¼	1¼	1¼	1½	1½

4 • 4½ sts per inch

	Child			Adult				
	S • 32"	M • 36"	L • 40"	XS • 44"	S • 48"	M • 52"	L • 56"	XL • 60"
BACK JACKET								
With smaller needles, cast on __ sts.	55•63	63•71	69•79	77•89	83•95	89•101	95•109	103•119
Work 1/1 rib for __ inches,	2	2	2½	2½	2½	3	3	3
increasing __ sts across last row of rib,	9	9	11	11	13	15	17	17
__ sts.	64•72	72•80	80•90	88•100	96•108	104•116	112•126	120•136
Change to larger needles and work in st st until piece meas __ inches.	7	8½	11	12	13	13	13½	14
Choose armhole style.								
Notched armhole: Bind off __ sts at beg of next 2 rows. Cont even. OR	8•9	8•8	10•11	10•12	10•11	10•11	11•12	10•12
Curved armhole: Bind off sts at each armhole edge in foll sequence:			3 / 4	3 / 4	3 / 4	3 / 4	4 / 4	3 / 4
	3 / 4	3 / 3	3 / 3	3 / 3	3 / 2	3 / 2	2 / 3	3 / 3
	2 / 2	2 / 2	2 / 2	2 / 2	2 / 2	2 / 2	2 / 2	2 / 2
	1x3 / 1x3	1x3 / 1x3	1x2 / 1x2	1x2 / 1x3	1x2 / 1x3	1x2 / 1x3	1x3 / 1x3	1x2 / 1x3
Cont even until armhole meas __ inches.	6	7½	8½	9½	10½	11½	12	13
Work __ sts for shoulder,	15•17	17•20	19•22	22•24	24•27	28•32	30•34	34•38
bind off center __ sts for neck, work to end. Place shoulder sts on hold for later three needle bind-off seaming.	18•20	22•24	22•24	24•28	28•32	28•30	30•34	32•36
FRONT JACKET								
Choose pocket design, and make pocket linings now.								
Horizontal pockets: With larger needles cast on __ sts.	14•16	16•18	18•20	20•23	24•27	24•27	24•27	24•27
Work st st for __ inches, place all sts on hold. OR	2	3	4	4½	5½	5½	5½	5½
Vertical pockets: With larger needles cast on __ sts.	16•18	20•23	20•23	24•27	28•32	28•32	28•32	28•32
Work st st for __ inches. Bind off all sts.	4	5	6	6½	7	7	7	7
FRONT: With smaller needles, cast on __ sts.	25•29	29•33	31•35	35•41	39•45	43•49	45•51	49•57
Work 1/1 rib for __ inches,	2	2	2½	2½	2½	3	3	3
increasing __ sts across last row of rib —	5	5	7	7	7	7	9	9
__ sts.	30•34	34•38	38•42	42•48	46•52	50•56	54•60	58•66
Change to larger needles and work in st st.								
Horizontal pockets: When piece meas __ inches,	4	5	6½	7	8	8½	8½	8½
from center front knit __ sts,	8•9	9•10	10•11	12•13	14•15	14•15	16•18	18•20
place next __ sts on hold. Place right side of pocket lining against wrong side of front, knit all lining sts from holder, knit remaining __ sts to side edge. (Reverse this sequence for left front). Cont working st st until piece meas same as back to armhole. OR	14•16	16•18	18•20	20•23	24•27	24•27	24•27	24•27
	8•9	9•10	10•11	10•12	8•10	12•14	14•15	16•19
Vertical pockets: When piece meas __ inches,	3	3	3½	3½	3½	4	4	4
from center front knit __ sts,	16•18	20•23	20•23	24•27	28•32	28•32	28•32	28•32
place rem __ sts on hold.	14•16	14•15	18•19	18•21	18•20	22•24	26•28	30•34
Work even for __ inches, place sts on hold. Take rem sts at side edge from holder and work even for __ inches. Reverse sequence for left front. Cont now working on all sts until piece meas same as back to armhole. Work armhole as for back.	3	4	5	5½	6	6	6	6
	3	4	5	5½	6	6	6	6
AT SAME TIME, choose neckline style.								
V-neck: When work meas __ inches, dec at neck edge 1 st every __ row	6	7½	9½	11	11½	11½	12	13
	6•5	5•5	6•6	6•5	6•5	6•6	6•5	6•5
__ times. Cont even until piece meas same as back. OR	7•8	9•10	9•9	10•12	12•14	12•13	13•14	14•16
Round neck: When work meas __ inches, at neck edge bind off in foll sequence:	10	13	16½	18½	20½	21	22	23½
			/ 3			/ 4	3 / 4	4 / 6
				3 / 3	3 / 3	3 / 3	3 / 3	3 / 3
	2x2 / 2x3	2x3 / 2x2	2x3 / 2x3	2x2 / 2x3	2x3 / 2x2	2x3 / 2x2	2x2 / 2x2	2x2 / 2x2
	1x3 / 1x2	1x3 / 1x3	1x3 / 1x3	1x3 / 1x3	1x3 / 1x3	1x3 / 1x3	1x3 / 1x3	1x3 / 1x3
Cont even until piece meas same as back. Place sts on hold for later three needle bind-off seaming.								

4 • 4½ sts per inch

	Child			Adult				
	S • 32"	M • 36"	L • 40"	XS • 44"	S • 48"	M • 52"	L • 56"	XL • 60"

SLEEVE

	S • 32"	M • 36"	L • 40"	XS • 44"	S • 48"	M • 52"	L • 56"	XL • 60"
With smaller needles, cast on __ sts.	31•35	33•37	35•39	39•43	41•47	43•49	45•51	47•55
Work 1/1 rib for __ inches,	2	2	2	3	3	3	3	3
increasing __ sts across last row —	5	5	5	5	5	7	7	7
__ sts.	36•40	38•42	40•44	44•48	46•52	50•56	52•58	54•62

Sleeve shaping:
Inc 1 stitch at beg and end of every

	S • 32"	M • 36"	L • 40"	XS • 44"	S • 48"	M • 52"	L • 56"	XL • 60"
__ row for ***straight*** sleeve cap	8•7	5•4	5•5	5•4	5•4	4•4	4•4	4•4
__ row for ***curved*** sleeve cap:	8•6	5•4	5•4	5•4	4•4	4•3	4•4	4•3
__ times —	6•7	11•13	14•16	16•19	19•21	21•24	22•25	25•27
__ sts.	48•54	60•68	68•76	76•86	84•94	92•104	96•108	104•116

When work measures

	S • 32"	M • 36"	L • 40"	XS • 44"	S • 48"	M • 52"	L • 56"	XL • 60"
__ inches for ***straight*** sleeve cap: bind off all sts.	10½	12½	15½	18	19	20	21	21½
__ inches for ***curved*** sleeve cap: bind off on each side in foll sequence:	10	12	15	17	17½	18	19	19½

	S • 32"	M • 36"	L • 40"	XS • 44"	S • 48"	M • 52"	L • 56"	XL • 60"
	3x1 | 3x1	3x1 | 3x3	3x2 | 4x1	3x2 | 4x1	3x1 | 4x1	3x2 | 4x1	4x1 | 4x1	3x2 | 4x1
	2x7 | 2x2	2x2 | 2x6	2x3 | 2x3	2x3 | 3x1	2x4 | 2x9	2x9 | 3x1	2x5 | 3x1	2x10 | 3x2
	| 1x2	1x2 | 3x1	1x3 | 3x1	1x4 | 2x9	1x3 | 3x3	3x2 | 2x9	1x3 | 2x10	4x2 | 2x8
	| 2x3	2x3 |	2x3 | 2x3	2x4 | 3x1	2x4 |	| 3x3	2x3 | 3x3	| 3x4
	| 3x1	3x2 |	3x1 | 3x2		3x2 |		4x2 |	

	S • 32"	M • 36"	L • 40"	XS • 44"	S • 48"	M • 52"	L • 56"	XL • 60"
Bind off remaining __ sts.	14•18	20•21	20•26	28•30	28•32	32•36	34•36	36•40

FINISHING

Work three needle bind off seaming for shoulders. Set sleeve in armhole. (For straight sleeve cap and notched armhole see instructions and diagram for Coat with Shawl Collar.) Sew side and sleeve seams. For following borders use smaller needles and pick up sts from right side.

V-neck border: Mark placement for buttonholes, with first at beg of v-neck shaping, the last ¾ inch from lower edge, and __ others spaced evenly between. Mark on right front for female, and on left front for male. Beg at lower right front edge, pick up __ sts along center front edge, __ sts along right front v-neck, __ sts across back neck, pick up sts along left front v-neck, and left center front edge as for right — __ sts. Work 1/1 rib for __ inches, bind off loosely in pattern. *(This requires a long circular needle, or the border may be worked in two parts, dividing and seaming at left shoulder seam)*

AT SAME TIME, when buttonhole border meas half of total width, work one row buttonholes at markers.

	S • 32"	M • 36"	L • 40"	XS • 44"	S • 48"	M • 52"	L • 56"	XL • 60"
(others)	1	1	2	3	3	3	3	3
sts along center front edge	24•27	30•34	38•43	44•50	46•52	46•52	48•54	52•59
sts along right front v-neck	29•32	35•40	41•46	43•49	49•55	53•60	56•63	58•65
sts across back neck	18•20	22•24	22•24	24•28	28•32	28•30	30•34	32•36
sts	124•138	152•172	180•202	198•226	218•246	226•254	238•268	252•284
rib inches	1¼	1¼	1½	1¾	2	2	2	2
(buttonhole at)	11•12	14•16	15•17	16•18	19•21	19•21	20•22	22•25

Round neck border: Pick up __ sts along right front neck curve, __ sts across back neck, and along left front neck curve as for right. Work 1/1 rib for __ inches. Bind off loosely in pattern. Mark placement for buttonholes, with the first ¾ inch from top edge, the last ¾ inch from lower edge, and __ others spaced evenly between. Mark on right front for female, and on left front for male. Pick up __ sts on each front edge, and work 1/1 rib for __ inches. Bind off loosely in pattern.

	S • 32"	M • 36"	L • 40"	XS • 44"	S • 48"	M • 52"	L • 56"	XL • 60"
right front neck curve	18•20	22•24	22•24	24•28	28•32	28•30	30•34	32•36
sts across back neck	40•44	50•56	52•58	56•64	66•74	66•72	70•78	76•86
rib inches	1	1	1	1¼	1¼	1¼	1½	1½
others	2	3	4	5	5	5	5	5
pick up sts each front edge	46•52	56•63	70•79	78•88	86•97	88•99	92•104	98•110
rib inches	1	1	1	1¼	1¼	1¼	1½	1½

AT SAME TIME, when buttonhole border meas half of total width, work one row buttonholes at markers. Sew on buttons.

Block garment using the wet towel method.

	Child			Adult				
	S • 32"	M • 36"	L • 40"	XS • 44"	S • 48"	M • 52"	L • 56"	XL • 60"

BACK JACKET

	S • 32"	M • 36"	L • 40"	XS • 44"	S • 48"	M • 52"	L • 56"	XL • 60"
With smaller needles, cast on __ sts.	41·49	47·55	51·61	57·67	61·73	67·81	71·85	77·93
Work 1/1 rib for __ inches,	2	2	2½	2½	2½	3	3	3
increasing __ sts across last row of rib,	7	7	9	9	11	11	13	13
__ sts.	48·56	54·62	60·70	66·76	72·84	78·92	84·98	90·106
Change to larger needles and work in st st until piece meas __ inches.	7	8½	11	12	13	13	13½	14

Choose armhole style.

Notched armhole: Bind off __ sts at beg of next 2 rows. Cont even.

	S • 32"	M • 36"	L • 40"	XS • 44"	S • 48"	M • 52"	L • 56"	XL • 60"
Notched	6·7	6·6	8·9	8·8	8·9	8·9	8·10	8·9

OR

Curved armhole: Bind off sts at each armhole edge in foll sequence:

	S • 32"	M • 36"	L • 40"	XS • 44"	S • 48"	M • 52"	L • 56"	XL • 60"
	2 | 3	2 | 2	3 | 4	3 | 3	3 | 4	3 | 4	3 | 3 (3)	3 | 4
	2 | 2	2 | 2	2 | 2	2 | 2	2 | 2	2 | 2	2 | 2	2 | 2
	1x2 | 1x2	1x2 | 1x2	1x3 | 1x3	1x3 | 1x3	1x3 | 1x3	1x3 | 1x3	1x3 | 1x2	1x3 | 1x3

	S • 32"	M • 36"	L • 40"	XS • 44"	S • 48"	M • 52"	L • 56"	XL • 60"
Cont even until armhole meas __ inches.	6	7½	8½	9½	10½	11½	12	13
Work __ sts for shoulder,	11·13	13·15	14·16	16·19	18·21	20·24	22·26	25·30
bind off center __ sts for neck, work to end. Place shoulder sts on hold for later three needle bind-off seaming.	14·16	16·20	16·20	18·22	20·24	22·26	24·26	24·28

FRONT JACKET

Choose pocket design, and make pocket linings now.

	S • 32"	M • 36"	L • 40"	XS • 44"	S • 48"	M • 52"	L • 56"	XL • 60"
Horizontal pockets: With larger needles cast on __ sts. Work st st for __ inches, place all sts on hold.	11·12	12·14	14·16	15·18	18·21	18·21	18·21	18·21
	2	3	4	4½	5½	5½	5½	5½
Vertical pockets: With larger needles cast on __ sts. Work st st for __ inches. Bind off all sts.	12·14	15·18	15·18	18·21	21·24	21·24	21·24	21·24
	4	5	6	6½	7	7	7	7
FRONT: With smaller needles, cast on __ sts.	19·23	23·27	23·29	27·31	29·35	33·39	33·41	39·45
Work 1/1 rib for __ inches,	2	2	2½	2½	2½	3	3	3
increasing __ sts across last row of rib—	3	3	5	5	5	5	7	5
__ sts. Change to larger needles and work in st st.	22·26	26·30	28·34	32·36	34·40	38·44	40·48	44·50
Horizontal pockets: When piece meas __ inches,	4	5	6½	7	8	8½	8½	8½
from center front knit __ sts,	6·7	6·7	7·8	9·10	10·12	10·12	12·14	13·15
place next __ sts on hold. Place right side of pocket lining against wrong side of front, knit all lining sts from holder, knit remaining __ sts to side edge.	11·12	12·14	14·16	15·18	18·21	18·21	18·21	18·21
	5·7	8·9	7·10	8·8	6·7	10·11	10·13	13·14

(Reverse this sequence for left front). Cont working st st until piece meas same as back to armhole.

OR

	S • 32"	M • 36"	L • 40"	XS • 44"	S • 48"	M • 52"	L • 56"	XL • 60"
Vertical pockets: When piece meas __ inches,	3	3	3½	3½	3½	4	4	4
from center front knit __ sts,	12·14	15·18	15·18	18·21	21·24	21·24	21·24	21·24
place rem __ sts on hold.	10·12	11·12	13·16	14·15	13·16	17·20	19·24	23·26
Work even for __ inches, place sts on hold. Take rem sts at side edge from holder and work even	3	4	5	5½	6	6	6	6
for __ inches. Reverse sequence for left front.	3	4	5	5½	6	6	6	6

Cont now working on all sts until piece meas same as back to armhole. Work armhole as for back.

AT SAME TIME, choose neckline style.

	S • 32"	M • 36"	L • 40"	XS • 44"	S • 48"	M • 52"	L • 56"	XL • 60"
V-neck: When work meas __ inches, dec at neck edge 1 st every __ row	6	7½	9½	11	11½	11½	12	13
	6·5	4·3	7·5	5·5	6·5	5·5	6·5	5·5
__ times. Cont even until piece meas same as back.	5·6	7·9	6·9	8·9	8·10	10·11	10·12	11·11

OR

Round neck: When work meas __ inches, at neck edge bind off in foll sequence:

	S • 32"	M • 36"	L • 40"	XS • 44"	S • 48"	M • 52"	L • 56"	XL • 60"
	2 | 2	2x2 | 2x3	2 | 2x3	2x3 | 2x3	2x3 | 2x2 (3)	3 | 3 2x2 | 2x3	3 | 3x2 2x2 | 2x2	3 | 3 2x2 | 2x2
	1x3 | 1x4	1x3 | 1x3	1x4 | 1x3	1x2 | 1x3	1x2 | 1x3	1x3 | 1x2	1x3 | 1x2	1x4 | 1x4

Cont even until piece meas same as back. Place sts on hold for later three needle bind-off seaming.

	Child			Adult				
3 • 3½ sts per inch	S • 32"	M • 36"	L • 40"	XS • 44"	S • 48"	M • 52"	L • 56"	XL • 60"

SLEEVE

	S • 32"	M • 36"	L • 40"	XS • 44"	S • 48"	M • 52"	L • 56"	XL • 60"
With smaller needles, cast on __ sts.	23·27	25·29	27·31	29·33	31·37	33·39	35·41	37·41
Work 1/1 rib for __ inches,	2	2	2	3	3	3	3	3
increasing __ sts across last row—	3	3	3	5	5	5	5	5
__ sts.	26·30	28·32	30·34	34·38	36·42	38·44	40·46	42·46

Sleeve shaping:
Inc 1 stitch at beg and end of every

	S • 32"	M • 36"	L • 40"	XS • 44"	S • 48"	M • 52"	L • 56"	XL • 60"
__ row for *straight* sleeve cap	7·6	6·4	6·4	6·4	5·4	4·4	5·4	4·3
__ row for *curved* sleeve cap:	7·6	5·4	6·4	6·4	5·4	4·3	4·4	4·3
__ times—	5·6	8·10	10·13	11·13	13·16	16·18	16·19	18·22
__ sts.	36·42	44·52	50·60	56·66	62·74	70·80	72·84	78·90

When work measures

	S • 32"	M • 36"	L • 40"	XS • 44"	S • 48"	M • 52"	L • 56"	XL • 60"
__ inches for *straight* sleeve cap: bind off all sts.	10½	12½	15½	18	19	20	21	21½
__ inches for *curved* sleeve cap: bind off on each side in foll sequence:	10	12	15	17	17½	18	19	19½
	2x6 | 3x1	2x7 | 3x1	3x1 | 4x1	3x1 | 3x2	3x1 | 4x1	4x1 | 5x1	3x2 | 3x2	3x2 | 4x1
	2x4	2x4	2x7 | 3x1	2x8 | 2x6	2x6 | 2x6	3x1 | 3x1	2x6 | 2x5	2x7 | 2x7
	3x1	3x2	2x5	4x1	3x2 | 3x3	2x5 | 2x3	3x2 | 3x4	3x2 | 3x4
			3x1			3x2 | 3x4		
Bind off remaining __ sts.	12·14	16·18	16·20	18·20	20·24	24·28	24·28	26·30

FINISHING

Work three needle bind off seaming for shoulders. Set sleeve in armhole. (For straight sleeve cap and notched armhole see instructions and diagram for Coat with Shawl Collar.) Sew side and sleeve seams. For following borders use smaller needles and pick up sts from right side.
V-neck border: Mark placement for buttonholes, with first at beg of v-neck shaping, the last ¾ inch from lower edge, and __ others spaced evenly between. Mark on right front for female, and on left front for male. Beg at lower right front edge, pick up __ sts along center front edge, __ sts along right front v-neck, __ sts across back neck, pick up sts along left front v-neck, and left center front edge as for right— __ sts. Work 1/1 rib for __ inches, bind off loosely in pattern. *(This requires a long circular needle, or the border may be worked in two parts, dividing and seaming at left shoulder seam)*
AT SAME TIME, when buttonhole border meas half of total width, work one row buttonholes at markers.

	S • 32"	M • 36"	L • 40"	XS • 44"	S • 48"	M • 52"	L • 56"	XL • 60"
(others spaced evenly)	1	1	2	3	3	3	3	3
sts along center front edge	18·21	23·26	28·33	33·39	35·40	35·40	36·42	39·45
sts along right front v-neck	22·25	26·31	31·36	32·38	37·43	40·47	42·49	43·50
sts across back neck	14·16	16·20	16·20	18·22	20·24	22·26	24·26	24·28
sts.	94·108	114·134	134·158	148·176	164·190	172·200	180·208	188·218
Work 1/1 rib for __ inches	1¼	1¼	1½	1¾	2	2	2	2

Round neck border: Pick up __ sts along right front neck curve, __ sts across back neck, and along left front neck curve as for right. Work 1/1 rib for __ inches. Bind off loosely in pattern.
Mark placement for buttonholes, with the first ¾ inch from top edge, the last ¾ inch from lower edge, and __ others spaced evenly between. Mark on right front for female, and on left front for male.
Pick up __ sts on each front edge, and work 1/1 rib for __ inches. Bind off loosely in pattern.
AT SAME TIME, when buttonhole border meas half of total width, work one row buttonholes at markers.
Sew on buttons.
Block garment using the wet towel method.

	S • 32"	M • 36"	L • 40"	XS • 44"	S • 48"	M • 52"	L • 56"	XL • 60"
Pick up sts along right front neck curve	8·9	10·12	11·13	12·14	14·16	14·17	15·18	17·19
sts across back neck	14·16	16·20	16·20	18·22	20·24	22·26	24·26	24·28
	30·34	36·44	38·46	42·50	48·56	50·60	54·62	58·66
Work 1/1 rib for __ inches	1	1	1	1¼	1¼	1¼	1½	1½
others spaced evenly	2	3	4	5	5	5	5	5
Pick up __ sts on each front edge	35·40	42·49	53·62	59·69	65·76	66·77	69·81	74·86
work 1/1 rib for __ inches	1	1	1	1¼	1¼	1¼	1½	1½

Coats

Coat with Shawl Collar	Child			Adult				
	S • 24"	M • 28"	L • 32"	XS • 36"	S • 40"	M • 44"	L • 48"	XL • 52"
5 • 6 sts per inch yardage	1150	1600	2100	2650	3000	3350	3600	3950
Cotton Fleece	6	8	10	13	14	16	17	19
Kaleidoscope	11	15	20	25	29	32	34	37
Nature Spun (S)	7	9	12	15	17	19	20	22
Top of the Lamb (S)	4	5	6	8	9	10	11	12
4 • 4½ sts per inch yardage	1000	1400	1800	2300	2600	2850	3100	3400
Country Classics (W)	6	8	10	13	14	15	17	18
Handpaint Originals	12	16	21	27	30	33	36	39
Lamb's Pride (W)	6	8	10	13	14	15	17	18
Lamb's Pride Superwash (W)	5	8	9	12	13	15	16	17
Nature Spun (W)	5	6	8	10	11	12	13	14
Prairie Silk	12	16	21	27	30	33	36	39
Top of the Lamb (W)	6	8	10	13	14	15	17	18
3 • 3½ sts per inch yardage	750	1050	1350	1700	1900	2100	2300	2500
Country Classics (B)	6	9	11	14	16	17	19	20
Lamb's Pride (B)	6	9	11	14	16	17	19	20
Lamb's Pride Superwash (B)	7	10	13	16	18	20	21	23

(Yardage and skein estimates are approximations only.)

Choose:

• coat with shawl collar

    notched armhole and straight sleeve

    cap, in-seam pocket

    garter stitch border at hem and cuff

    back vent

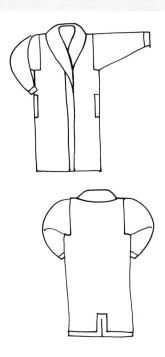

Collar only	Child			Adult				
	S • 24"	M • 28"	L • 32"	XS • 36"	S • 40"	M • 44"	L • 48"	XL • 52"
5 • 6 sts per inch yardage	200	200	250	350	350	400	450	450
Cotton Fleece	1	1	2	2	2	2	3	3
Kaleidoscope	2	2	3	4	4	4	5	5
Nature Spun (S)	2	2	2	2	2	3	3	3
Top of the Lamb (S)	1	1	1	1	1	2	2	2
4 • 4½ sts per inch yardage	175	175	200	275	300	350	400	400
Country Classics (W)	1	1	2	2	2	2	3	3
Handpaint Originals	2	2	3	4	4	4	5	5
Lamb's Pride (W)	1	1	2	2	2	2	3	3
Lamb's Pride Superwash (W)	1	1	1	2	2	2	2	2
Nature Spun (W)	1	1	1	2	2	2	2	2
Prairie Silk	2	2	3	4	4	4	5	5
Top of the Lamb (W)	1	1	2	2	2	2	3	3
3 • 3½ sts per inch yardage	150	150	175	225	250	275	300	300
Country Classics (B)	2	2	2	2	2	3	3	3
Lamb's Pride (B)	2	2	2	2	2	3	3	3
Lamb's Pride Superwash (B)	2	2	2	3	3	3	3	3

(Yardage and skein estimates are approximations only.)

This chart indicates yarn needs for the shawl collar only. If you opt to knit the collar in a contrast yarn, adjust yardage needs for coat body by subtracting collar yardage from total yardage in chart on page 108

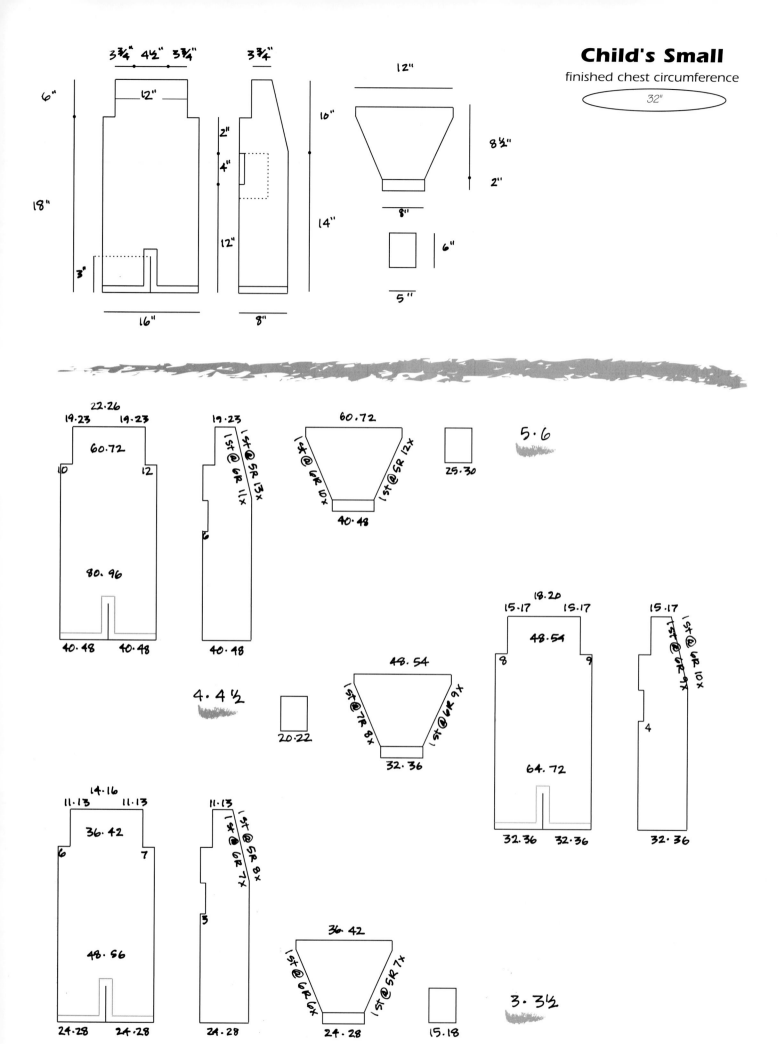

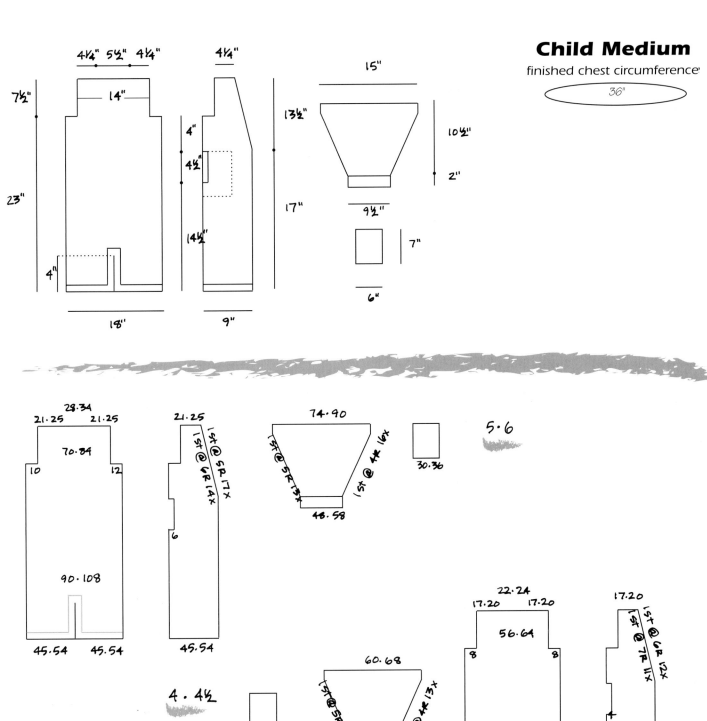

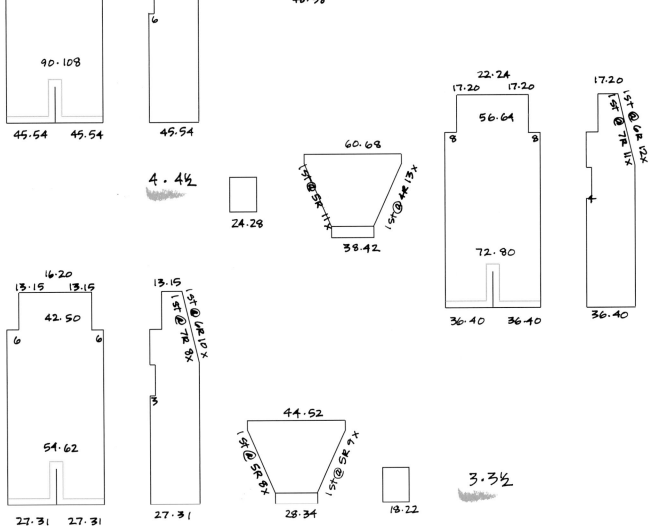

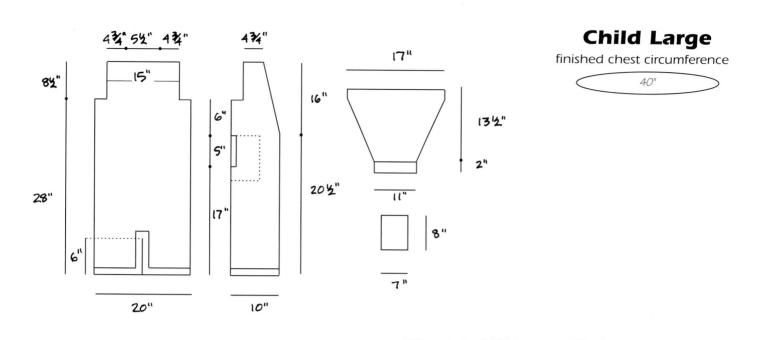

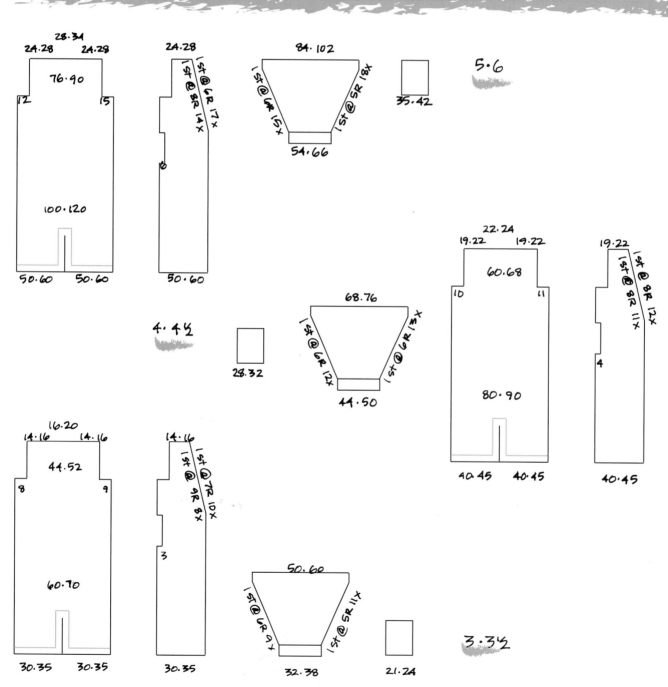

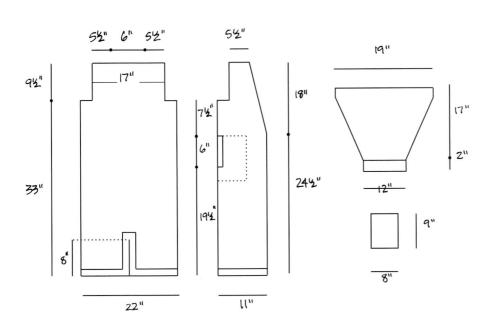

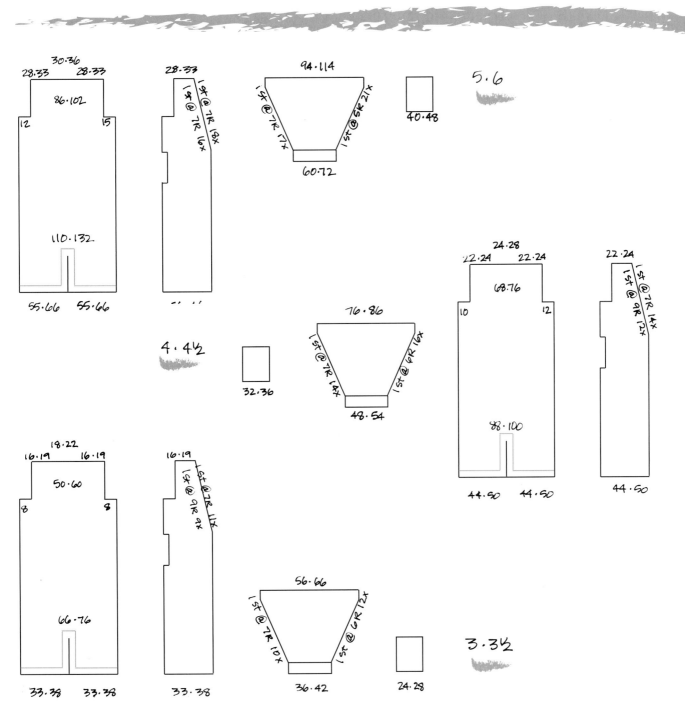

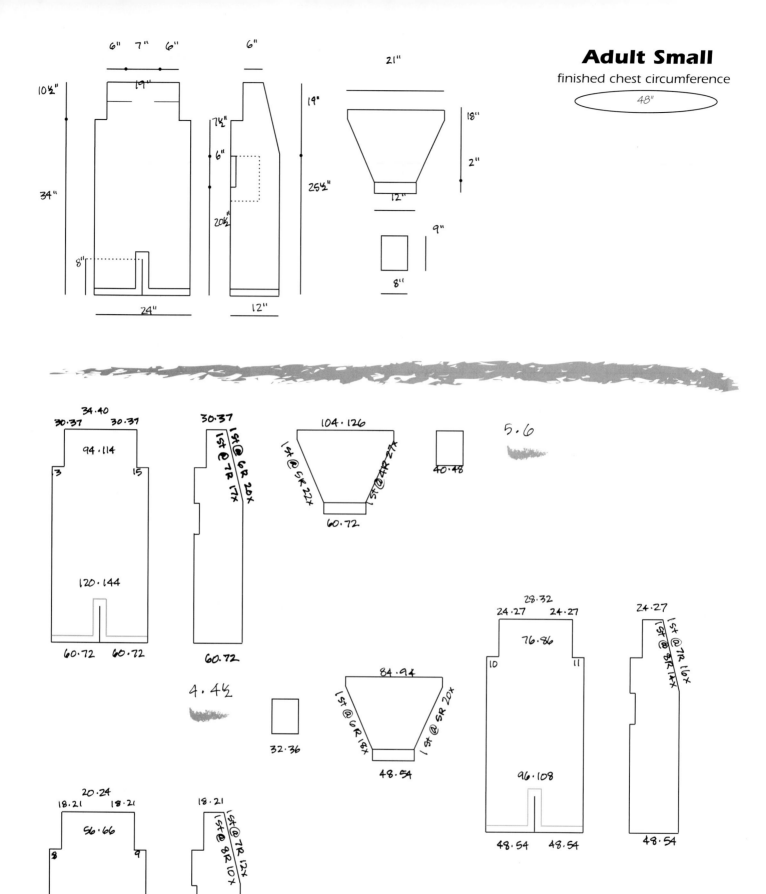

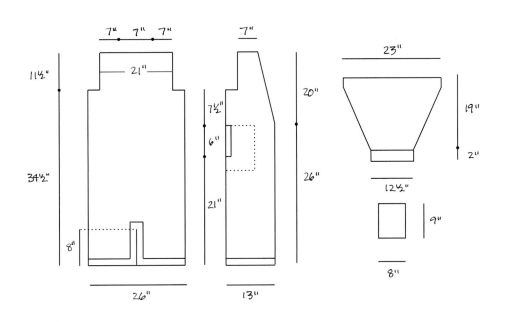

Adult Medium

finished chest circumference

52"

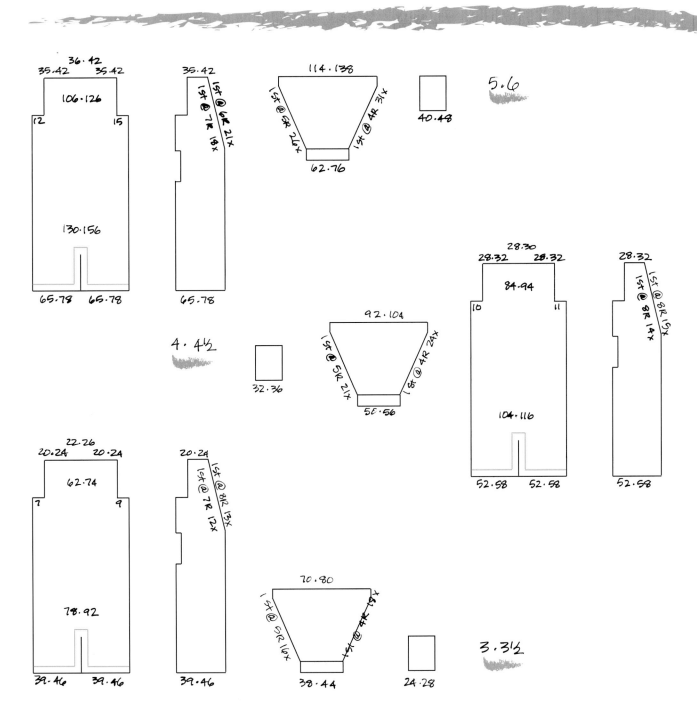

56"

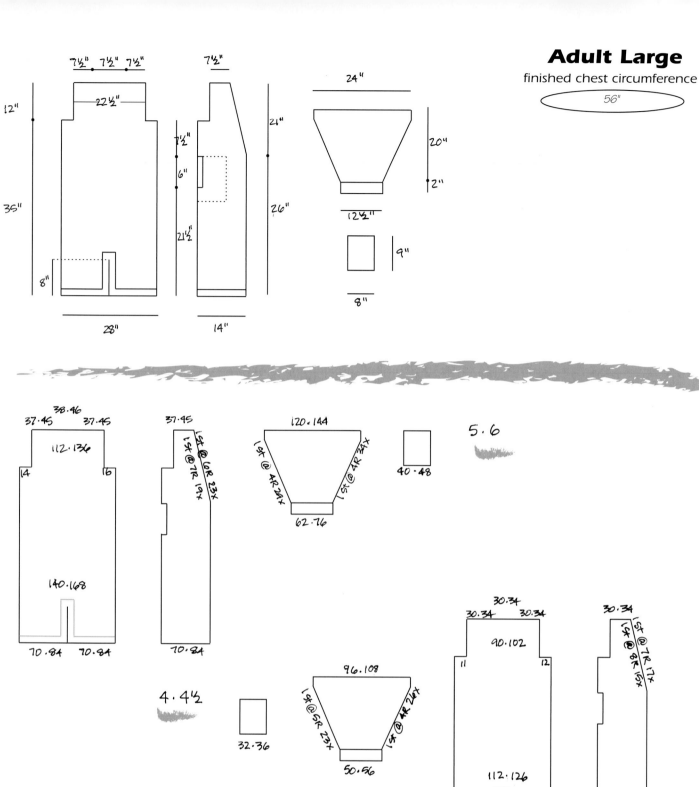

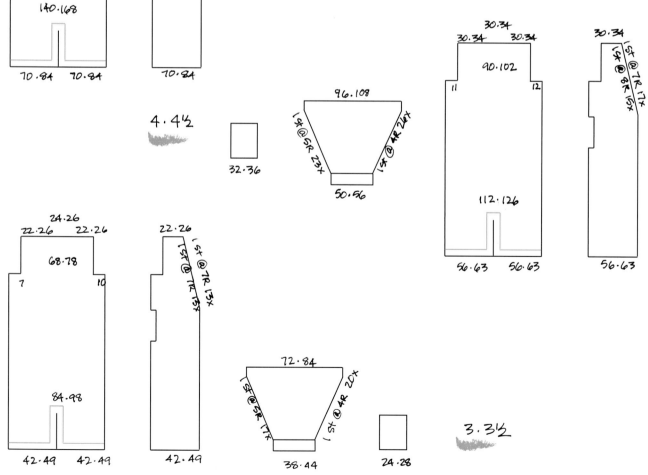

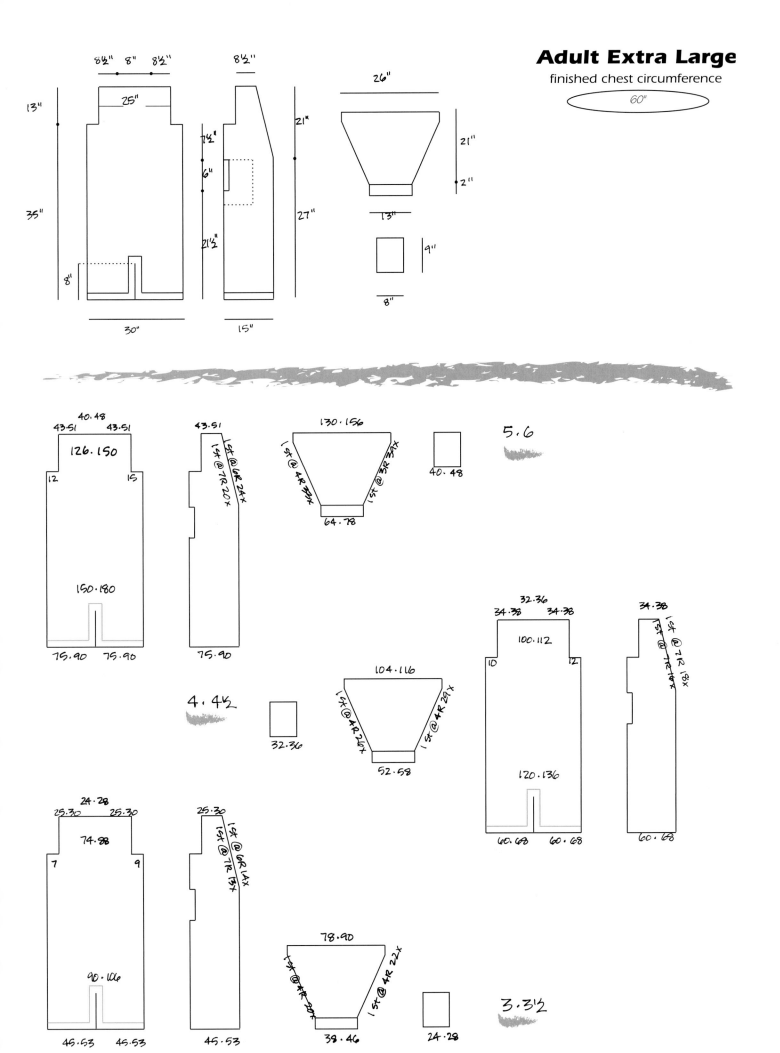

	Child			Adult				
	S • 32"	M • 36"	L • 40"	XS • 44"	S • 48"	M • 52"	L • 56"	XL • 60"

BACK COAT (with shawl collar)
Lower left back:
With smaller needles, cast on __ sts.
Work garter stitch for __ inches. Change to larger needles and knit across row, turn. (WS) Purl to last 5 sts, knit 5. Repeat last two rows until piece meas __ inches from beg, end right side facing. Break yarn. Place sts on spare needle same size or smaller.

40·48	45·54	50·60	55·66	60·72	65·78	70·84	75·90
1½	1½	1½	2½	2½	2½	2½	2½
3	4	6	8	8	8	8	8

Lower right back:
With smaller needles, cast on __ sts.
Work garter stitch for __ inches. Change to larger needles and knit across row, turn. (WS) Knit 5 sts, purl to end of row. Repeat last two rows until piece meas __ inches from beg, ending with right side facing. Do not break yarn. To join pieces, knit across lower right back sts immediately followed by lower left back sts in one continuous row, turn. Purl __ sts, knit 10 sts, purl to end. Repeat last two rows until piece meas __ inches from beg. Change to st st and work until piece meas __ inches.
Notched armhole: Bind off __ sts at each armhole edge. Cont even on __ sts until armhole meas __ inches.
Work __ sts for shoulder, bind off center __ sts for neck, work to end. Place shoulder sts on hold for later finishing.

40·48	45·54	50·60	55·66	60·72	65·78	70·84	75·90
1½	1½	1½	2½	2½	2½	2½	2½
3	4	6	8	8	8	8	8
35·43	40·49	45·55	50·61	55·67	60·73	65·79	70·85
4	5	7	9	9	9	9	9
18	23	28	33	34	34½	35	35
10·12	10·12	12·15	12·15	13·15	12·15	14·16	12·15
60·72	70·84	76·90	86·102	94·114	106·126	112·136	126·150
6	7½	8½	9½	10½	11½	12	13
19·23	21·25	24·28	28·33	30·37	35·42	37·45	43·51
22·26	28·34	28·34	30·36	34·40	36·42	38·46	40·48

FRONT COAT (with shawl collar)
With smaller needles, cast on __ sts.
Work garter stitch for __ inches.
Change to larger needles and work in st st until piece meas __ inches, to lower edge of pocket opening. Bind off 6 sts at side edge, cont in st st until pocket opening meas __ inches from bind off. Using cable cast on method, cast on 6 sts at side edge. **AT SAME TIME** when piece meas __ inches, **Shape V-neck:** Dec at neck edge 1 st every __ row __ times.
AT SAME TIME, when work meas same as back to armhole, bind off __ sts at armhole edge. Cont even until piece meas same as back. Place all sts on hold for later three needle bind-off seaming.

40·48	45·54	50·60	56·66	60·72	65·78	70·84	75·90
1½	1½	1½	2½	2½	2½	2½	2½
12	14½	17	19½	20½	21	21½	21½
4	4½	5	6	6	6	6	6
14	17	20½	24½	25½	26	26	27
6·5	6·5	8·6	7·7	7·6	7·6	7·6	7·6
11·13	14·17	14·17	16·18	17·20	18·21	19·23	20·24
10·12	10·12	12·15	12·15	13·15	12·15	14·16	12·15

SLEEVE
With smaller needles, cast on __ sts.
Work garter stitch for 2 inches. Change to larger needles and work in st st, increasing 1 st each end of row every __ row __ times.
Work even on __ sts until sleeve meas __ inches. Bind off all sts.

40·48	48·58	54·66	60·72	60·72	62·76	62·76	64·78
6·5	5·4	6·5	7·5	5·4	5·4	4·4	4·3
10·12	13·16	15·18	17·21	22·27	26·31	29·34	33·39
60·72	74·90	84·102	94·114	104·126	114·138	120·144	130·156
10½	12½	15½	19	20	21	22	23

POCKET LINING
Cast on __ sts. Work st st until piece measures __ inches from beg. Bind off.

25·30	30·36	35·42	40·48	40·48	40·48	40·48	40·48
6	7	8	9	9	9	9	9

FINISHING
Work 3 needle bind off seam for shoulders.
Collar/border: Beg at lower edge of right front, pick up __ sts along center front, __ sts on neck edge, and __ sts on one half of back neck— __ sts. Knit 2 rows (CB).

70·84	85·102	102·123	122·148	128·153	130·156	130·156	135·162
50·55	68·82	81·97	92·112	96·116	102·122	106·128	106·128
11·13	14·16	14·16	15·18	18·21	18·21	18·22	20·24
131·152	167·200	197·236	229·278	242·290	250·299	254·306	261·314

5 • 6 sts per inch	Child			Adult				
	S • 32"	M • 36"	L • 40"	XS • 44"	S • 48"	M • 52"	L • 56"	XL • 60"

FINISHING (cont)

	S • 32"	M • 36"	L • 40"	XS • 44"	S • 48"	M • 52"	L • 56"	XL • 60"
Short row as folls: K __ sts, wrap, turn, k to end.	61·68	82·98	95·113	107·130	114·137	120·143	124·150	126·152
K __ sts, wrap, turn, k to end.	56·62	77·92	90·107	102·124	109·131	115·137	119·144	121·146
K __ sts, wrap; turn, k to end. Cont in like fashion,	51·56	72·86	85·101	97·118	104·125	110·131	114·138	116·140
knitting __ sts fewer on every other row until you	5·6	5·6	5·6	5·6	5·6	5·6	5·6	5·6
have completed k __, wrap, turn, k to end.	17·20	22·26	23·25	23·26	26·29	28·31	28·30	26·32
Knit even on all sts for __ inches more. Bind off	2	2	2	2	3	3	3	3

loosely.

Hide wraps as needed.

AT SAME TIME, when border at center front meas one half of total width, work 1 one-row buttonhole __ inches from lower edge on right front for female. This garment is designed primarily for the female, yet this coat could be suitable for a male, with an appropriate color and texture of yarn. Buttonholes would then be made on the left front, with the first (top) __ inches from lower edge, and __ more, spaced about 4 inches apart. Pocket garter st border: Pick up __ sts along pocket opening edge. Work garter st until equal to side edge. Bind off. Sew pocket border selvage to coat front at each upper and lower edge of pocket opening. Place right side of pocket lining against wrong side of coat front, matching side edges and top of pocket lining at upper edge of opening. From wrong side whipstitch pocket lining to front, leaving border edge open.

	S • 32"	M • 36"	L • 40"	XS • 44"	S • 48"	M • 52"	L • 56"	XL • 60"
buttonhole __ inches from lower edge on right	14	17	20½	24½	25½	26	26	27
with the first (top) __ inches from lower edge	14	17	20½	24½	25½	26	26	27
and __ more, spaced about 4 inches apart	2	2	3	4	4	4	4	4
Pick up __ sts	20·24	22·27	25·30	30·36	30·36	30·36	30·36	30·36

Set in sleeves, sewing straight edge of sleeve cap to the selvage edge only of armhole, from notched corner to notched corner. Seam bound off edge of armhole (a) to sleeve seam edge (b). Sew side seam, being careful to catch pocket lining and leave pocket border free. Sew sleeve seam. Sew center back collar seam.

Sew on button(s). Block, using wet towel method.

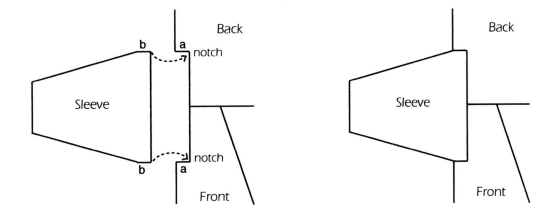

	Child			Adult				
	S • 32"	M • 36"	L • 40"	XS • 44"	S • 48"	M • 52"	L • 56"	XL • 60"

BACK COAT (with shawl collar)

Lower left back:
With smaller needles, cast on __ sts.
Work garter stitch for __ inches. Change to larger needles and knit across row, turn. (WS) Purl to last 5 sts, knit 5. Repeat last two rows until piece meas __ inches from beg, end right side facing. Break yarn. Place sts on spare needle same size or smaller.

Lower right back:
With smaller needles, cast on __ sts.
Work garter stitch for __ inches. Change to larger needles and knit across row, turn. (WS) Knit 5 sts, purl to end of row. Repeat last two rows until piece meas __ inches from beg, ending with right side facing. Do not break yarn. To join pieces, knit across lower right back sts immediately followed by lower left back sts in one continuous row, turn. Purl __ sts, knit 10 sts, purl to end. Repeat last two rows until piece meas __ inches from beg. Change to st st and work until piece meas __ inches.
Notched armhole: Bind off __ sts at each armhole edge. Cont even on __ sts until armhole meas __ inches.
Work __ sts for shoulder, bind off center __ sts for neck, work to end. Place shoulder sts on hold for later finishing.

	S • 32"	M • 36"	L • 40"	XS • 44"	S • 48"	M • 52"	L • 56"	XL • 60"
cast on (LLB)	32·36	36·40	40·45	44·50	48·54	52·58	56·63	60·68
garter inches	1½	1½	1½	2½	2½	2½	2½	2½
meas inches	3	4	6	8	8	8	8	8
cast on (LRB)	32·36	36·40	40·45	44·50	48·54	52·58	56·63	60·68
garter inches	1½	1½	1½	2½	2½	2½	2½	2½
meas inches	3	4	6	8	8	8	8	8
Purl __ sts	27·31	31·35	35·40	39·45	43·49	47·53	51·58	55·63
meas inches	4	5	7	9	9	9	9	9
st st inches	18	23	28	33	34	34½	35	35
Bind off sts	8·9	8·8	10·11	10·12	10·11	10·11	11·12	10·12
Cont even on sts	48·54	56·64	60·68	68·76	76·86	84·94	90·102	100·112
armhole inches	6	7½	8½	9½	10½	11½	12	13
shoulder sts	15·17	17·20	19·22	22·24	24·27	28·32	30·34	34·38
neck sts	18·20	22·24	22·24	24·28	28·32	28·30	30·34	32·36

FRONT COAT (with shawl collar)

With smaller needles, cast on __ sts.
Work garter stitch for __ inches.
Change to larger needles and work in st st until piece meas __ inches, to lower edge of pocket opening. Bind off 4 sts at side edge, cont in st st until pocket opening meas __ inches from bind off. Using cable cast on method, cast on 4 sts at side edge. **AT SAME TIME** when piece meas __ inches,
Shape V-neck: Dec at neck edge 1 st every __ row __ times.
AT SAME TIME, when work meas same as back to armhole, bind off __ sts at armhole edge.
Cont even until piece meas same as back. Place all sts on hold for later three needle bind-off seaming.

	S • 32"	M • 36"	L • 40"	XS • 44"	S • 48"	M • 52"	L • 56"	XL • 60"
cast on sts	32·36	36·40	40·45	44·50	48·54	52·58	56·63	60·68
garter inches	1½	1½	1½	2½	2½	2½	2½	2½
meas inches	12	14½	17	19½	20½	21	21½	21½
pocket inches	4	4½	5	6	6	6	6	6
meas inches	14	17	20½	24½	25½	26	26	27
every __ row	6·6	7·6	8·8	9·7	8·7	8·8	8·7	7·7
times	9·10	11·12	11·12	12·14	14·16	14·15	15·17	16·18
bind off sts	8·9	8·8	10·11	10·12	10·11	10·11	11·12	10·12

SLEEVE

With smaller needles, cast on __ sts.
Work garter stitch for 2 inches. Change to larger needles and work in st st, increasing 1 st each end of row every __ row __ times.
Work even on __ sts until sleeve meas __ inches. Bind off all sts.

	S • 32"	M • 36"	L • 40"	XS • 44"	S • 48"	M • 52"	L • 56"	XL • 60"
cast on sts	32·36	38·42	44·50	48·54	48·54	50·56	50·56	52·58
every __ row	7·6	5·4	6·6	7·6	6·5	5·4	5·4	4·4
times	8·9	11·13	12·13	14·16	18·20	21·24	23·26	26·29
even on sts	48·54	60·68	68·76	76·86	84·94	92·104	96·108	104·116
meas inches	10½	12½	15½	19	20	21	22	23

POCKET LINING

Cast on __ sts. Work st st until piece measures __ inches from beg. Bind off.

	S • 32"	M • 36"	L • 40"	XS • 44"	S • 48"	M • 52"	L • 56"	XL • 60"
Cast on sts	20·22	24·28	28·32	32·36	32·36	32·36	32·36	32·36
inches	6	7	8	9	9	9	9	9

FINISHING

Work 3 needle bind off seam for shoulders.
Collar/border: Beg at lower edge of right front, pick up __ sts along center front, __ sts on neck edge, and __ sts on one half of back neck— __ sts. Knit 2 rows (CB).

	S • 32"	M • 36"	L • 40"	XS • 44"	S • 48"	M • 52"	L • 56"	XL • 60"
pick up sts	56·63	68·76	82·92	98·110	102·114	104·117	104·117	108·122
sts on neck edge	40·45	54·61	64·73	74·84	78·86	82·92	86·96	86·96
sts on back neck	9·10	11·12	11·12	12·14	14·16	14·16	15·16	16·18
total sts	105·118	133·149	157·177	184·208	194·216	200·225	205·229	210·236

	Child			Adult				
	S • 32"	M • 36"	L • 40"	XS • 44"	S • 48"	M • 52"	L • 56"	XL • 60"

FINISHING (cont)

Short row as folls: K __ sts, wrap, turn, k to end.
K __ sts, wrap, turn, k to end.
K __ sts, wrap; turn, k to end. Cont in like fashion, knitting __ sts fewer on every other row until you have completed k __, wrap, turn, k to end.
Knit even on all sts for __ inches more. Bind off loosely.
Hide wraps as needed.

AT SAME TIME, when border at center front meas one half of total width, work 1 one-row buttonhole __ inches from lower edge on right front for female. This garment is designed primarily for the female, yet this coat could be suitable for a male, with an appropriate color and texture of yarn. Buttonholes would then be made on the left front, with the first (top) __ inches from lower edge, and __ more, spaced about 4 inches apart.
Pocket garter st border: Pick up __ sts along pocket opening edge. Work garter st until equal to side edge. Bind off. Sew pocket border selvage to coat front at each upper and lower edge of pocket opening. Place right side of pocket lining against wrong side of coat front, matching side edges and top of pocket lining at upper edge of opening. From wrong side whipstitch pocket lining to front, leaving border edge open.

Set in sleeves, sewing straight edge of sleeve cap to the selvage edge only of armhole, from notched corner to notched corner. Seam bound off edge of armhole (a) to sleeve seam edge (b). Sew side seam, being careful to catch pocket lining and leave pocket border free. Sew sleeve seam. Sew center back collar seam.
Sew on button(s). Block, using wet towel method.

	Child			Adult				
	S • 32"	M • 36"	L • 40"	XS • 44"	S • 48"	M • 52"	L • 56"	XL • 60"
	49•55	65•73	75•85	86•98	92•102	96•108	101•112	102•114
	45•51	61•69	71•81	82•94	88•98	92•104	97•108	98•110
	41•47	57•65	67•77	78•90	84•94	88•100	93•104	94•106
	4	4	4	4	4	4	4	4
	17•15	17•17	19•17	18•18	20•22	20•20	21•20	22•22
	2	2	2	2	3	3	3	3
	14	17	20 1/2	24 1/2	25 1/2	26	26	27
	2	2	3	4	4	4	4	4
	16•18	18•20	20•22	24•27	24•27	24•27	24•27	24•27

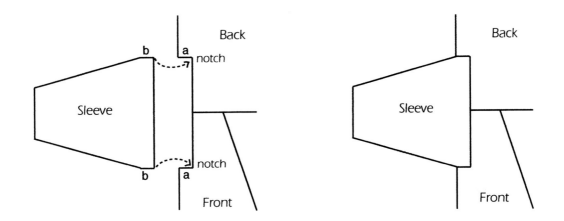

3 • 3½ sts per inch

	Child			Adult				
	S • 32"	M • 36"	L • 40"	XS • 44"	S • 48"	M • 52"	L • 56"	XL • 60"

BACK COAT (with shawl collar)
Lower left back:
With smaller needles, cast on __ sts.
Work garter stitch for __ inches. Change to larger
needles and knit across row, turn. (WS) Purl to last
5 sts, knit 5. Repeat last two rows until piece meas
__ inches from beg, end right side facing.
Break yarn. Place sts on spare needle same size
or smaller.

24•28	27•31	30•35	33•38	36•42	39•46	42•49	45•53
1½	1½	1½	2½	2½	2½	2½	2½
3	4	6	8	8	8	8	8

Lower right back:
With smaller needles, cast on __ sts.
Work garter stitch for __ inches. Change to larger
needles and knit across row, turn. (WS) Knit 5 sts,
purl to end of row. Repeat last two rows until piece
meas __ inches from beg, ending with right side
facing. Do not break yarn. To join pieces, knit across
lower right back sts immediately followed by lower
left back sts in one continuous row, turn. Purl __ sts,
knit 10 sts, purl to end. Repeat last two rows until
piece meas __ inches from beg. Change to st st and
work until piece meas __ inches.
Notched armhole: Bind off __ sts at each armhole
edge. Cont even on __ sts until armhole meas
__ inches.
Work __ sts for shoulder,
bind off center __ sts for neck, work to end. Place
shoulder sts on hold for later finishing.

24•28	27•31	30•35	33•38	36•42	39•46	42•49	45•53
1½	1½	1½	2½	2½	2½	2½	2½
3	4	6	8	8	8	8	8
19•23	22•26	25•30	28•33	31•37	34•41	37•44	40•48
4	5	7	9	9	9	9	9
18	23	28	33	34	34½	35	35
6•7	6•6	8•9	8•8	8•9	7•9	7•10	7•9
36•42	42•50	44•52	50•60	56•66	62•74	68•78	74•88
6	7½	8½	9½	10½	11½	12	13
11•13	13•15	14•16	16•19	18•21	20•24	22•26	25•30
14•16	16•20	16•20	18•22	20•24	22•26	24•26	24•28

FRONT COAT (with shawl collar)
With smaller needles, cast on __ sts.
Work garter stitch for __ inches.
Change to larger needles and work in st st until
piece meas __ inches, to lower edge of pocket
opening. Bind off 3 sts at side edge, cont in st st
until pocket opening meas __ inches from bind off.
Using cable cast on method, cast on 3 sts at side
edge. **AT SAME TIME** when piece meas __ inches,
Shape V-neck: Dec at neck edge 1 st every __ row
__ times.
AT SAME TIME, when work meas same as back to
armhole, bind off __ sts at armhole edge.
Cont even until piece meas same as back. Place all
sts on hold for later three needle bind-off seaming.

24•28	27•31	30•35	33•38	36•42	39•46	42•49	45•53
1½	1½	1½	2½	2½	2½	2½	2½
12	14½	17	19½	20½	21	21½	21½
4	4½	5	6	6	6	6	6
14	17	20½	24½	25½	26	26	27
6•5	7•6	9•7	9•7	8•7	7•8	7•7	7•6
7•8	8•10	8•10	9•11	10•12	12•13	13•13	13•14
6•7	6•6	8•9	8•8	8•9	7•9	7•10	7•9

SLEEVE
With smaller needles, cast on __ sts.
Work garter stitch for 2 inches. Change to larger
needles and work in st st, increasing 1 st each end
of row every __ row
__ times.
Work even on __ sts until sleeve meas
__ inches. Bind off all sts.

24•28	28•34	32•38	36•42	36•42	38•44	38•44	38•46
6•5	5•5	6•5	7•6	6•5	5•4	5•4	4•4
6•7	8•9	9•11	10•12	13•16	16•18	17•20	20•22
36•42	44•52	50•60	56•66	62•74	70•80	72•84	78•90
10½	12½	15½	19	20	21	22	23

POCKET LINING
Cast on __ sts. Work st st until piece measures
__ inches from beg. Bind off.

| 15•18 | 18•22 | 21•24 | 24•28 | 24•28 | 24•28 | 24•28 | 24•28 |
| 6 | 7 | 8 | 9 | 9 | 9 | 9 | 9 |

FINISHING
Work 3 needle bind off seam for shoulders.
Collar/border: Beg at lower edge of right front,
pick up __ sts along center front,
__ sts on neck edge,
and __ sts on one half of back neck—
__ sts. Knit 2 rows (CB).

42•49	51•59	61•71	74•86	76•90	78•92	78•92	81•94
30•35	41•48	48•56	56•64	58•68	60•72	64•74	64•74
7•8	8•9	8•9	9•10	10•12	10•12	11•13	12•14
79•92	100•116	117•136	139•160	144•170	148•176	153•179	157•182

	Child			Adult				
	S • 32"	M • 36"	L • 40"	XS • 44"	S • 48"	M • 52"	L • 56"	XL • 60"

FINISHING (cont)

	S • 32"	M • 36"	L • 40"	XS • 44"	S • 48"	M • 52"	L • 56"	XL • 60"
Short row as folls: K __ sts, wrap, turn, k to end.	37·43	49·57	56·65	65·74	68·80	70·84	75·87	76·88
K __ sts, wrap, turn, k to end.	34·40	46·54	53·62	62·71	65·77	77·81	72·84	73·85
K __ sts, wrap; turn, k to end. Cont in like fashion,	31·37	40·51	50·59	59·68	62·74	74·78	69·81	70·82
knitting __ sts fewer on every other row until you	3	3	3	3	3	3	3	3
have completed k __, wrap, turn, k to end.	10·10	13·15	14·17	14·17	14·17	16·18	18·18	19·19
Knit								
even on all sts for __ inches more. Bind off loosely.	2	2	2	2	3	3	3	3
Hide wraps as needed.								

AT SAME TIME, when border at center front meas one half of total width, work 1 one-row buttonhole __ inches from lower edge on right front for female. This garment is designed primarily for the female, yet this coat could be suitable for a male, with an appropriate color and texture of yarn. Buttonholes would then be made on the left front, with the first (top) __ inches from lower edge, and __ more, spaced about 4 inches apart. Pocket garter st border: Pick up __ sts along

	S • 32"	M • 36"	L • 40"	XS • 44"	S • 48"	M • 52"	L • 56"	XL • 60"
(buttonhole from lower edge, right front)	14	17	20½	24½	25½	26	26	27
(first top from lower edge)	14	17	20½	24½	25½	26	26	27
(and __ more)	2	2	3	4	4	4	4	4
(pick up sts along pocket)	12·14	14·16	15·18	18·21	18·21	18·21	18·21	18·21

pocket opening edge. Work garter st until equal to side edge. Bind off. Sew pocket border selvage to coat front at each upper and lower edge of pocket opening. Place right side of pocket lining against wrong side of coat front, matching side edges and top of pocket lining at upper edge of opening. From wrong side whipstitch pocket lining to front, leaving border edge open.

Set in sleeves, sewing straight edge of sleeve cap to the selvage edge only of armhole, from notched corner to notched corner. Seam bound off edge of armhole (a) to sleeve seam edge (b). Sew side seam, being careful to catch pocket lining and leave pocket border free. Sew sleeve seam. Sew center back collar seam.

Sew on button(s). Block, using wet towel method.

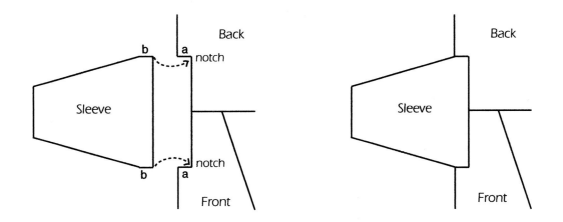

Coat with Lapel Collar	Child			Adult				
	S • 24"	M • 28"	L • 32"	XS • 36"	S • 40"	M • 44"	L • 48"	XL • 52"
6½ • 7 sts per inch yardage								
for pocket lining only								
Cotton Fine	1	1	1	2	2	2	2	2
Nature Spun (F)	1	1	1	1	1	1	1	1
Wildfoote	1	1	1	2	2	2	2	2
5 • 6 sts per inch yardage	1100	1550	2050	2600	3000	3300	3550	3900
Cotton Fleece	6	8	10	13	14	16	17	19
Kaleidoscope	11	15	20	25	29	31	34	37
Nature Spun (S)	6	9	12	15	17	18	20	22
Top of the Lamb (S)	4	5	6	8	9	10	11	12
4 • 4½ sts per inch yardage	950	1350	1750	2250	2550	2850	3050	3350
Country Classics (W)	5	8	10	12	14	15	17	18
Handpaint Originals	11	16	20	26	29	33	35	39
Lamb's Pride (W)	5	8	10	12	14	15	17	18
Lamb's Pride Superwash (W)	5	7	9	12	13	15	16	17
Nature Spun (W)	4	6	8	10	11	12	13	14
Prairie Silk	11	16	20	26	29	33	35	39
Top of the Lamb (W)	5	8	10	12	14	15	17	18
3 • 3½ sts per inch yardage	700	1000	1300	1700	1900	2150	2300	2500
Country Classics (B)	6	8	11	14	16	18	19	20
Lamb's Pride (B)	6	8	11	14	16	18	19	20
Lamb's Pride Superwash (B)	7	10	12	16	18	20	21	23

(Yardage and skein estimates are approximations only.)

Choose:

• coat with lapel collar

    curved armhole and shaped sleeve cap

    vertical slit pocket

    shaped pocket lining

    finished hems

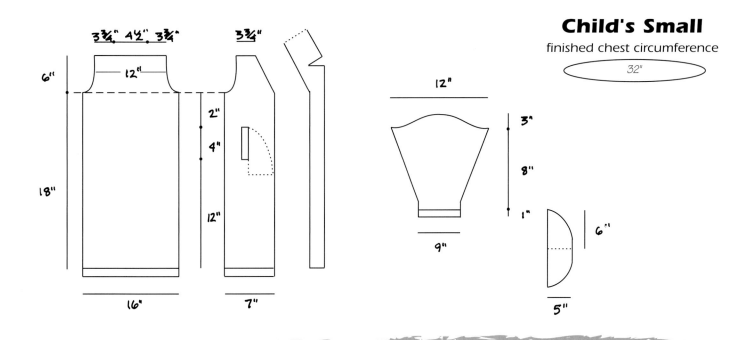

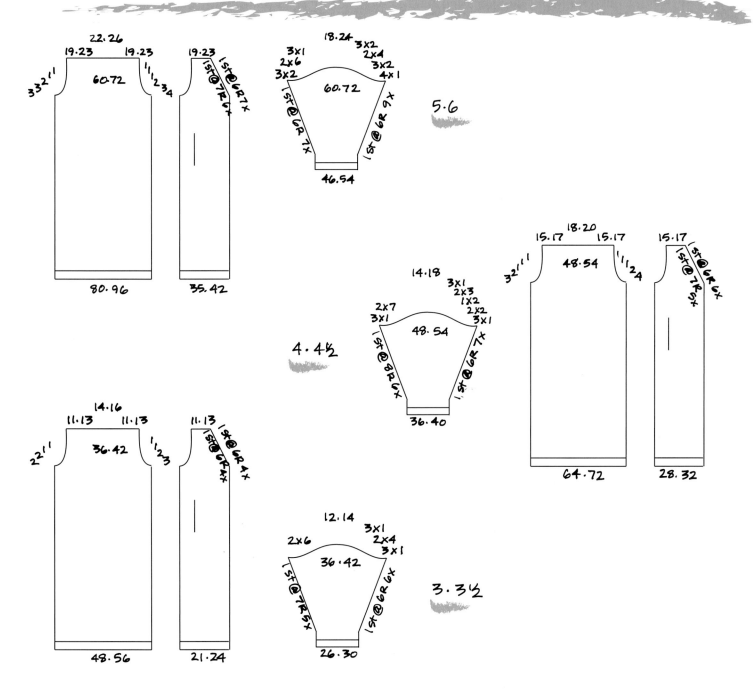

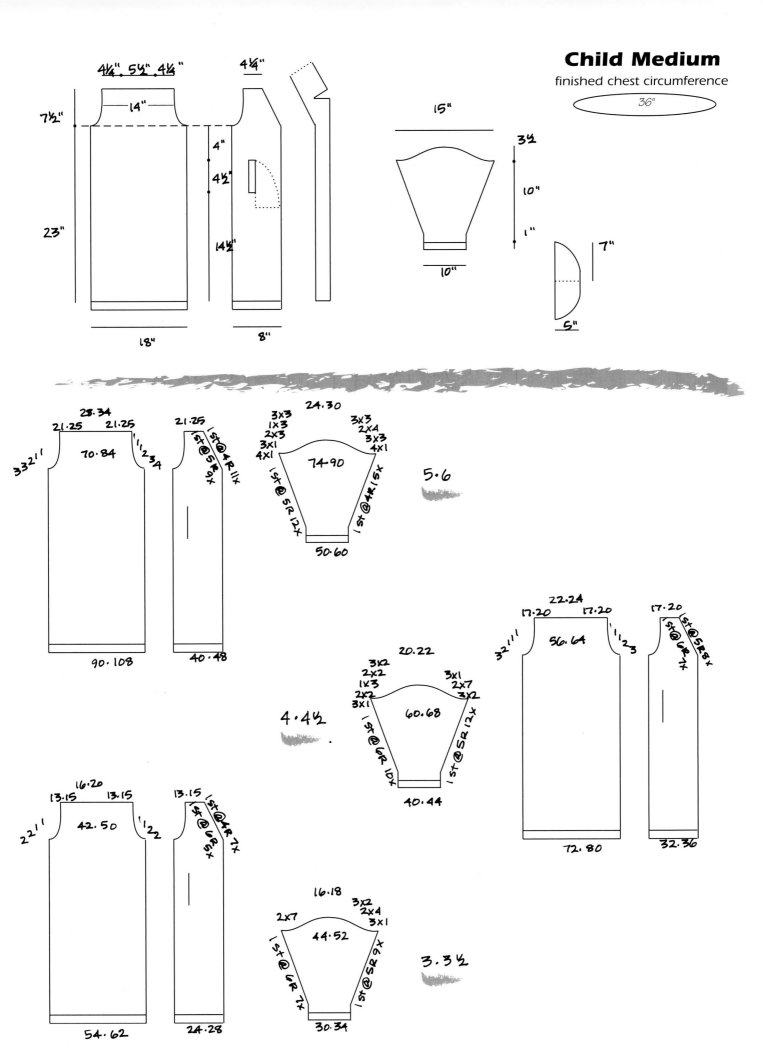

4¼" . 5½" . 4¼"

4¼"

14"

7½"

4"

4½"

23"

14½"

18"

8"

15"

3½

10"

1"

10"

7"

5"

28·34
21·25   21·25

33 2/11   70·84   ''2 3/4

21·25   1 st @ 5 R 9x

1 st @ 4 R 11x

24·30
3x3   3x3
1x3   2x4
2x3   3x3
3x1   4x1
4x1

74·90

1 st @ 4 R 15x

1 st @ 5 R 12x

50·60

5·6

90·108   40·48

4·4½

22·24
17·20   17·20

32 2/11   56·64   ''2 3

17·20   1 st @ 5 R 8x

1 st @ 6 R 7x

20·22
3x2   3x1
2x2   2x7
1x3   3x2
2x2
3x1

60·68

1 st @ 6 R 10x   1 st @ 5 R 12x

40·44

72·80   32·36

16·20
13·15   13·15

22 1/11   42·50   ''2 2

13·15   1 st @ 4 R 7x

1 st @ 6 R 5x

16·18
3x2
2x4
2x7   3x1

44·52

1 st @ 6 R 7x   1 st @ 5 R 9x

3·3½

54·62   24·28   30·34

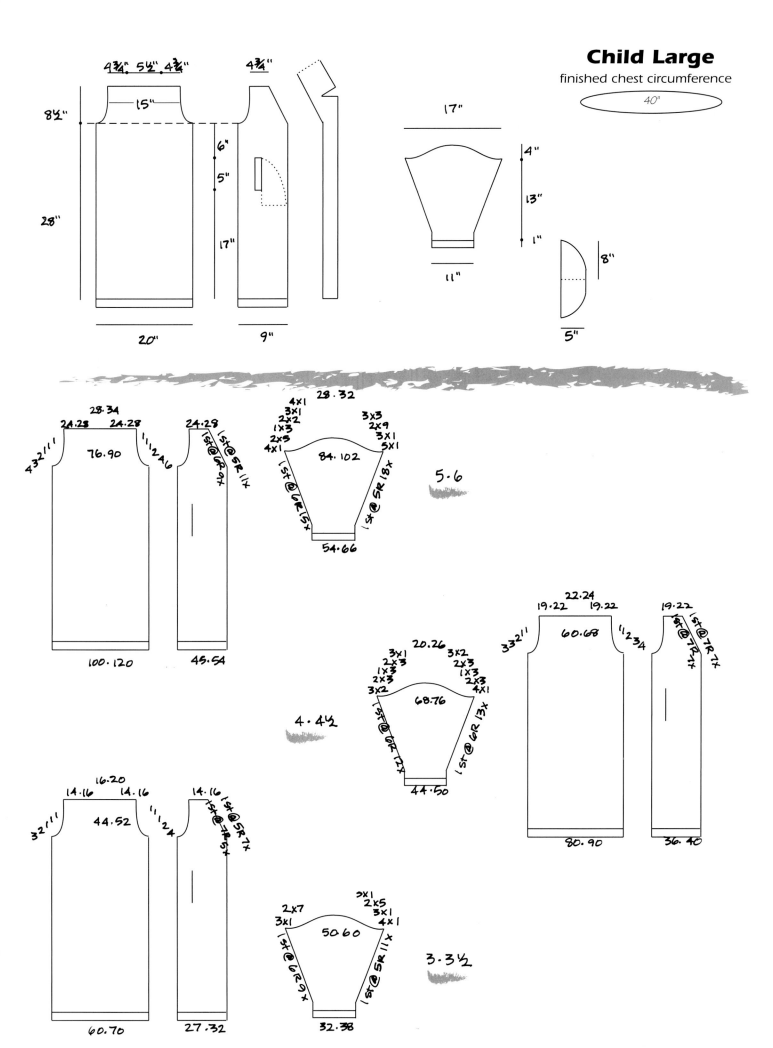

4¾" 5½" 4¾"

15"

4¾"

8½"

28"

6"

5"

17"

20"

9"

17"

4"

13"

1"

11"

8"

5"

28·34
24·28 24·28
4 3/2 11   1 1/2 A 6
76·90
100·120

24·28 1st@5R 11x
1st@6R 9x
45·54

28·32
4x1
3x1
2x2
1x3
2x5
4x1
1st@6R 15x

3x3
2x9
3x1
5x1
1st@5R 18x
84·102
54·66

5·6

4·4½

3·3½

22·24
19·22   19·22
3 3/2 11   1 1/2 34
60·68
80·90

19·22 1st@7R 7x
1st@7R 7x
36·40

20·26
3x1   3x2
2x3   2x3
1x3   1x3
2x3   2x3
3x2   4x1
1st@6R 12x
1st@6R 13x
68·76
44·50

16·20
14·16   14·16
3 3/2 11   1 1/2 4
44·52
60·70

14·16 1st@5R 7x
1st@7R 5x
27·32

2x7   3x1
3x1   2x5
                3x1
                4x1
1st@6R 9x
1st@5R 11x
50·60
32·38

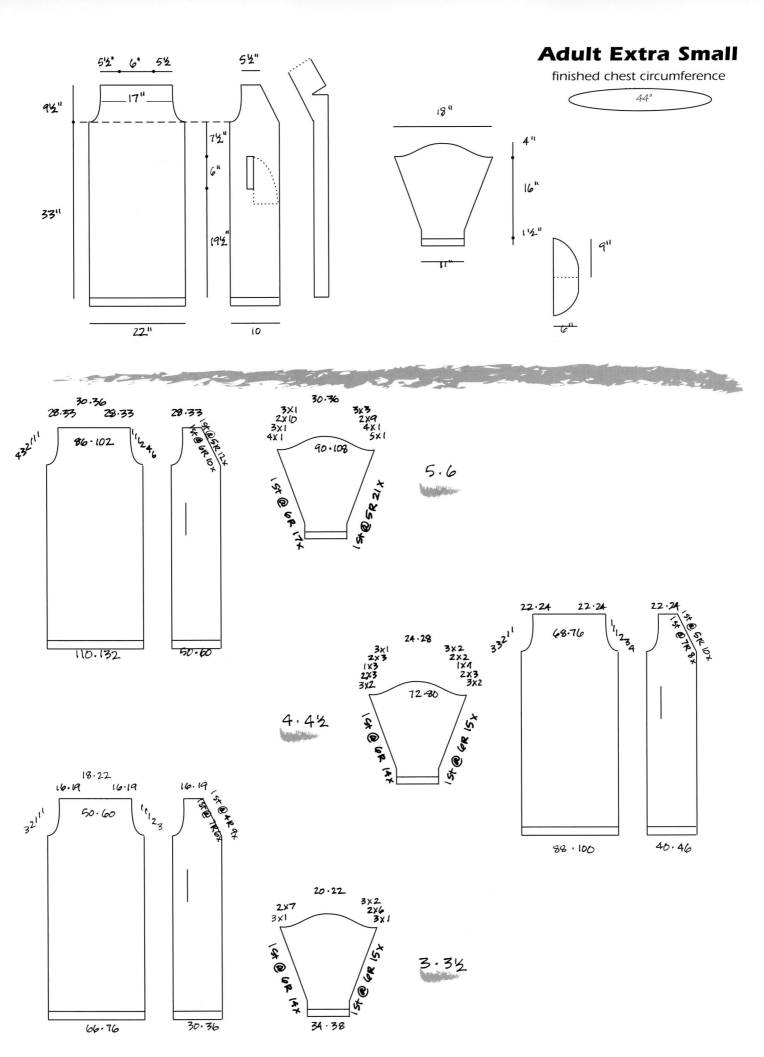

Adult Extra Small

finished chest circumference

44"

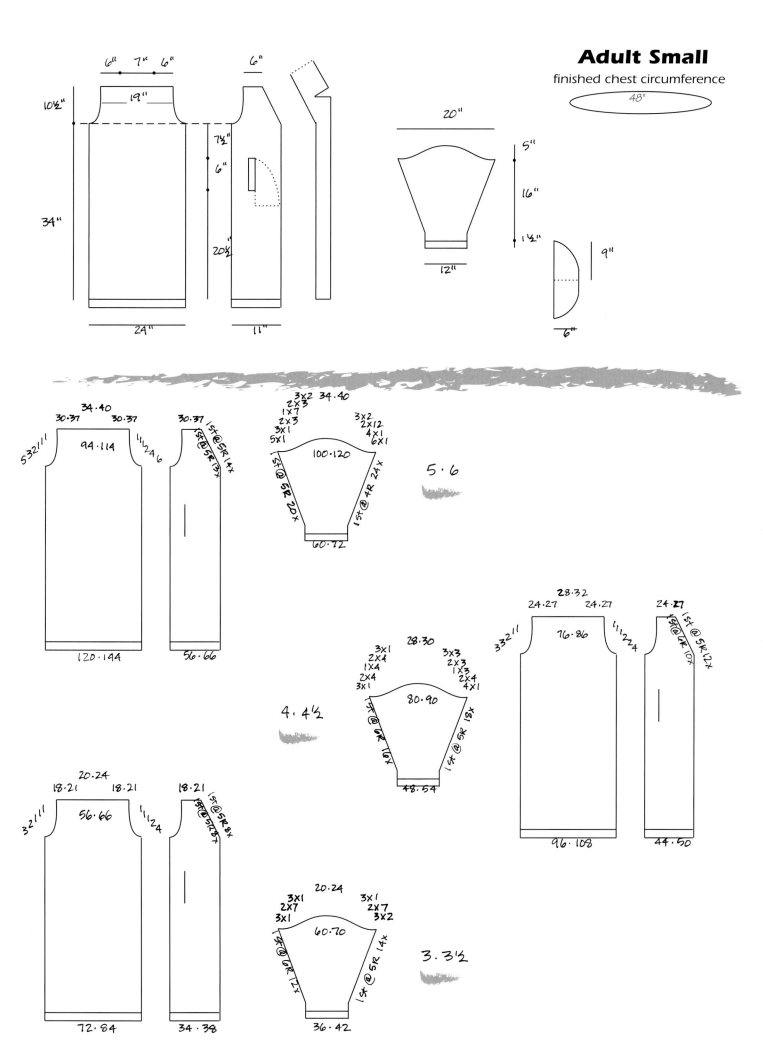

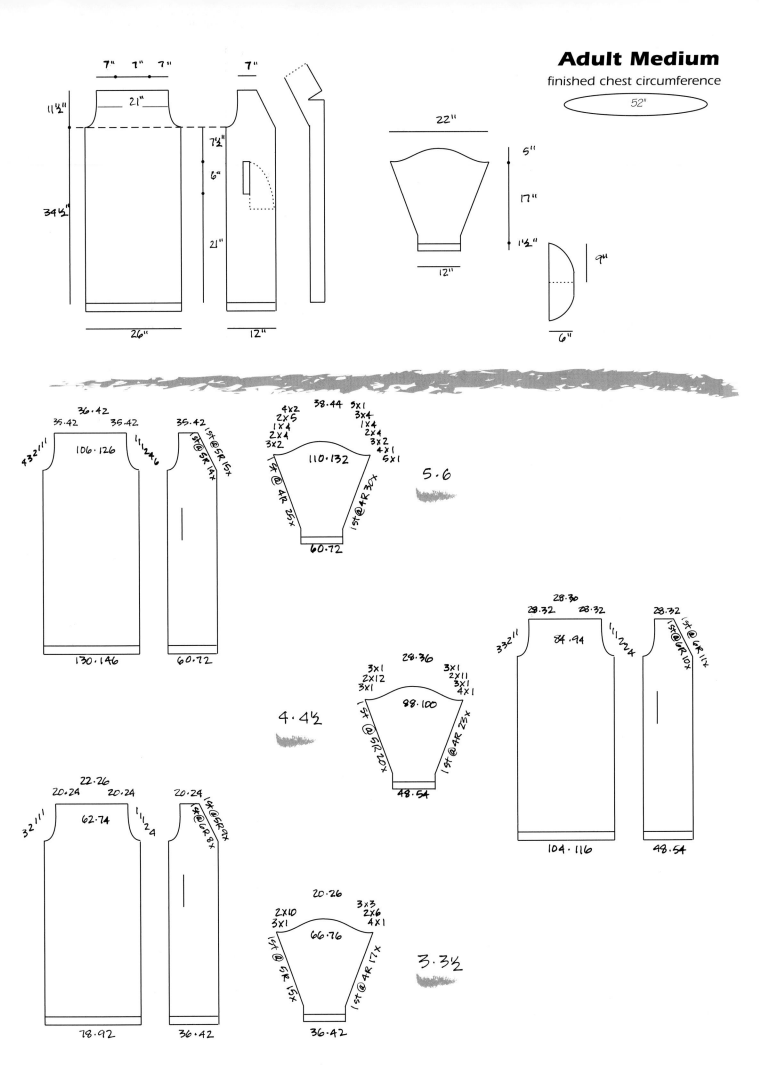

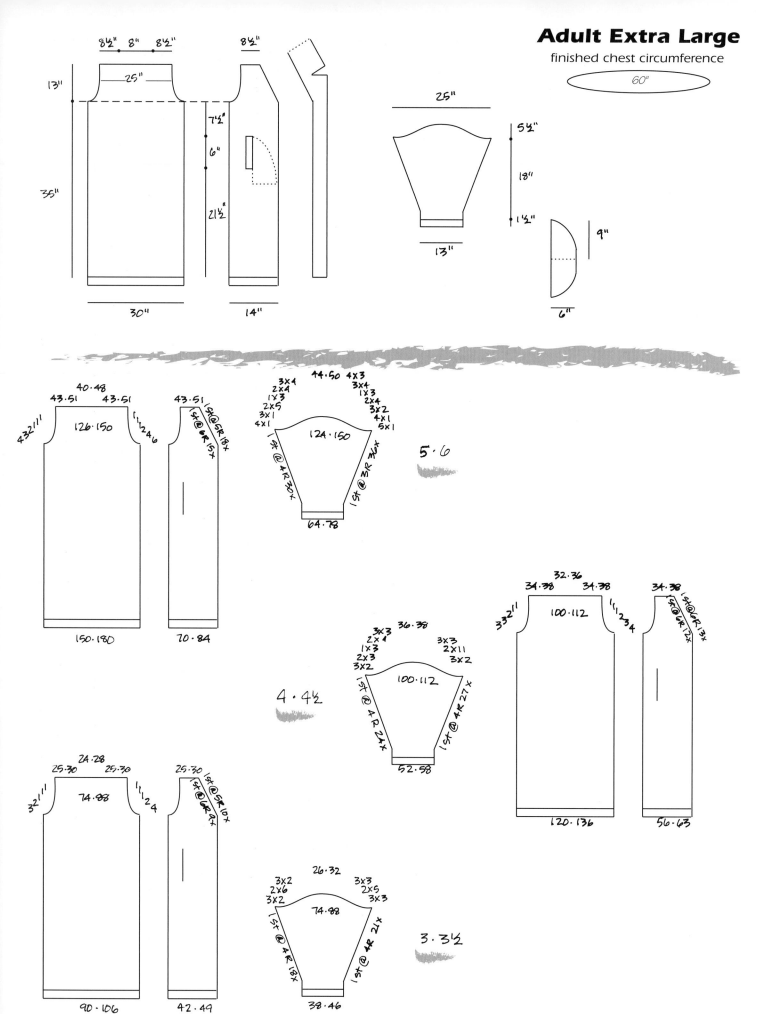

5 • 6 sts per inch

	Child			Adult				
	S • 32"	M • 36"	L • 40"	XS • 44"	S • 48"	M • 52"	L • 56"	XL • 60"
BACK COAT (with lapel collar)								
Cast on __ sts.	80·96	90·108	100·120	110·132	120·144	130·146	140·168	150·180
Work st st stitch for __ inches, ending with wrong side facing. Knit across WS row for turning ridge.	1½	1½	1¾	2	2	2	2	2
Cont in st st until piece meas __ inches from turning ridge.	18	23	28	33	34	34½	35	35
Shape curved armhole: Bind off at each armhole edge in foll sequence	3 / 4	3 / 4	4 / 6	4 / 6	5 / 6	4 / 6	6 / 6	4 / 6
	3 / 3	3 / 3	3 / 4	3 / 4	3 / 4	3 / 4	3 / 4	3 / 4
	2 / 2	2 / 2	2 / 2	2 / 2	2 / 2	2 / 2	2 / 2	2 / 2
	1x2 / 1x3	1x2 / 1x3	1x3 / 1x3	1x3 / 1x3	1x3 / 1x3	1x3 / 1x3	1x3 / 1x4	1x3 / 1x3
Cont even on __ sts	60·72	70·84	76·90	86·102	94·114	106·126	112·136	126·150
until armhole meas __ inches.	6	7½	8½	9½	10½	11½	12	13
Work __ sts for shoulder,	19·23	21·25	24·28	28·33	30·37	35·42	37·49	43·51
bind off center __ sts for neck, work to end. Place shoulder sts on hold for later finishing.	22·26	28·34	28·34	30·36	34·40	36·42	38·46	40·48
FRONT COAT (with lapel collar)								
Cast on __ sts.	35·42	40·48	45·54	50·60	56·66	60·72	65·78	70·84
Work st st stitch for __ inches, ending with wrong side facing. Knit across WS row for turning ridge.	1½	1½	1¾	2	2	2	2	2
Cont in st st until piece meas __ inches from turning ridge.	12	14½	17	19½	20½	21	21½	21½
Make pocket opening: From center front, work __ sts, place rem sts on hold. Work even for __ inches,	20·24	25·30	27·33	30·36	35·42	35·42	37·45	37·45
place sts on hold. Take rem sts at side edge from	4	4½	5	6	6	6	6	6
holder and work even for __ inches. Cont now	4	4½	5	6	6	6	6	6
working on all sts until piece meas __ inches from turning ridge. Shape curved armhole as for back.	18	23	28	33	34	34½	35	35
AT SAME TIME, shape v-neck: dec 1 st at neck edge every __ row	7·6	5·4	6·5	6·5	5·5	5·5	6·4	6·5
__ times.	6·7	9·11	9·11	10·12	13·14	14·15	14·17	15·18
Cont even on __ sts until piece meas same as back. Place shoulder sts on hold for later three needle bind-off seaming.	19·23	21·25	24·28	28·33	30·37	35·42	37·45	43·51
SLEEVE								
Cast on __ sts.	46·54	50·60	54·66	56·66	60·72	60·72	62·74	64·78
Work st st stitch for __ inches, ending with wrong side facing. Knit across WS row for turning ridge.	1¼	1¼	1¼	1½	1½	1½	1½	1½
Shaping: Cont in st st, inc 1 stitch at beg and end of every __ row	6·6	5·4	6·5	6·5	5·4	4·4	4·3	4·3
__ times—	7·9	12·15	15·18	17·21	20·24	25·30	26·32	30·36
__ sts.	60·72	74·90	84·102	90·108	100·120	110·132	114·138	124·150
When work meas __ inches from turning ridge, bind off on each side in foll sequence:	8	10	13	16	16	17	17	18
	3x2 / 4x1	4x1 / 4x1	4x1 / 5x1	4x1 / 5x1	5x1 / 6x1	3x2 / 5x1	4x2 / 7x1	4x1 / 5x1
	2x6 / 3x2	3x1 / 3x3	2x5 / 3x1	3x1 / 4x1	3x1 / 4x1	2x4 / 4x1	2x4 / 4x1	3x1 / 4x1
	3x1 / 2x4	2x3 / 2x4	1x3 / 2x9	2x10 / 2x9	2x3 / 2x12	1x4 / 3x2	1x4 / 3x2	2x5 / 3x2
	/ 3x2	1x3 / 3x3	2x2 / 3x3	3x1 / 3x3	1x7 / 3x2	2x5 / 2x4	2x5 / 2x4	1x3 / 2x4
		3x3 /	3x1 /	4x1 /	2x3 /	4x2 / 1x4	4x2 / 1x4	2x4 / 1x3
			4x1 /		3x2 /	/ 3x4	/ 3x4	3x4 / 3x4
						/ 5x1	/ 5x1	/ 4x3
Bind off rem __ sts.	18·24	24·30	28·32	30·36	34·40	38·44	38·46	44·50
FINISHING Work 3 needle bind off seaming for shoulders. On each front neck edge, place marker __ inches down from shoulder seam.	2	2	2½	3	3	3	3½	3½

	Child			Adult				
	S • 32"	M • 36"	L • 40"	XS • 44"	S • 48"	M • 52"	L • 56"	XL • 60"

FINISHING

Left Front Border/Lapel/Collar

Cast on __ sts. Work garter stitch as folls:
Row 1(RS): knit. Row 2: With yarn in front, slip 1 purlwise, bring yarn to back, knit to end. *(The slipped stitch edge is the finished center front edge.)*

	S	M	L	XS	S	M	L	XL
Cast on __ sts	12·14	12·14	12·14	16·18	16·18	16·18	16·18	16·18

Repeat last 2 rows until piece meas __ inches, slightly stretched. Place marker.

	S	M	L	XS	S	M	L	XL
piece meas __ inches	18	23	28	33	34	34½	35	35

NOTE: *For male garment, work buttonholes in left front, see placement as for right front.*

Shape lapel: With RS facing, knit 1, make 1, knit to end. Repeat row 2. Cont to increase in this way every one inch __ times more—
__ sts.
When work meas __ inches from marker, with WS facing, bind off __ sts, knit to end.
Place rem __ sts on hold.

	S	M	L	XS	S	M	L	XL
every one inch __ times more	5	8	8	9	12	12	13	14
__ sts	18·20	21·23	21·23	26·28	29·31	29·31	30·32	31·33
work meas __ inches from marker	4	5½	6	6½	7½	8½	8½	9½
bind off __ sts	12·14	12·14	12·14	16·18	16·18	16·18	16·18	16·18
Place rem __ sts on hold	6	9	9	10	13	13	14	15

Right Front Border/Lapel/Collar

Cast on __ sts. Work garter stitch as folls:
Row 1 (RS): With yarn in front, slip 1 purlwise, bring yarn to back, knit to end. Row 2: knit. Repeat last 2 rows until piece meas __ inches, slightly stretched.
One row buttonhole row: slip 1, knit __, work buttonhole as folls: yarn to front, slip next st, yarn to back. [Slip next st; on right needle pass second st over first st and off end of needle] __ times. Slip last bound off st back to left needle. Turn work.
Cable cast on __ sts (one more than you bound off), turn work. With yarn in back, slip first st from left needle, pass extra cast on st over it to close and secure the buttonhole. Knit to end. Repeat buttonhole row every __ inches
__ times more—
__ buttonholes total. Cont even until work meas __ inches, place marker.

	S	M	L	XS	S	M	L	XL
Cast on __ sts	12·14	12·14	12·14	16·18	16·18	16·18	16·18	16·18
piece meas __ inches	5½	9	9½	12	13	13½	14	14
slip 1, knit __	3·4	3·4	3·4	5·6	5·6	5·6	5·6	5·6
__ times	4	4	4	4	4	4	4	4
Cable cast on __ sts	5	5	5	5	5	5	5	5
buttonhole row every __ inches	3½	3½	3½	4	4	4	4	4
__ times more	3	4	5	5	5	5	5	5
__ buttonholes total	4	5	6	6	6	6	6	6
work meas __ inches	18	23	28	33	34	34½	35	35

Shape lapel: With RS facing, slip 1, knit __ sts, make 1, knit 1. Knit 1 row. Cont to increase before last st in row every one inch __ times more—
__ sts.
When work meas __ inches from marker, with RS facing, bind off __ sts, knit to end, do not turn. Place lapel border adjacent to marker placement on right front neck edge, pick up __ sts along right front neck edge, __ sts along back neck, and along left front neck edge to marker as for right, knit sts from hold on left front lapel. (See diagram below.) Turn. *Yarn in front, slip first at purlwise, yarn to back, knit to end. Repeat from * until collar meas __ inches from picked up edge, ending with underside of collar facing. Bind off all sts loosely.

	S	M	L	XS	S	M	L	XL
slip 1, knit __ sts	10·12	10·12	10·12	14·16	14·16	14·16	14·16	14·16
every one inch __ times more	5	8	8	9	12	12	13	14
__ sts	18·20	21·23	21·23	26·28	29·31	29·31	30·32	31·33
work meas __ inches from marker	4	5½	6	6½	7½	8½	8½	9½
bind off __ sts	12·14	12·14	12·14	16·18	16·18	16·18	16·18	16·18
pick up __ sts along right front neck	10·12	10·12	12·14	15·18	15·18	15·18	17·21	17·21
__ sts along back neck	20·22	26·28	26·28	28·30	32·34	34·36	36·38	38·40
collar meas __ inches	3	3	3	4	4	4	4	4

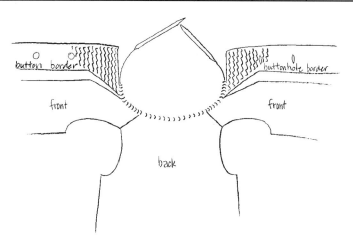

button border   buttonhole border

front   front

back

4 • 4½ sts per inch

	Child			Adult				
	S • 32"	M • 36"	L • 40"	XS • 44"	S • 48"	M • 52"	L • 56"	XL • 60"
BACK COAT (with lapel collar)								
Cast on __ sts.	64·72	72·80	80·90	88·100	96·108	104·116	112·126	120·136
Work st st stitch for __ inches, ending with wrong side facing. Knit across WS row for turning ridge.	1½	1½	1¾	2	2	2	2	2
Cont in st st until piece meas __ inches from turning ridge.	18	23	28	33	34	34½	35	35
Shape curved armhole: Bind off at each armhole edge in foll sequence	3|4 2|2 1x3|1x3	3|3 2|2 1x3|1x3	3|4 3|3 2|2 1x3|1x3	3|4 3|3 2|2 1x2|1x2	3|4 3|2 2|2 1x2|1x3	3|4 3|2 2|2 1x2|1x3	4|4 2|3 2|2 1x3|1x3	3|4 3|3 2|2 1x2|1x3
Cont even on __ sts	48·54	56·64	60·68	68·76	76·86	84·94	90·102	100·112
until armhole meas __ inches.	6	7½	8½	9½	10½	11½	12	13
Work __ sts for shoulder,	15·17	17·20	19·22	22·24	24·27	28·32	30·34	34·38
bind off center __ sts for neck, work to end. Place shoulder sts on hold for later finishing.	18·20	22·24	22·24	24·28	28·32	28·30	30·34	32·36
FRONT COAT (with lapel collar)								
Cast on __ sts.	28·32	32·36	36·40	40·46	44·50	48·54	52·58	56·63
Work st st stitch for __ inches, ending with wrong side facing. Knit across WS row for turning ridge.	1½	1½	1¾	2	2	2	2	2
Cont in st st until piece meas __ inches from turning ridge.	12	14½	17	19½	20½	21	21½	21½
Make pocket opening: From center front, work __ sts, place rem sts on hold. Work even for __ inches, place sts on hold. Take rem sts at side edge from holder and work even for __ inches. Cont now working on all sts until piece meas __ inches from turning ridge.	16·18 4 4 18	20·22 4½ 4½ 23	22·24 5 5 28	24·27 6 6 33	28·31 6 6 34	28·31 6 6 34½	30·33 6 6 35	30·33 6 6 35
Shape curved armhole as for back.								
AT SAME TIME, shape v-neck: dec 1 st at neck edge every __ row	7·6	6·5	7·7	7·5	6·5	6·6	6·6	6·6
__ times.	5·6	7·8	7·7	8·10	10·12	10·11	11·12	12·13
Cont even on __ sts until piece meas same as back. Place shoulder sts on hold for later three needle bind-off seaming.	15·17	17·20	19·22	22·24	24·27	28·32	30·34	34·38
SLEEVE								
Cast on __ sts.	36·40	40·44	44·50	44·50	48·54	48·54	50·56	52·58
Work st st stitch for __ inches, ending with wrong side facing. Knit across WS row for turning ridge.	1¼	1¼	1¼	1½	1½	1½	1½	1½
Shaping: Cont in st st, inc 1 stitch at beg and end of every __ row	8·6	6·5	6·6	6·6	6·5	5·4	4·4	4·4
__ times—	6·7	10·12	12·13	14·15	16·18	20·23	21·24	24·27
__ sts.	48·54	60·68	68·76	72·80	80·90	88·100	92·104	100·112
When work meas __ inches from turning ridge, bind off on each side in foll sequence:	8	10	13	16	16	17	17	18
	3x1|3x1 2x7|2x2	3x1|3x2 2x2|2x7 1x2| 2x2| |3x2	3x2|4x1 2x3|2x3 1x3|3x1 2x3|2x3 3x1|3x2	3x2|3x2 2x3|2x3 1x3|1x3 2x3|2x3 3x1|3x2	3x1|4x1 2x4|2x4 1x3|1x4 2x4|2x3 3x1|3x3	3x1|4x1 2x12|3x1 3x1|2x11 |3x1	3x2|4x1 2x9|3x1 3x2|2x9 |3x3	3x2|3x2 2x3|2x11 1x3|3x3 2x4 3x3
Bind off rem __ sts.	14·18	20·22	20·26	24·28	28·30	28·36	32·36	36·38
FINISHING Work 3 needle bind off seaming for shoulders. On each front neck edge, place marker __ inches down from shoulder seam.	2	2	2½	3	3	3	3½	3½

	Child			Adult				
	S • 32"	M • 36"	L • 40"	XS • 44"	S • 48"	M • 52"	L • 56"	XL • 60"

FINISHING

Left Front Border/Lapel/Collar

Cast on __ sts. Work garter stitch as folls:
Row 1 (RS): knit. Row 2: With yarn in front, slip 1 purlwise, bring yarn to back, knit to end. *(The slipped stitch edge is the finished center front edge.)* Repeat last 2 rows until piece meas __ inches, slightly stretched. Place marker.

NOTE: for male garment, work buttonholes in left front, see placement as for right front.

Shape lapel: With RS facing, knit 1, make 1, knit to end. Repeat row 2. Cont to increase in this way every one inch __ times more—
__ sts.
When work meas __ inches from marker, with WS facing, bind off __ sts, knit to end.
Place rem __ sts on hold.

	S • 32"	M • 36"	L • 40"	XS • 44"	S • 48"	M • 52"	L • 56"	XL • 60"
Cast on	9	9	9	12	12	12	12	12
piece meas	18	23	28	33	34	34½	35	35
increase times more	3	4	4	5	6	6	7	7
sts	13	14	14	18	19	19	20	20
when work meas	4	5½	6	6½	7½	8½	8½	9½
bind off	9	9	9	12	12	12	12	12
rem sts	4	5	5	6	7	7	8	8

Right Front Border/Lapel/Collar

Cast on __ sts. Work garter stitch as folls:
Row 1 (RS): With yarn in front, slip 1 purlwise, bring yarn to back, knit to end. Row 2: knit. Repeat last 2 rows until piece meas __ inches, slightly stretched.
One row buttonhole row: slip 1, knit __, work buttonhole as folls: yarn to front, slip next st, yarn to back. [Slip next st; on right needle pass second st over first st and off end of needle] __ times. Slip last bound off st back to left needle. Turn work. Cable cast on __ sts (one more than you bound off), turn work. With yarn in back, slip first st from left needle, pass extra cast on st over it to close and secure the buttonhole. Knit to end. Repeat buttonhole row every __ inches
__ times more—
__ buttonholes total. Cont even until work meas __ inches, place marker.
Shape lapel: With RS facing, slip 1, knit __ sts, make 1, knit 1. Knit 1 row. Cont to increase before last st in row every one inch __ times more—
__ sts.
When work meas __ inches from marker, with RS facing, bind off __ sts, knit to end, do not turn. Place lapel border adjacent to marker placement on right front neck edge, pick up __ sts along right front neck edge, __ sts along back neck, and along left front neck edge to marker as for right, knit sts from hold on left front lapel. (See diagram below.) Turn. *Yarn in front, slip first st purlwise, yarn to back, knit to end. Repeat from * until collar meas __ inches from picked up edge, ending with underside of collar facing. Bind off all sts loosely.

	S • 32"	M • 36"	L • 40"	XS • 44"	S • 48"	M • 52"	L • 56"	XL • 60"
Cast on	9	9	9	12	12	12	12	12
piece meas	5½	9	9½	12	13	13½	14	14
slip/times	2	2	2	3	3	3	3	3
every inches	3½	3½	3½	4	4	4	4	4
times more	3	4	5	5	5	5	5	5
buttonholes total	4	5	6	6	6	6	6	6
work meas	18	23	28	33	34	34½	35	35
knit sts	7	7	7	10	10	10	10	10
increase times more	3	4	4	5	6	6	7	7
sts	13	14	14	18	19	19	20	20
when work meas	4	5½	6	6½	7½	8½	8½	9½
bind off	9	9	9	12	12	12	12	12
pick up right front neck	7	7	8	10	10	10	12	12
back neck sts	14·16	16·20	16·20	18·22	20·24	22·26	24·26	24·28
collar meas	3	3	3	4	4	4	4	4

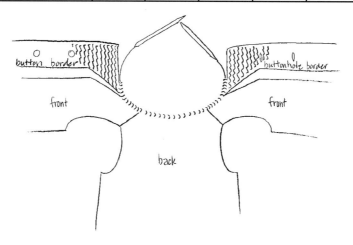

3 • 3½ sts per inch

	Child			Adult				
	S • 32"	M • 36"	L • 40"	XS • 44"	S • 48"	M • 52"	L • 56"	XL • 60"
BACK COAT (with lapel collar)								
Cast on __ sts.	48•56	54•62	60•70	66•76	72•84	78•92	84•98	90•106
Work st st stitch for __ inches, ending with wrong side facing. Knit across WS row for turning ridge.	1½	1½	1¾	2	2	2	2	2
Cont in st st until piece meas __ inches from turning ridge.	18	23	28	33	34	34½	35	35
Shape curved armhole: Bind off at each armhole edge in foll sequence	2 | 3	2 | 2	3 | 4	3 | 3	3 | 4	3 | 4	3 / 3 | 3	3 | 4
	2 | 2	2 | 2	2 | 2	2 | 2	2 | 2	2 | 2	2 | 2	2 | 2
	1x2 | 1x2	1x2 | 1x2	1x3 | 1x3	1x3 | 1x3	1x3 | 1x3	1x3 | 1x3	1x2 | 1x2	1x3 | 1x3
Cont even on __ sts	36•42	42•50	44•52	50•60	56•66	62•74	68•78	74•88
until armhole meas __ inches.	6	7½	8½	9½	10½	11½	12	13
Work __ sts for shoulder,	11•13	13•15	14•16	16•19	18•21	20•24	22•26	25•30
bind off center __ sts for neck, work to end. Place shoulder sts on hold for later finishing.	14•16	16•20	16•20	18•22	20•24	22•26	24•26	24•28
FRONT COAT (with lapel collar)								
Cast on __ sts.	21•24	24•28	27•32	30•36	34•38	36•42	39•46	42•49
Work st st stitch for __ inches, ending with wrong side facing. Knit across WS row for turning ridge.	1½	1½	1¾	2	2	2	2	2
Cont in st st until piece meas __ inches from turning ridge.	12	14½	17	19½	20½	21	21½	21½
Make pocket opening: From center front, work __ sts, place rem sts on hold. Work even for __ inches,	12•14	15•17	16•19	18•21	21•24	21•24	22•26	22•26
place sts on hold. Take rem sts at side edge from	4	4½	5	6	6	6	6	6
holder and work even for __ inches. Cont now	4	4½	5	6	6	6	6	6
working on all sts until piece meas __ inches from turning ridge. Shape curved armhole as for back.	18	23	28	33	34	34½	35	35
AT SAME TIME, shape v-neck: dec 1 st at neck edge every __ row	6•6	6•4	7•5	7•4	5•5	6•5	5•5	6•5
__ times.	4•4	5•7	5•7	6•9	8•8	8•9	10•10	9•10
Cont even on __ sts until piece meas same as back. Place shoulder sts on hold for later three needle bind-off seaming.	11•13	13•15	14•16	16•19	18•21	20•24	22•26	25•30
SLEEVE								
Cast on __ sts.	26•30	30•34	32•38	34•38	36•42	36•42	38•44	38•46
Work st st stitch for __ inches, ending with wrong side facing. Knit across WS row for turning ridge.	1¼	1¼	1¼	1½	1½	1½	1½	1½
Shaping: Cont in st st, inc 1 stitch at beg and end of every __ row	7•6	6•5	6•5	7•5	6•5	5•4	5•4	4•4
__ times—	5•6	7•9	9•11	10•13	12•14	15•17	15•18	18•21
__ sts.	36•42	44•52	50•60	54•64	60•70	66•76	68•80	74•88
When work meas __ inches from turning ridge, bind off on each side in foll sequence:	8	10	13	16	16	17	17	18
	2x6 | 3x1	2x7 | 3x1	3x1 | 4x1	3x1 | 3x1	3x1 | 3x2	3x1 | 4x1	3x1 | 4x1	3x2 | 3x3
	2x4	2x4	2x7 | 3x1	2x7 | 2x6	2x7 | 2x7	2x10 | 2x6	2x3 | 3x1	2x6 | 2x5
	3x1	3x2	2x5	3x2	3x1 | 3x1	3x3	1x3 | 2x5	3x2 | 3x3
			3x1				2x2 | 3x3	
							3x2	
Bind off rem __ sts.	12•14	16•18	16•20	20•22	20•24	20•26	24•28	26•32
FINISHING								
Work 3 needle bind off seaming for shoulders. On each front neck edge, place marker __ inches down from shoulder seam.	2	2	2½	3	3	3	3½	3½

3 • 3½ sts per inch

	Child			Adult				
	S • 32"	M • 36"	L • 40"	XS • 44"	S • 48"	M • 52"	L • 56"	XL • 60"

FINISHING

Left Front Border/Lapel/Collar

	S•32"	M•36"	L•40"	XS•44"	S•48"	M•52"	L•56"	XL•60"
Cast on __ sts. Work garter stitch as folls: Row 1(RS): knit. Row 2: With yarn in front, slip 1 purlwise, bring yarn to back, knit to end. *(The slipped stitch edge is the finished center front edge.)*	8	8	8	10	10	10	10	10
Repeat last 2 rows until piece meas __ inches, slightly stretched. Place marker.	18	23	28	33	34	34½	35	35
NOTE: for male garment, work buttonholes in left front, see placement as for right front.								
Shape lapel: With RS facing, knit 1, make 1, knit to end. Repeat row 2. Cont to increase in this way every one inch __ times more—	3	4	4	5	6	6	7	7
__ sts.	12	13	13	16	17	17	18	18
When work meas __ inches from marker, with WS	4	5½	6	6½	7½	8½	8½	9½
facing, bind off __ sts, knit to end.	8	8	8	10	10	10	10	10
Place rem __ sts on hold.	4	5	5	6	7	7	8	8

Right Front Border/Lapel/Collar

	S•32"	M•36"	L•40"	XS•44"	S•48"	M•52"	L•56"	XL•60"
Cast on __ sts. Work garter stitch as folls: Row 1 (RS): With yarn in front, slip 1 purlwise, bring yarn to back, knit to end. Row 2: knit. Repeat last 2 rows until piece meas __ inches, slightly stretched.	8	8	8	10	10	10	10	10
	5½	9	9½	12	13	13½	14	14
One row buttonhole row: slip 1, knit __, work	1	1	1	2	2	2	2	2
buttonhole as folls: yarn to front, slip next st, yarn to back. [Slip next st; on right needle pass second st over first st and off end of needle] __ times. Slip last bound off st back to left needle. Turn work.	4	4	4	4	4	4	4	4
Cable cast on __ sts (one more than you bound off), turn work. With yarn in back, slip first st from left needle, pass extra cast on st over it to close and secure the buttonhole. Knit to end. Repeat buttonhole row every __ inches	5	5	5	5	5	5	5	5
	3½	3½	3½	4	4	4	4	4
__ times more—	3	4	5	5	5	5	5	5
__ buttonholes total. Cont even until	4	5	6	6	6	6	6	6
work meas __ inches, place marker.	18	23	28	33	34	34½	35	35
Shape lapel: With RS facing, slip 1, knit __ sts,	6	6	6	8	8	8	8	8
make 1, knit 1. Knit 1 row. Cont to increase before last st in row every one inch __ times more—	3	4	4	5	6	6	7	7
__ sts.	12	13	13	16	17	17	18	18
When work meas __ inches from marker, with RS	4	5½	6	6½	7½	8½	8½	9½
facing, bind off __ sts, knit to end, do not turn. Place lapel border adjacent to marker placement on right front neck edge, pick up __ sts along right front neck	8	8	8	10	10	10	10	10
	7	7	8	10	10	10	12	12
edge, __ sts along back neck, and along left front neck edge to marker as for right, knit sts from hold on left front lapel. (See diagram below.) Turn. *Yarn in front, slip first st purlwise, yarn to back, knit to end. Repeat from * until collar meas __ inches from picked up edge, ending with underside of collar facing. Bind off all sts loosely.	12·14	14·16	14·16	16·18	18·20	20·22	22·24	22·24
	3	3	3	4	4	4	4	4

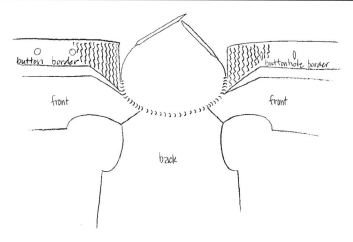

FINISHING

Pocket borders (make 2)
Cast on __ sts for 5•6 sts per inch

	Child			Adult				
Cast on __ sts for 5•6 sts per inch	5•6	5•6	5•6	6•7	6•7	6•7	6•7	6•7
4•4 ½ sts per inch	4	4	4	5	5	5	5	5
3•3 ½ sts per inch	3	3	3	4	4	4	4	4

Slip 1, knit to end. Knit 1 row. Repeat last 2 rows until border meas __ inches, bind off. (Slipped st edge is finished edge.)

	Child			Adult				
border meas __ inches	4	4½	5	6	6	6	6	6

Pocket Lining (make 2 reverse image)
With fingering yarn, and needles for 8 ½ sts per inch gauge, cast on __ sts. Knit 1 row, purl 1 row, turn. With knit side facing, cable cast on __ sts, knit across row, purl 1 row. Cont to cable cast on in foll sequence:

	Child			Adult				
cast on __ sts	4	4	4	8	8	8	8	8
cable cast on __ sts	3	3	3	4	4	4	4	4
	3x2	3x2	3x2	3x3	3x3	3x3	3x3	3x3
	2x5	2x5	2x5	2x5	2x5	2x5	2x5	2x5

For all sizes: inc 1 st EOR 14 times
inc 1 st every 4th row 6 times. Place marker at last increase.
Work even until pocket meas __ inches from beg.
Place marker to indicate the half fold.

	Child			Adult				
pocket meas __ inches from beg	6	7	8	9	9	9	9	9

To make the mirror image from the halfway point, knit even for same number of rows as there are between the two markers.
For all sizes: dec 1 st every 4th row 6 times, dec 1 st EOR 14 times. Bind off 2 sts 5 times, 3 sts 3 times, 4 sts once (end for Child sizes), and 8 sts once (end for Adult sizes.)
Fold in half at marker, knit side together, and single crochet layers together along curved edge (d). Single crochet from fold along selvage edge (c), leaving __ inches free to attach to pocket slit opening. (See diagrams below.)

	Child			Adult				
leaving __ inches free	4	4½	5	6	6	6	6	6

Make second pocket lining the reverse image by casting sts on, knit 1 row, turn. Cable cast on with the purl side facing, following the same sequence as above.

Sewing together: Place lower edge of front garter stitch border even with hem turning ridge and sew border to front using an invisible weaving seam working from right side of garment. Set sleeves in armholes. Sew side and sleeve seams. Sew pocket borders to pocket opening side nearest CF. On inside of garment, sew pocket lining to pocket slit opening., matching pocket lining edge (a) to slit pocket side (a), and matching (b) to (b). (See diagrams below.) Reverse for left front. Fold hem to wrong side at turning ridge, and whipstitch in place. Sew on buttons.

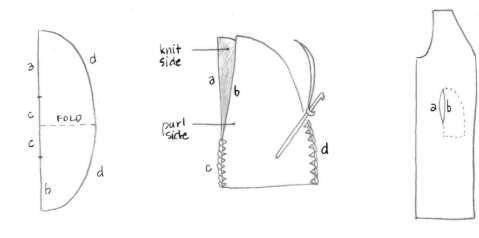

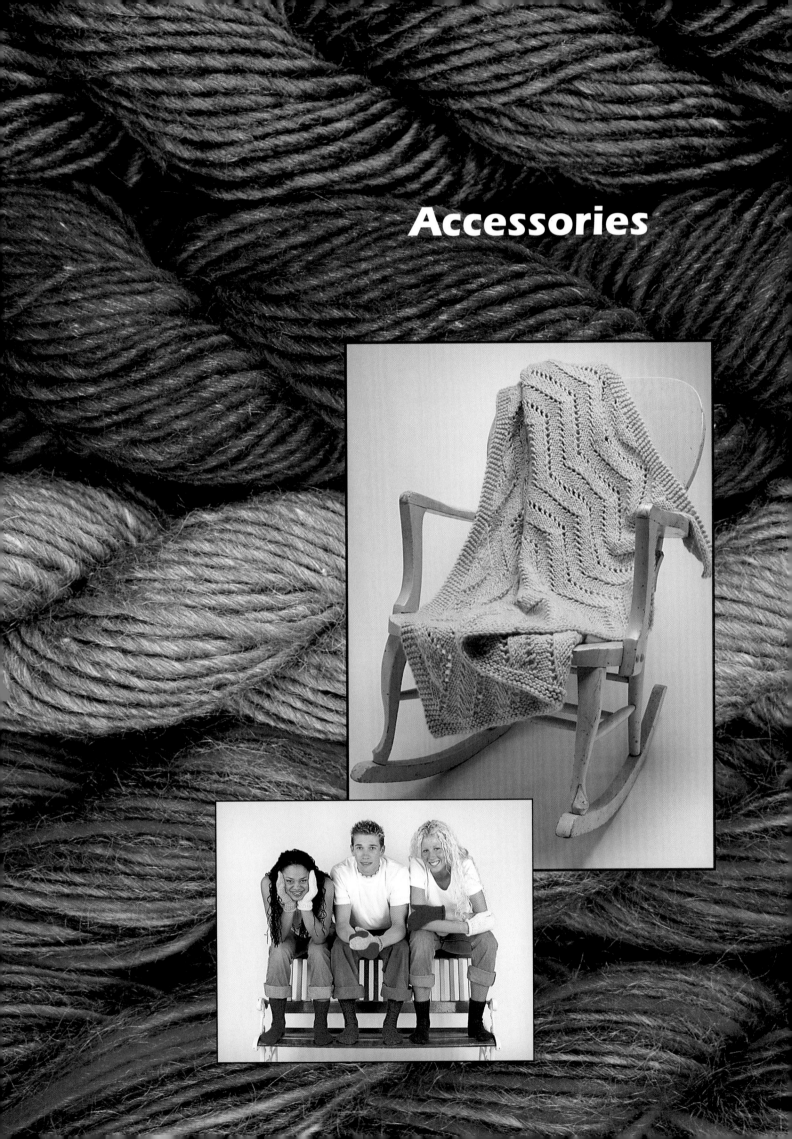

Accessories

Hats	Child/Adult		
	S • 18"	M • 20"	L • 22"
5 • 6 sts per inch yardage	175	225	275
Cotton Fleece	1	1 or 2	2
Kaleidoscope	2	3	3
Nature Spun (S)	1	2	2
Top of the Lamb (S)	1	1	1
4 • 4½ sts per inch yardage	175	225	250
Country Classics (W)	1	2	2
Handpaint Originals	2	3	3
Lamb's Pride (W)	1	2	2
Lamb's Pride Superwash (W)	1	2	2
Nature Spun (W)	1	1	1 or 2
Prairie Silk	2	3	3
Top of the Lamb (W)	1	2	2
3 • 3½ sts per inch yardage	125	150	175
Country Classics (B)	1	2	2
Lamb's Pride (B)	1	2	2
Lamb's Pride Superwash (B	2	2	2

(Yardage and skein estimates are approximations only.)

Basic Hat Building

1 With smaller dpn or circular needle, cast on sts.
2 Work ribbing for desired length.
3 Change to larger needles, cont in st st until work measures desired length to crown shaping.
4 Shape crown by decreasing at regular stitch intervals every other row until last round is k 2 tog around. Cut yarn and draw end through all loops to secure.

BASIC STOCKING HAT

With smaller dpn, cast on __ sts:

		S • 18"	M • 20"	L • 22"
	for 5•6 sts per inch	90•108	100•120	110•132
	for 4•4 ½ sts per inch	72•80	80•90	88•99
	for 3•3 ½ sts per inch	54•64	60•70	66•77

Being careful not to twist cast on edge, join and place marker to indicate beg of round. Work 1/1 rib for __ inches. Change to larger needles and cont in st st until piece meas __ inches from beg.

		S • 18"	M • 20"	L • 22"
		2	2½	2½
		6	7	7½

Shape crown: knit __ sts:

		S • 18"	M • 20"	L • 22"
	for 5•6 sts per inch	8•10	8•10	9•10
	for 4•4 ½ sts per inch	7•8	8•8	9•9
	for 3•3 ½ sts per inch,	4•6	4•5	4•5

k 2 tog, repeat to end of round. Knit one round even.

Knit __ sts:

		S • 18"	M • 20"	L • 22"
	for 5•6 sts per inch	7•9	7•9	8•9
	for 4•4 ½ sts per inch	6•7	7•7	8•8
	for 3•3 ½ sts per inch,	3•5	3•4	3•4

k 2 tog, repeat to end of round. Knit one round even. Cont decreasing with one fewer st between decs until __ sts remain:

		S • 18"	M • 20"	L • 22"
	for 5•6 sts per inch	9•9	10•10	10•11
	for 4•4 ½ sts per inch	8•8	8•9	8•9
	for 3•3 ½ sts per inch.	9•8	10•10	11•11

Cut yarn, leaving a length for finishing, and thread yarn needle.
Draw through all remaining loops to secure.
Weave in ends on wrong side.

SPORT FIT 'BEANIE'

With smaller dpn, cast on __ sts:

		S • 18"	M • 20"	L • 22"
	for 5•6 sts per inch	90•108	100•120	110•132
	for 4•4 ½ sts per inch	72•80	80•90	88•99
	for 3•3 ½ sts per inch	54•64	60•70	66•77

Being careful not to twist cast on edge, join and place marker to indicate beg of round. Work 1/1 rib for __ inches. Change to larger needles and cont in st st until piece meas __ inches from beg.

		S • 18"	M • 20"	L • 22"
		1½	1¾	2
		4	5	6

Shape crown: knit __ sts:

		S • 18"	M • 20"	L • 22"
	for 5•6 sts per inch	8•10	8•10	9•10
	for 4•4 ½ sts per inch	7•8	8•8	9•9
	for 3•3 ½ sts per inch,	4•6	4•5	4•5

k 2 tog, repeat to end of round. Knit one round even.

Knit __ sts:

		S • 18"	M • 20"	L • 22"
	for 5•6 sts per inch	7•9	7•9	8•9
	for 4•4 ½ sts per inch	6•7	7•7	8•8
	for 3•3 ½ sts per inch,	3•5	3•4	3•4

k 2 tog, repeat to end of round. Knit one round even. Cont decreasing with one fewer st between decs until __ sts remain:

		S • 18"	M • 20"	L • 22"
	for 5•6 sts per inch	9•9	10•10	10•11
	for 4•4 ½ sts per inch	8•8	8•9	8•9
	for 3•3 ½ sts per inch.	9•8	10•10	11•11

Cut yarn, leaving a length for finishing, and thread yarn needle.
Draw through all remaining loops to secure.
Weave in ends on wrong side.

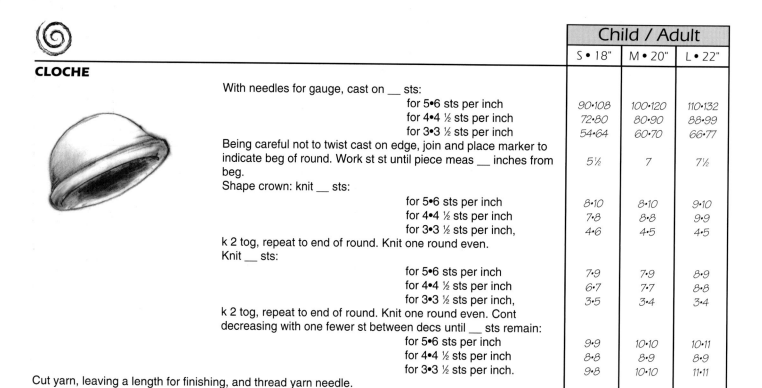

CLOCHE

	Child / Adult		
	S • 18"	M • 20"	L • 22"

With needles for gauge, cast on __ sts:

for 5•6 sts per inch	90•108	100•120	110•132
for 4•4 ½ sts per inch	72•80	80•90	88•99
for 3•3 ½ sts per inch	54•64	60•70	66•77

Being careful not to twist cast on edge, join and place marker to indicate beg of round. Work st st until piece meas __ inches from beg.

	5 ½	7	7 ½

Shape crown: knit __ sts:

for 5•6 sts per inch	8•10	8•10	9•10
for 4•4 ½ sts per inch	7•8	8•8	9•9
for 3•3 ½ sts per inch,	4•6	4•5	4•5

k 2 tog, repeat to end of round. Knit one round even.

Knit __ sts:

for 5•6 sts per inch	7•9	7•9	8•9
for 4•4 ½ sts per inch	6•7	7•7	8•8
for 3•3 ½ sts per inch,	3•5	3•4	3•4

k 2 tog, repeat to end of round. Knit one round even. Cont decreasing with one fewer st between decs until __ sts remain:

for 5•6 sts per inch	9•9	10•10	10•11
for 4•4 ½ sts per inch	8•8	8•9	8•9
for 3•3 ½ sts per inch.	9•8	10•10	11•11

Cut yarn, leaving a length for finishing, and thread yarn needle.
Draw through all remaining loops to secure.
Weave in ends on wrong side.

Socks	Child			Adult		
	S	M	L	S	M	L
6½ • 7 sts per inch yardage	150	225	275	325	425	525
Cotton Fine	1	1	2	2	2	3
Nature Spun (F)	1	1	1	2	2	2
Wildfoote	1	2	2	2	2	3
5 • 6 sts per inch yardage	125	175	225	250	325	400
Cotton Fleece	1	1	2	2	2	2
Kaleidoscope	2	2	3	3	3	4
Nature Spun (S)	1	1	2	2	2	3
Top of the Lamb (S)	1	1	1	1	1	2
4 • 4½ sts per inch yardage	125	150	200	250	300	350
Country Classics (W)	1	1	2	2	2	3
Handpaint Originals	2	2	3	3	4	4
Lamb's Pride (W)	1	1	2	2	2	3
Lamb's Pride Superwash (W)	1	1	1	2	2	2
Nature Spun (W)	1	1	2	2	2	2
Prairie Silk	2	2	3	3	4	4
Top of the Lamb (W)	1	1	2	2	2	3
3 • 3½ sts per inch yardage	100	125	150	175	225	275
Country Classics (B)	1	1	2	2	2	3
Lamb's Pride (B)	1	1	2	2	2	3
Lamb's Pride Superwash (B	1	2	2	2	3	3

(Yardage and skein estimates are approximations only.)

Basic Sock Building

1 Cast on sts and divide onto three needles.

2 Knit ribbing for crew sock until it measures desired length.

3 Back of heel: Work back and forth on one half of the cast on sts, leaving the other half for knitting the instep later.

4 To turn the heel: When the back of heel is complete, short row as follows: knit two thirds of the sts less one, SSK (last st of center third and first st of last third), k 1, turn. Slip 1 purlwise, purl to last st of center third, p 2 tog (last st of center third and first st of remaining third on the purl side), p 1, turn. Slip 1 knitwise and work the sts before and after the gaps SSK on the knit side and p2tog on the purl side. Repeat until all sts have been worked off, end having completed a right side row, working yarn is at left side of heel. Divide sts on 2 dpn so that beg of round will be at center of heel.

5 To shape heel gusset: Pick up sts along side of heel. Continue on next needle (instep), then pick up and knit the same number of sts on other side of heel. Knit to center back of heel, rounds begin here. Stitches should be divided as follows: ½ of heel sts and left gusset on needle #1, instep sts on needle #2, right gusset and ½ heel sts on needle #3. Knit one round even. To decrease: knit to last 3 sts on first needle, k 2 tog, k 1; knit across second needle; k 1, ssk, knit to end of round on third needle. Knit one round even. Repeat last two rounds until stitch count is back to original number of cast on. Knit even until sock measures length desired minus about 2 inches for toe shaping.

6 To shape toe: Knit to last 3 sts on first needle, k 2 tog, k 1. On second needle k 1, ssk, knit to last 3 sts, k 2 tog, k 1. On third needle k 1, ssk, knit to end. Knit one or two rounds even. Repeat last two rounds until 16 stitches remain. Knit sts from needle #1 onto needle #3. Stitches are now on two needles. Graft, using kitchener stitch.

BASIC SOCKS

		Child			Adult		
		S	M	L	S	M	L
Sock circumference (C) __ inches		5½	6½	7	7½	8½	9½
Total length of sock (L) __ inches		5	6½	8	9½	10½	11½
Number of sts per inch V							
With dpn, cast on __ sts.	4	22	26	28	30	34	38
	5	28	32	36	38	44	48
	6	32	38	42	46	52	58
	7	38	46	50	52	60	66
	8	44	52	56	60	68	76
	9	50	58	64	68	76	86

Being careful not to twist cast on edge, join and place marker to indicate beg of round. Work 1/1 rib for __ inches, or desired length.

		Child			Adult		
		S	M	L	S	M	L
		3	4½	6	7	8	9

Place one half of total number of sts on one needle to be worked as heel. Place rem sts on 2 needles for instep, to be worked later. Work back and forth on heel sts as folls: (RS) [Slip 1, k 1] repeat across, turn. (WS) Slip 1, purl to end. Repeat last two rows for __ inches:

		S	M	L	S	M	L
		1¼	1½	1¾	2	2¼	2½

Turning heel: Knit __ sts:

sts/inch V		S	M	L	S	M	L
	4	6	8	8	9	10	12
	5	8	10	11	12	14	15
	6	10	12	13	14	16	18
	7	12	14	16	16	19	21
	8	14	16	18	19	22	24
	9	16	18	20	22	24	28

SSK, k 1, turn.
Slip 1, purl __ sts:

sts/inch V		S	M	L	S	M	L
	4	2	4	3	4	5	6
	5	3	5	5	6	7	7
	6	5	6	6	6	7	8
	7	6	6	8	7	9	10
	8	7	7	9	9	11	11
	9	8	8	9	11	11	14

P 2 tog, p 1, turn.
Slip 1, k __ sts.

sts/inch V		S	M	L	S	M	L
	4	3	5	4	5	6	7
	5	4	6	6	7	8	8
	6	6	7	7	7	8	9
	7	7	7	9	8	10	11
	8	8	8	10	10	12	12
	9	9	9	10	12	12	15

SSK, k 1, turn.
Slip 1, purl __ sts:

sts/inch V		S	M	L	S	M	L
	4	4	6	5	6	7	8
	5	5	7	7	8	9	9
	6	7	8	8	8	9	10
	7	8	8	10	9	11	12
	8	9	9	11	11	13	13
	9	10	10	11	13	13	16

P 2 tog, p 1, turn. Cont in this fashion, always working together the 2 sts on each side of the gap, until all sts have been worked. Knit 1 row on all sts. Divide heel sts onto 2 needles (#1 and #3), place all instep sts onto 1 needle (#2)

		Child			Adult	
	S	M	L	S	M	L

SOCKS (cont)

Heel gusset: With needle #1, pick up approx ___ sts along side of heel:

sts/inch ∨						
4	6	6	7	8	9	10
5	6	8	9	10	11	12
6	8	9	10	12	14	15
7	9	10	12	14	16	18
8	10	12	14	16	18	20
9	12	14	16	18	20	22

Work across instep sts on needle #2. With empty needle pick up same number sts long other side of heel, knit across heel sts on needle #3, ending at center back heel. Knit one round even, working into back of loops on picked up sts.

Shape gussett: Knit until 3 sts remain on needle #1, k 2 tog, k1. Knit across instep sts. On needle #3, k 1, SSK, knit to end of round. Knit one round even. Cont to dec in this fashion every other round until there are the same number sts as cast on. Knit even until foot length meas from back of heel ___ inches, or approx 2 inches less than desired length.

	3½	4¾	6	7½	8½	9½

Shape toe: Work to last 3 sts on needle #1, k 2 tog, k 1. On needle #2, k 1, ssk, work to last 3 sts on needle, k 2 tog, k 1. On needle #3, k 1, ssk, knit to end of round. Knit one round even. [Work dec round, work one rnd even] until 8 sts remain. Place sts on 2 needles and graft together, using kitchener stitch.

Basic Mitten Building

1 Cast on stitches and divide onto
three double pointed needles.
Use a needle one or two sizes
smaller for a tighter fit for cuff.
2 Work ribbing for desired length.
3 Change to larger needles and
work in st st, shaping the thumb
gore with regularly spaced
increases. Place thumb stitches
on hold.
4 Continue on palm stitches until
mitten measures 1½ inches less
than desired length. Decrease
at regular intervals every other
row until last round is k 2 tog
around. Cut yarn and draw end through all loops to secure.
5 Place thumb stitches on dpn and work in round until ½ inch less than desired length.
Decrease at regular intervals. Cut yarn and draw end through all loops to secure.

(make 2!)

Mittens	Child			Adult	
	S • 5"	M • 5.5"	L • 6"	M • 7"	L • 8"
5 • 6 sts per inch yardage	75	100	125	150	175
Cotton Fleece	1	1	1	1	1
Kaleidoscope	1	1	2	2	2
Nature Spun (S)	1	1	1	1	1
Top of the Lamb (S)	1	1	1	1	1
4 • 4½ sts per inch yardage	75	100	125	150	175
Country Classics (W)	1	1	1	1	1
Handpaint Originals	1	2	2	2	2
Lamb's Pride (W)	1	1	1	1	1
Lamb's Pride Superwash (W)	1	1	1	1	1
Nature Spun (W)	1	1	1	1	1
Prairie Silk	1	2	2	2	2
Top of the Lamb (W)	1	1	1	1	1
3 • 3½ sts per inch yardage	50	75	100	125	150
Country Classics (B)	1	1	1	1	2
Lamb's Pride (B)	1	1	1	1	2
Lamb's Pride Superwash (B	1	1	1	2	2

(Yardage and skein estimates are approximations only.)

	Child			Adult	
	S • 5"	M • 5.5"	L • 6"	M • 7"	L • 8"

MITTENS

With same or smaller dpn, cast on __ sts:

	Child			Adult	
for 5•6 sts per inch	24•30	28•32	30•36	36•42	40•48
for 4•4 ½ sts per inch	20•22	22•24	24•28	28•32	32•36
for 3•3 ½ sts per inch	16•18	16•18	18•22	22•24	24•28

Cuff option 1: Knit st st for __ inch.

Work 1/1 rib for __ inches.

	Child			Adult	
Knit st st	3/4	3/4	1	1	1
Work 1/1 rib	1¼	1¼	1½	1½	1¾

OR

Cuff option 2: Work 1/1 rib for __ inches.

	Child			Adult	
	2	2	2	2½	3

Change to larger needles, and cont even in st st for one round.

Shape thumb gore: Inc 1 st in first st (first thumb st), inc 1 st in next st (last thumb st), place marker.

Knit __ rounds even:

	Child			Adult	
for 5•6 sts per inch	2•2	2•2	3•3	4•3	4•4
for 4•4 ½ sts per inch	2•3	3•3	3•3	4•3	4•4
for 3•3 ½ sts per inch	2•2	2•2	2•2	3•3	3•3

Inc 1 in first thumb st, k 2, inc 1 in last thumb st; repeat from * to *.

Cont to inc in first and last thumb sts, having 2 sts more between incs after each inc round; repeat * to * rounds even, until __ sts in thumb gore:

	Child			Adult	
for 5•6 sts per inch	8•10	8•10	10•12	12•16	14•16
for 4•4 ½ sts per inch	6•8	6•8	8•8	10•12	10•12
for 3•3 ½ sts per inch	6•6	6•6	6•8	8•8	8•8

Mitten should meas approx __ inches above rib.

	Child			Adult	
	1½	1¾	2¼	2¾	3¼

Slip thumb sts to strand of yarn to hold. At end of last round of hand sts, cast on 2 sts. Stitch count is same as original number cast on.

Knit even for hand until mitten meas __ inches above rib.

	Child			Adult	
	3	4	5	6	6½

For sizes working on 18 or 22 sts, dec 2 sts evenly spaced in next round.

Mitten tip shaping: k __ sts

	Child			Adult	
for 5•6 sts per inch	4•4	5•6	4•4	4•4	6•6
for 4•4 ½ sts per inch	3•3	3•4	4•5	5•6	6•4
for 3•3 ½ sts per inch	2•2	2•2	2•3	3•4	4•5

k 2 tog, around.

Knit two rounds even for gauges 5•6 sts per inch, knit one round even for gauges 4•4 ½ and 3•3 ½ sts per inch.

K __ sts

	Child			Adult	
for 5•6 sts per inch	3•3	4•5	3•3	3•3	5•5
for 4•4 ½ sts per inch	2•2	2•3	3•4	4•5	5•4
for 3•3 ½ sts per inch	1•1	1•1	1•2	2•3	3•4

k 2 tog, around. Knit round(s) even.

Cont dec with 1 fewer sts between decs, followed by even rounds, until 1 st between decs rem. K 2 tog around.

Cut yarn, leaving a length for finishing, and thread yarn needle.

Draw through all remaining loops to secure.

Weave in end on wrong side.

Thumb: Place the thumb gore sts onto two needles. With a third needle, pick up __ sts on the cast on sts at inside of thumb—

	Child			Adult	
for 5•6 sts per inch	2•2	3•3	2•3	3•2	2•3
for 4•4 ½ sts per inch	2•3	3•2	2•3	2•2	3•3
for 3•3 ½ sts per inch	1•1	1•2	2•1	1•3	2•3

__ sts total for thumb:

	Child			Adult	
for 5•6 sts per inch	10•12	11•13	12•15	15•18	16•19
for 4•4 ½ sts per inch	8•9	9•10	10•11	12•14	13•15
for 3•3 ½ sts per inch	7•7	7•8	8•9	9•11	10•11

Knit around until thumb meas __ inches above cast on sts.

	Child			Adult	
	1¼	1½	1¾	2	2¼

Dec round: *K 1, k 2 tog,* around. Knit any remaining sts in round.

Knit 1 round even.

K 2 tog around. Knit any remaining sts in round. Finish as for tip of mitten.

Make second mitten the same.

Scarves	Child (6 x 40)		Adult (8 x 54)	
6½ • 7 sts per inch yardage				
Cotton Fine	2		3	
Nature Spun (F)	1		2	
Wildfoote	1		3	
5 • 6 sts per inch yardage				
Cotton Fleece	1		2	
Kaleidoscope	2		4	
Nature Spun (S)	2		2	
Top of the Lamb (S)	1		2	
4 • 4½ sts per inch yardage				
Country Classics (W)	1		2	
Handpaint Originals	2		4	
Lamb's Pride (W)	1		2	
Lamb's Pride Superwash (W)	1		2	
Nature Spun (W)	1		2	
Prairie Silk	2		4	
Top of the Lamb (W)	1		2	
3 • 3½ sts per inch yardage				
Country Classics (B)	1		3	
Lamb's Pride (B)	1		3	
Lamb's Pride Superwash (B	2		4	

(Yardage and skein estimates are approximations only.)

Basic Scarf

Cast on sts. Work in seed stitch or garter for desired length. Bind off.

Experiment with gauges on your choice of yarn. Use recommended gauges as guides only. A looser gauge will produce more drape, a more compact gauge will produce more body to the knitted fabric.

SCARF

	Child 6 x 40"	Adult 8 x 54"
With needles for gauge, cast on __ sts:		
for 6½ • 7 sts per inch	40 • 42	52 • 56
for 5 • 6 sts per inch	30 • 36	40 • 48
for 4 • 4½ sts per inch	24 • 28	32 • 36
for 3 • 3½ sts per inch	18 • 20	24 • 28
Work in seed stitch for __ inches, or desired length. Bind off. Weave in ends	40	54

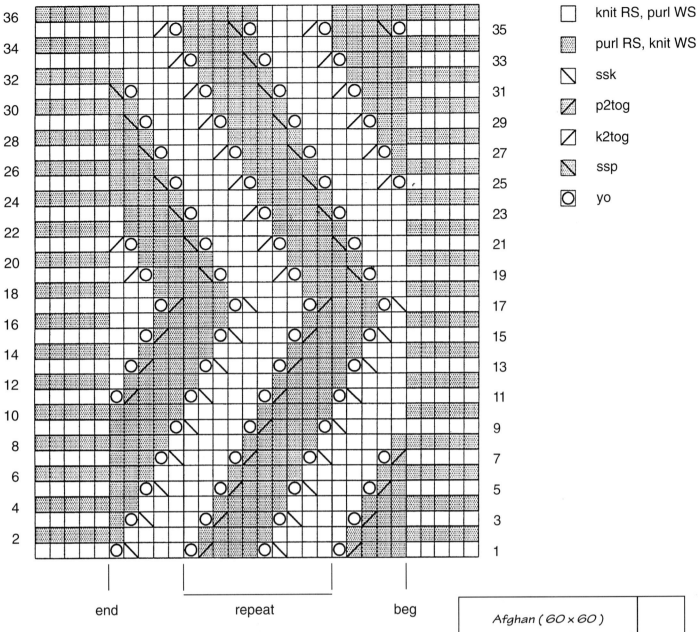

	knit RS, purl WS
	purl RS, knit WS
	ssk
	p2tog
	k2tog
	ssp
	yo

end   repeat   beg

Afghan (60 x 60)	
5 • 6 sts per inch yardage	
Cotton Fleece	14
Kaleidoscope	28
Nature Spun (S)	17
Top of the Lamb (S)	9
4 • 4½ sts per inch yardage	
Country Classics (W)	14
Handpaint Originals	30
Lamb's Pride (W)	14
Lamb's Pride Superwash (W)	13
Nature Spun (W)	11
Prairie Silk	30
Top of the Lamb (W)	14
3 • 3½ sts per inch yardage	
Country Classics (B)	15
Lamb's Pride (B)	15
Lamb's Pride Superwash (B	17

(Yardage and skein estimates are approximations only.)

Zig Zag Reversible Afghan

Text instructions are given for graph as follows, with number of repeats for bracketed pattern given for bulky/worsted/sport:

Row 1: k5, p3, p2tog, yo, [k3, ssk, yo, p3, p2tog, yo] 13/18/23x, k3, ssk, yo, k5.
Row 2: k6, p4, [p1, k5, p4] 13/18/23x, p1, k9.
Row 3: k5, p2, p2tog, yo, k1, [k2, ssk, yo, p3, p2tog, yo, k1] 13/18/23x, k2, ssk, yo, p1, k5.
Row 4: k7, p3, [p2, k5, p3] 13/18/23x, p2, k8.
Row 5: k5, p1, p2tog, yo, k2, [k1, ssk, yo, p3, p2tog, yo, k2] 13/18/23x, k1, ssk, yo, p2, k5.
Row 6: k8, p2, [p3, k5, p2] 13/18/23x, p3 k7.
Row 7: k5, p2tog, yo, k3, [ssk, yo, p3, p2tog, yo, k3] 13/18/23x, ssk, yo, p3, k5.
Row 8: k9, p1, [p4, k5, p1] 13/18/23x, p4, k6.
Row 9: k9, ssk, [yo, p3, p2tog, yo, k3, ssk] 13/18/23x, yo, p4, k5.
Row 10: k10, [p5, k5]13/18/23x, p5, k5.
Row 11: k8, ssk, yo, [p3, p2tog, yo, k3, ssk, yo] 13/18/23x, p3, p2tog, yo, k5.
Row 12: k5, p1, k4, [k1, p5, k4] 13/18/23x, k1, p4, k5.
Row 13: k7, ssk, yo, p1, [p2, p2tog, yo, k3, ssk, yo, p1] 13/18/23x, p2, p2tog, yo, k6.
Row 14: k5, p2, k3, [k2, p5, k3] 13/18/23x, k2, p3, k5.
Row 15: k6, ssk, yo, p2, [p1, p2tog, yo, k3, ssk, yo, p2] 13/18/23x, p1, p2tog, yo, k7.
Row 16: k5, p3, k2, [k3, p5, k2] 13/18/23x, k3, p2, k5.
Row 17: k5, ssk, yo, p3, [p2tog, yo, k3, ssk, yo, p3] 13/18/23x, p2tog, yo, k8.
Row 18: k5, p3, k2, [k3, p5, k2] 13/18/23x, k3, p2, k5.
Row 19: k7, yo, ssp, p1, [p2, yo, ktog, k3, yo, ssp, p1] 13/18/23x, p2, yo, k2tog, k6.
Row 20: k5, p2, k3, [k2, p5, k3] 13/18/23x, k2, p3, k5.
Row 21: k8, yo, ssp, [p3, yo, k2tog, k3, yo, ssp]13/18/23x, p3, yo, k2tog, k5.
Row 22: k5, p1, k4, [k1, p5, k4] 13/18/23x, k1, p4, k5.
Row 23: k9, yo, [ssp, p3, yo, k2tog, k3, yo] 13/18/23x, ssp, p3, k6.
Row 24: k10, [p5, k5] 13/18/23x, p5, k5.
Row 25: k5, yo, k2tog, k3, [yo, ssp, p3, yo, k2tog, k3] 13/18/23x, yo, ssp, p3, k5.
Row 26: k9, p1, [p4, k5, p1] 13/18/23x, p4, k6.
Row 27: k5, p1, yo, k2tog, k2, [k1,yo, ssp, p3, yo, k2tog, k2] 13/18/23x, k1, yo, ssp, p2, k5.
Row 28: k8, p2, [p3, k5, p2] 13/18/23x, p3, k7.
Row 29: k5, p2, yo, k2tog, k1, [k2, yo, ssp, p3, yo, k2tog, k1] 13/18/23x, k2, yo, ssp, p1, k5.
Row 30: k7,p3, [p2, k5, p3] 13/18/23x, p2, k8.
Row 31: k5, p3,yo, k2tog, [k3, yo, ssp, p3, yo, k2tog] 13/18/23x, k3, yo, ssp, k5.
Row 32: k6, p4, [p1, k5, p4] 13/18/23x, p1, k9.
Row 33: k5, p4, yo, [k2tog, k3, yo, ssp, p3, yo] 13/18/23x, k2tog, k9.
Row 34: k5, p5, [k5, p5] 13/18/23x, k10.
Row 35: k5, yo, ssp, p3, [yo, k2tog, k3, yo, ssp, p3] 13/18/23x, yo, k2tog, k8.
Row 36: k5, p5, [k5, p5] 13/18/23x, k10.

Cast on stitches, 150 for bulky yarns/200 for worsted/250 for sport. Work 6 rows garter stitch (knit every row). Follow graph, reading right to left on odd numbered RS rows, left to right on even numbered WS rows. First and last 5 sts in each row are garter stitch border as indicated; begin zig zag pattern at line marked beg and work first 5 sts, work next 10 sts pattern repeat 13 times for bulky/ 18 for worsted/23 for sport. Work last 5 sts of zig zag pattern, then 5 sts of border. Continue repeating entire graph until piece measures 59 inches. Work 5 rows garter stitch, bind off on row 6 of garter stitch.

Burly Spun Afghan

With size 13 needles, and a gauge of 2 sts per inch, the afghan size will be approximately 60 x 60 inches.

Takes 12 skeins.

Cast on 125 stitches. Repeat bracketed pattern
across rows.
Rows 1 and 5:   [k5, p3], ending k5.
Rows 2 and 4:   p5, [k3, p5].
Row 3:   [k5, p1 yo, p2tog], k5.
Rows 6 and 12:   p.
Rows 7 and 11:   [k1, p3, k4], k1, p3, k1.
Rows 8 and 10:   p1, k3, p1, [p4, k3, p1].
Row 9:   [k1, p1, yo, p2tog, k4], k1, p1, yo, p2tog, k1.

Repeat rows 1 — 12 until work measures 60 inches.
Bind off.
Single crochet around edges for finish.

Guide to Techniques

The techniques offered here cover the basics for all the knitting patterns presented in this book. While not as detailed as my own Knitter's Companion, and certainly not as complete as the Vogue Knitting volume, you will find all the techniques I have used in creating the garments and accessories. Use this chapter as a refresher course.

BASICS

Gauge, or tension, is necessary information to knit for accuracy in size. Knit a four inch square sample swatch with your choice of yarn and needles. Knit stockinette or the pattern stitch you will be using. Measure inside the selvage, since the edge stitches are always somewhat misshapen. Lay a ruler or tape measure under a row of knit stitches, and count the number of stitches in the four inches, including fractions. Divide this number by 4 to get your stitch per inch gauge. Too few stitches means your work is loose, try smaller needles. Too many stitches means your work is tight, try bigger needles.

Long-Tail Cast On begins with a slip knot and a long tail on a knitting needle held in your right hand. Lay the tail over your left thumb and the working yarn (attached to the ball) over your left index finger, catching the yarn in your palm with your remaining fingers. Holding your hand and needle in a vertical position, insert the needle upward into the loop on the front of the thumb, over and around the yarn on the index fin-

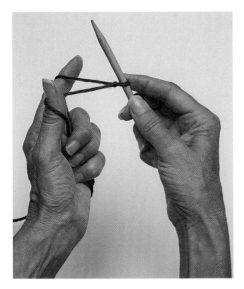

ger, and down through the loop on the thumb. Remove your thumb from the loop and adjust the tension of the new cast on stitch by replacing your thumb under the tail yarn, and gently pulling on the needle. Repeat until you have the desired number of stitches.

Cable Cast On begins with a slip knot and a tail just long enough

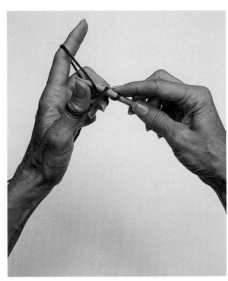

for finishing purposes. Hold the needle in your left hand and with free needle knit into the first stitch, leaving the stitch on the left needle. Pull a loop forward and place it on the left needle. *Insert the right needle between the two stitches, wrap as if to knit, pull the loop forward and place on the left needle. Repeat from *until you have the desired number of stitches. This is used on one row buttonholes.

Knit — Continental Style Hold the needle with the cast on stitches in your left hand, with the working yarn held in back over your index finger and in your palm against the needle for tension. Insert right nee-

dle into the first stitch from front to back, and over and behind the yarn. Pull the working yarn through the stitch to the front, forming a new stitch on the right needle and slipping the stitch off the left needle.

Purl — Continental Style Hold the needle with the cast on stitches in your left hand, with the working yarn held in front over your index finger and in your palm against the needle for tension. Insert right

needle into the first stitch from back to front. With left index finger, lay working yarn over the right needle from front to back, then down between needles. Pull working yarn through to the back, forming a new stitch on the right needle and slipping the stitch off the left needle.

    Bind Off. Work two stitches, knitting over knit stitches and purling over purl stitches.With two sitches on right needle, pass the right stitch over the left and off the end of the needle. Work the next

stitch, repeat the pass. Continue until the desired number of stitches have been bound off. If you bind off all stitches, cut the working yarn and pull cut end through the last stitch to secure it.

SHAPING

Make One Increase. While many other increase methods may be used, Make One is easily done and very subtle. Simply twist a loop with the working yarn and place it on the right needle as a new stitch. This works the same on the knit side and the purl side.

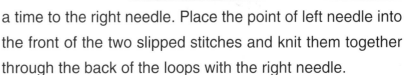

SSK is a left slanting decrease worked on the knit side.

Slip two stitches knitwise one at a time to the right needle. Place the point of left needle into the front of the two slipped stitches and knit them together through the back of the loops with the right needle.

SSP is a decrease worked on the purl side that is left slanting on the knit side. Slip two stitches knitwise one at a time to the right needle. Return them to the left needle, keeping them twisted. Purl the two stitches together through the back of the loops. (The right needle is at an awkward angle at first to enter the stitches from back to front.)

K2tog is a right slanting decrease worked on the knit side. Place right needle into two stitches at the same time knitwise, and knit them as one.

P2tog is a decrease worked on the purl side and is right slanting on the knit side. Place right needle into two stitches at the same time purlwise, and purl them as one.

Short rowing is a method of shaping where only part of the row is worked, increasing the number of rows in one area without binding off unworked stitches. The number of stitches remains constant. Work the partial row to the turning point, slip the next stitch purlwise. Transfer the working yarn between the needles to its opposite side, pass the same stitch back to the left needle, transfer the working yarn back between the needles to its original side, and turn the work. Repeat as instructions indicate. On the return rows, hide the wraps by working them together with the stitches that have been wrapped.

Yarn over is an open increase in which you lay the yarn over the needle front to back. If the previous stitch is a knit, then first bring the yarn forward between the needles, then lay it over the needle. If the previous stitch is a purl, the yarn is already in the front ready to lay over the needle. If the next stitch is a knit, then yarn is already in back to continue knitting. If the next stitch is a purl, then bring yarn forward between the needles to continue purling.

CONNECTING

Invisible Weaving Seam is used on stockinette stitch for vertical seams such as side or sleeve seams. Working from the right side, insert a threaded tapestry needle into a knit stitch on the selvage edge catching the horizontal bar, and then under a corresponding bar on the opposite side. Continue to alternate sides, pulling the seaming yarn in the direction of the seam. When seam is complete, whipstitch on back side and weave tail end in.

Slip Stitch Crochet Seam is used on horizontal and curved seams such as shoulders and armholes. With right sides together and working one stitch at a time, insert a crochet hook through both layers of knitting one stitch's width in from the edge. Yarn over the hook and draw a loop through both layers, then yarn over the hook again and draw a loop through the first to secure the end. *Insert hook into next stitch through both layers, yarn over the hook and draw a loop through the layers and through the loop on the hook. Repeat from * until seam is complete. Avoid pulling too tightly or puckers will be evident. Cut working yarn

Kitchener Stitch is used to graft stitches together for the appearance of continuous knitting. Use this method to seam the toes of socks. Place the stitches to be grafted onto two needles. Break working yarn and thread tapestry needle, leaving a length suitable for finishing a short seam. Hold two needles parallel together in left hand, wrong sides facing together. *Insert tapestry needle into first stitch on front needle knitwise, slip it off the needle. Insert tapestry needle into second stitch on front needle purlwise, leave it on the needle, pull yarn through. Insert tapestry needle into first stitch on back needle purlwise, slip it off the needle. Insert tapestry needle into second stitch on back needle knitwise, leave it on the needle, pull yarn through. Repeat from * until all stitches are used. Weave end in on wrong side.

Three Needle Bind Off is an efficient way to bind off two edges and seam them simultaneously, producing a professional, flat seam. Use this method for seaming shoulders, where stitch number is the same on each piece. With knitting still on needles and right sides facing together, hold two needles parallel together in left hand. Place a third needle, one or two sizes larger, into the first stitch on each needle knitwise and knit them together as one. Repeat, there will be two stitches on the right needle. Pass the right stitch over the left and off the end of the needle. Continue to knit together as one the first stitch on each needle, and binding off until one stitch remains. Cut yarn and draw end through last loop to secure.

EDGING

Picking Up Stitches along an edge and knitting them creates finished borders. Always pick up stitches with the right side facing, working from right to left with a separate ball of yarn. Insert needle under oneor two strands of edge stitches, wrap as if to knit and pull newly made stitch to right side and leave it on the needle. To make counting easier, I will divide the knitted edge into fourths and mark with open markers. I pick up ¼ of my total stitches needed in each section, placing the marker on the needle as I go.

Single Crochet Edge is a stabilizing edge that does not add significant width. Working right to left, begin by inserting hook into knitted edge one stitch in. Yarn over hook and draw up a loop. Yarn over hook again and draw loop through loop on hook. *Insert hook into next stitch, yarn over hook and draw up a loop through knit layer, yarn over hook and draw a loop through both loops on hook. Repeat from * until edge has been covered. Cut yarn and draw end through last loop to secure.

Slipped Stitch Edge on a garter stitch border, as on the coat with lapel, is a clean finish, leaving neat, even stitches along the edge. At the beginning of the row, with yarn in front, slip first stitch purlwise, yarn to back and knit to end. On the next row, knit all stitches including the slipped stitch. (On the right border of the coat, you will slip the first stitch on the right side. On the left border of the coat, you will slip the first stitch on the wrong side.)

DETAILING

The Eyelet Buttonhole is virtually hidden in a border of single rib, especially if you work it following a knit stitch, not a purl. Simply yarn over, k2tog.

The One Row Buttonhole is a visible, neat and firm buttonhole. Work to where you want the buttonhole placed, bring yarn to front, slip the next stitch purlwise, yarn to back. *Slip next stitch, pass second stitch over first and off end of needle. Repeat from * 3 times. Replace last bound off stitch to left needle, turn work. Cable cast on 5 stitches, or one more than you bound off. (See Cable Cast On.) Turn work. With yarn in back, slip the first stitch from the left needle and pass the extra cast on stitch over it to close the buttonhole.

Whipstitch Hem Fold hem to wrong side of work at turning ridge and pin in place. Insert a threaded tapestry needle into a stitch on the wrong side of the knitting, and then into the cast on edge of the hem. Do not pull tightly or too much indentation will be visible on the right side. Right to left, or left to right, I like to slant my whipstitch the same direction as that of the cast on edge I'm covering.

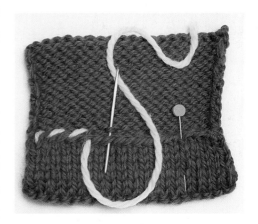

Blocking is the process of wetting the knitted work to ensure evenness and stability. For best results, block the pieces before you sew them together. My favorite is the wet towel method, safe for all types of yarns. Run a large bath or beach towel through the rinse/spin cycle in a washing machine. Roll the knitted pieces up in the towel, place in a large plastic bag and leave for several hours. The pieces will then be uniformly damp and ready to pin to the blocking surface. Use an out-of-the-way place on the carpet, and measure to match the dimensions given in the pattern. Pin every few inches and let dry completely.

ABBREVIATIONS	
approx	approximately
beg	beginning
bo	bind off
cb	center back
cf	center front
cont	continue
dpn	double pointed needles
eor	every other row
foll	following
k	knit
k2tog	knit two together
meas	measures
p	purl
p2tog	purl two together
patt	pattern
rem	remaining
rnd	round
rs	right side
SC	single crochet
ssk	slip, slip, knit
ssp	slip, slip, purl
st st	stockinette stitch
sts	stitches
ws	wrong side

PATTERN STITCHES	
st st	knit one row, purl one row. Repeat
1/1 rib	row 1: k1, p1. row 2: k1, p1 In subsequent rows knit over knit stitches, and purl over purl stitches.
seed stitch	row 1: k1, p1. row 2 p1, k1. In subsequent rows knit over purl stitches and purl over knit stitches.
garter stitch	knit every row

KNITTING NEEDLE CONVERSION TABLE

US	0	1	2	3	4	5	6	7	8	9	10	10½	11	13	15
Metric (mm)	2	2¼ 2½	2¾ 3	3¼	3½	3¾	4	4½	5	5½	6	6½ 7 7½	8	9	10
UK	14	13	12 11 10		9	8	7	6	5	4	3 2 1	0	00	000	